Stirring up Liberation Theologies

Stirring up Liberation Theologies

Edited by Jione Havea

scm press

© Editor and contributors 2024

Published in 2024 by SCM Press
Editorial office
3rd Floor, Invicta House,
110 Golden Lane,
London EC1Y 0TG, UK
www.scmpress.co.uk

SCM Press is an imprint of Hymns Ancient & Modern Ltd
(a registered charity)

Hymns Ancient & Modern® is a registered trademark of
Hymns Ancient & Modern Ltd
13A Hellesdon Park Road, Norwich,
Norfolk NR6 5DR, UK

All rights reserved. No part of this publication may be reproduced,
stored in a retrieval system, or transmitted,
in any form or by any means, electronic, mechanical,
photocopying or otherwise, without the prior permission of
the publisher, SCM Press.

The editor and contributors have asserted their right under the Copyright,
Designs and Patents Act 1988 to be identified as the Authors of this Work

British Library Cataloguing in Publication data
A catalogue record for this book is available
from the British Library

ISBN: 978-0-334-06516-6

Typeset by Regent Typesetting

Contents

Acknowledgements vii
Contributors ix

1 Re(l)ease: Ends of Liberation 1
  Jione Havea

release

2 What Do You Do When the God of Liberation Fails to
  Liberate? 15
  Miguel A. De La Torre

3 Decolonizing Priesthood: Affirming the Priestly Role of
  Women in the Hebrew Bible 27
  Jasmine Devadason

4 Hermeneutics of the Land: Evangelical Women and the
  Landless Workers Movement in Brazil 40
  Angelica Tostes and Delana Corazza

5 'Seh Yuh Sorry!': Jamaica Talks Back to the British Empire 55
  Anna Kasafi Perkins

(re)*lease*

6 Liberation as Praxis: Structural Poverty and Public
  Prophetic Theology 69
  Sithembiso S. Zwane

7 'We Can't Stay Home, Our Children Must Eat': African
  Women, Street Markets and Survival during Covid-19 84
  Lilian Cheelo Siwila

8	Mark's *Ochlos* as Minjung: An Overseas Foreign Workers' (OFW) Reading *Dong Hyeon Jeong*	98
9	Post-Trauma Narrative: A Path to Liberation in the Bible and Beyond *Diana Paulding*	117
10	Post-Liberation, Stress and African Youth *Thandi Soko-de Jong*	131

(rel)*ease*

11	Our Practices Preach: The Church-Industrial Complex and The United Church of Christ *Sheryl Johnson*	153
12	Liberation at the Cusp of Apocalypse: A Small Move from Making More to Making Beauty *S. Lily Mendoza*	169
13	*Being Moved*: Pina Bausch's Incarnational Dance and Divine Desire's Queer Choreography *Ángel F. Méndez-Montoya*	185
14	Liberation of Things: Accessing to the Agency of Thing *Iljoon Park*	197

unending

| 15 | freedom is for freeing
Michael N. Jagessar | 213 |

Names and Subjects Index   221

Acknowledgements

Work on this book was supported by Council for World Mission through its DARE programme (Discernment and Radical Engagement).

Cover and Figure 1.1
Yanto Gombo, *Papuan Woman* (acrylic on canvas 2021)
Courtesy of the artist

All Scripture quotations, unless otherwise marked, are from the New Revised Standard Version, Updated Edition. Copyright © 2021 National Council of Churches of Christ in the United States of America. Used by permission. All rights reserved worldwide.

Scripture quotations marked NASB 1995 are from the New American Standard Bible®, Copyright © 1960, 1971, 1977, 1995 by The Lockman Foundation. All rights reserved.

Scripture quotations marked NIVUK are from the Holy Bible, New International Version® Anglicised, NIV® Copyright © 1979, 1984, 2011 by Biblica, Inc.® Used by permission. All rights reserved worldwide.

Contributors

DELANA CORAZZA is a social scientist with background in Architecture and Urbanism (FAU-USP). She is currently a doctoral candidate in Geography at UNESP and is a researcher and coordinator on the research project 'Evangelicals, Politics and Grassroots Work' at Tricontinental: Institute for Social Research (Brazil).

MIGUEL A. DE LA TORRE serves as Professor of Social Ethics and Latinx Studies at Iliff School of Theology in Denver. A Fulbright scholar, he has taught in Indonesia, Mexico, South Africa, Costa Rica, Cuba and Germany. He served as president of the Society of Christian Ethics and director to the American Academy of Religion. A scholar-activist, De La Torre has also published in popular media, served on civic organizations and wrote the screenplay to a documentary on immigration (http://www.trailsofhopeandterrorthemovie.com/) that won over seven awards.

JASMINE DEVADASON is from the Church of South India and currently works with the North West & Mann Region of the Methodist Church (UK). Her PhD dissertation at the University of Manchester examined the book of Job from a Dalit woman's perspective. Her interests are on the Hebrew Bible, Dalit feminist liberation hermeneutics and postcolonial hermeneutics. She incorporates contemporary and contextual issues in her teaching, writing and preaching. She is involved in local, national and global organizations that work with grassroots groups.

JIONE HAVEA is co-parent for Diya Lākai, native pastor (Methodist Church in Tonga), migrant to the cluster of islands now known as Australia and senior research fellow with Trinity Methodist Theological College (Aotearoa New Zealand) and with Centre for Religion, Ethics and Society (Charles Sturt University, Australia). Jione is energized by opportunities to collaborate and excuses for theological (broadly conceived) revol-u-ting.

MICHAEL N. JAGESSAR is from Guyana where the natives kept Eldorado out of the reach of the Colonials by spinning excitingly deceptive stories. After 'pirates plundered the Caribbean' extracting most of the region's wealth and the IMF became a new form of piracy, Michael followed the trail of the wealth, which landed him in Britain (1999). Michael's religious heritages include Islam, Hinduism and Christianity, and he gets excited over cricket, Caribbean spirit-filled punch, creolized Caribbean curry and the ever-elusive Anancy/Anansi (patron saint of the Caribbean).

DONG HYEON JEONG is Assistant Professor of New Testament Interpretation at Garrett-Evangelical Theological Seminary. He served as a missionary in the Philippines for two years with his parents, who have been missionaries themselves since 1987. He is an ordained elder of the United Methodist Church. His book is entitled *Embracing the Nonhuman in the Gospel of Mark*.

SHERYL JOHNSON is a white settler, born on Treaty 1 territory in what is colonially known as Winnipeg, Canada. She is a recent graduate of the PhD program at Graduate Theological Union in Berkeley, California, where she studied Christian Ethics supervised by Dr Cynthia Moe-Lobeda. Sheryl currently serves as a Professor of Theology and Chair of the DMin programme at St Stephen's College and as a part-time minister at a progressive UCC congregation.

ÁNGEL F. MÉNDEZ-MONTOYA was born in Mexicali, BC, Mexico. He was a professional dancer and co-founder of the company U.X. Onodanza (Mexico City) and earned his PhD in Philosophical Theology from the University of Virginia. He is currently a full-time professor and researcher at the Department of Religious Sciences at the Universidad Iberoamericana in Mexico City. He has published in various anthologies and in national and international journals.

S. LILY MENDOZA is Professor of Culture and Communication at Oakland University in Rochester, Michigan, USA and Director of the Center for Babaylan Studies, a non-profit organization committed to decolonization and indigenization among diasporic Filipinos on Turtle Island. She hails originally from the Philippines in the traditional homeland of the Ayta and other indigenous peoples. Her latest (co-edited) book publication is *Decolonizing Ecotheology: Indigenous and Subaltern Challenges* (2022).

CONTRIBUTORS

ILJOON PARK is a research professor at Wonkwang University (Korea). His research addresses the subjects of being-human in contemporary philosophies, cognitive science, evolutionary theories, evolutionary psychology, artificial life and so on. His publications include 'A Postnaturalist idea of ec-stasy: an East–West Dialogue in a Tran-human age' in *Nature's Transcendence and Immanence: A Comparative Interdisciplinary Ecstatic Naturalism* (2018) and 'com/passion as the bodily extension: a theological critique of the interpretations of plasticity' in *Madang* 33 (2020).

DIANA PAULDING is a PhD candidate at the University of Exeter (UK). Her research looks at the impact of the individual voice on narratives about cultural trauma in the book of Job, and how this can inform Christians and the church today. She is a member of the United Reformed Church (URC) and is on the leadership team for yo*ur*church, the URC's first digital church. She was a representative for URC Youth on the 2019 Educational Visit to Israel and the Occupied Palestinian Territories, is a trustee of Sabeel Kairos UK and serves on the URC's Faith and Order committee.

ANNA KASAFI PERKINS is Senior Programme Officer, University of the West Indies and Adjunct Faculty, St Michael's Theological College, Kingston, Jamaica. She teaches and researches in ethics, justice, popular culture, sexuality, theology, scripture. She is a member of the National Bioethics Committee of Jamaica and the Legal Aid Council of Jamaica. Her recent publications are *Ethics Amidst COVID-19* (2020), co-authored with R. Clive Landis, and *Rough Riding: Tanya Stephens and the Power of Music to Transform Society* (2021), co-edited with Adwoa Onuora and Ajamu Nangwaya.

LILIAN CHEELO SIWILA is Associate Professor in the School of Religion, Philosophy and Classics, and Head of discipline for Theology and Gender Studies, Academic Leader for Community Engagement, at University of KwaZulu-Natal (South Africa). She is a member of the Circle of Concerned African Women Theologians, and several ecumenical bodies. Her research interests include religion, gender, culture, indigenous knowledge on ecology, African indigenous churches, sexual and reproductive health rights. She has published with internationally recognized journals and books, including four edited book volumes.

THANDI SOKO-DE JONG is a Malawian-Dutch activist-theologian. She is a PhD candidate at the Protestant Theological University in the Netherlands on Intercultural theology. She is a tutor at the Foundation Academy of Amsterdam, a columnist, and is involved with various networks and working groups, including the Werkgroep Heilzame Verwerking Slavernijverleden, and serves as a board member of the MissieNederland (formerly Evangelical Alliance). Her motivation for activist-theology stems from her interest in examining and interrogating theologies that inform and sustain social injustice.

ANGELICA TOSTES is a researcher at Tricontinental: Institute for Social Research, an institute connected to popular movements in the Global South, coordinator of the research project 'Evangelicals, Politics and Grassroots Work', and Course Coordinator at Ecumenical Center for Evangelization and Popular Education in Brazil (CESEEP). She is a feminist theologian and interfaith activist, a member of the Global Interfaith Network for People of All Sexes, Sexual Orientation, Gender Identity, and Expression. She is interested in interreligious dialogue, feminist and queer theologies and evangelicals in Brazilian politics.

SITHEMBISO S. ZWANE is a lecturer in the Theology and Development Programme and Director of the Ujamaa Centre for Biblical and Theological Community Development and Research in the School of Religion, Philosophy and Classics (SRPC), at the University of KwaZulu-Natal (South Africa). He is a member of the Evangelical Lutheran Church of Southern Africa (ELCSA), and his work draws on liberation theology praxis and Contextual Bible Study (CBS) to engage with the socio-economic challenges in the public realm.

I

Re(l)ease: Ends of Liberation

JIONE HAVEA

Release – let out, let go, let loose – is the key goal (*end*) of liberation. In the exodus narrative, the elected descendants of Abraham, Isaac and Jacob[1] were led out of Egypt, but they were not let go. They were let out from bondage to Pharaoh and then they were given regulations after regulations, after regulations, to keep them organized and bonded to YHWH. They were released from the arms of Pharaoh, and retaken (read: *re-leased*) into the arms of YHWH. Their release was partial.

Regulations are mechanisms for keeping order in a community and, for devotees, regulations are freeing. Regulations define limits and mandate affairs, to be in order and appropriate. But regulations, like doctrines, are also tools for controlling minds and spirits. Like doctrines, including the Doctrine of Discovery – issued in the interest of the Christian mission – regulations seek to control and tame minds and spirits and, of course bodies. Put differently, regulations can also enslave.

Yanto Gombo's *Papuan Woman* (see Figure 1.1) places a human head upon the landscape of West Papua. West Papua is the 'other half' (on the western side) of the island where Papua New Guinea is (on the eastern side) – they share the same island, but Papua New Guinea gained independence from Australia in 1975 while West Papua is still occupied by Indonesia (since 1969). Papua New Guinea is recognized – but not fully respected – in geopolitics, while West Papua is not even an itch in the eyes of the world's powers.

The head of *Papuan Woman* begins to crack up, to break open, because of the roots that are invading and occupying it, and a Band-Aid is not enough. The Band-Aid is useless. Hopeless. The landscape is littered with bullets and other rubbish of human civilization, including an article of clothing hanging from the stump – suggesting that she had been raped. The eyes of the human head are closed, and tears run down her cheeks.

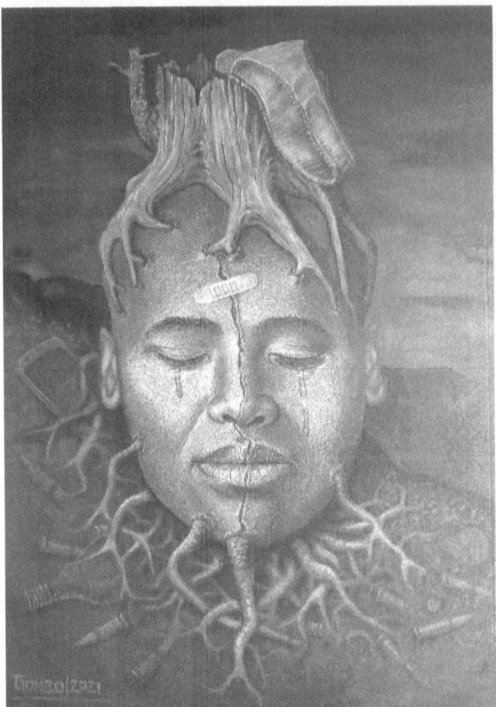

Figure 1.1: *Yanto Gombo,* Papuan Woman *(acrylic on canvas 2021), courtesy of the artist*

The human head is prominent in this work, but the land is also being invaded and occupied. Raped. The *Papuan Woman* depicts the enslavement of the human mind and of the land – in West Papua, the home (is)land of Gombo, people and land are connected in the native world view as well as in the experience and reality of being cracked and raped. The invasion of one is the invasion of the other also. The *tears* (pun intended) of one means the *tearing* (crying, ripping) of the other. In West Papua, and in other occupied (is)lands of Pasifika and beyond,[2] the occupation of land and sea tears and enslaves people also. For occupied (is)lands, there is no liberation. Liberation has *ended*.

Returning to the exodus narrative: the descendants of Sarah, Rebekah, Leah and Rachel were led out of Egypt and driven towards a specific destination – Canaan, also known as Palestine (which is still under occupation) – appointed for them by YHWH. The land to which they were led was not of their choosing, a land that was occupied when their ancestor first arrived: 'When they had come to the land of Canaan, Abram passed through the land to the place at Shechem, to the oak of Moreh. *At that time the Canaanites were in the land*' (Gen. 12.5b–6). For some 40 years, and the passing of one human generation, the people who were led out of Egypt were driven around the wilderness to arrive as inheritors of YHWH's promise and, of course – to be invaders of Canaan. Their partial release was a threat to the freedom of the native people of the land at their destination, not to mention the threat that they posed to the freedom of the people of the land in the wilderness.

Release, as the goal (end) of liberation, is a freeing process but it is not baggage-free. *Release* favours subjects who have been suppressed.

Initially, the suppressed people would experience some (rel)*ease*. They then celebrate and dance, as Miriam led when her people crossed the Sea of Reeds (Exod. 15). They were released from one authority – Pharaoh – but they ended up being (re)*leased* to another authority – YHWH. In the course of the exodus narrative (spreading across the books of Exodus to Deuteronomy), the release of Miriam's people led to the displacement (read: dis-ease) of the people of the land in the wilderness and in Canaan.

At the end of the exodus narrative, the dynamics of release – *release*, (rel)*ease*, (re)*lease* – entangle so tightly that none of the subjects involved in the process was at ease. The goal (end) of liberation was in danger of coming to *end* (stop, finish, kaput) – for Miriam's people, for the people in their way (wilderness) and at their destination (Canaan), and for YHWH. Lest we forget, the liberation of the land was also threatened.

This collection engages the dynamics of release in the context of Liberation Theologies. Liberation Theologies have set out on many journeys, and they have many stories, in different settings, geographically and academically, which this collection presumes but does not set out to retell. On the other hand, this collection aims to *stir up* interest in extending the reach of Liberation Theologies wherever readers are located.

Flow of the book

The chapters are presented in three clusters under the frames of *release*, (re)*lease*, and (rel)*ease*. The clusters flow from (1) seeking to *release* our minds from some of the theological traps (read: to emancipate ourselves from mental/theological slavery, as the late prophet Bob Marley invited in 'Redemption Song') that life has called into question towards identifying (2) alternative set-ups (potential traps?) to which we may (re)*lease* our stirred up theological minds and (3) alternative expressions of theological (rel)*ease*. An *unending* reflection closes – by opening up – the collection.

release

There are four theological and cultural traps interrogated in the first cluster of chapters: uncritical hope in God as saviour, uncritical adoption of the crusades of patriarchy (e.g. priesthood as man's only business), uncritical treating of the land as commodity and proverbial cash-cow, and uncritical regard for empire as salvific and scot-free.

First, Miguel A. De La Torre (Chapter 2) challenges the politics of hope. To hope is not some wishful desire but an expected joy that God will bring about God's purposes. Jürgen Moltmann argued for a hope based in a God who keeps promises, a God who is a step ahead of humanity making all things new. Moltmann's hope is based on God's promise which validates the gospel and assures us of an eternal and blissful afterlife, safeguards a future with meaning and purpose, fortifies a sense of security, provides tranquillity of mind and, most important, secures a sense of peace amid life's vicissitudes. But what do we do when the God of liberation fails to liberate? When God's promises fall short, a theology must be constructed that limits who is destined for liberation and, by extension, salvation.

This chapter wonders if the God of Moltmann, the God of Eurocentrism, the God who justified colonialism and slavery, has become the God of people on/under the margins – people who have many faces and stories across the world – to their detriment. When global oppression and repression continue, is the God of modernity capable of saving/liberating those who fall short of whiteness? Does embracing the God of the colonizer contribute to the oppression of those on the margins of empire? What does it mean to move beyond this white God of modernity? In short, this chapter explores what a postcolonial God rooted among the world's disenfranchised would look like, and more importantly, how this new understanding would contribute to how social justice is defined and how ethics and praxis are formulated.

Second, Jasmine Devadason (Chapter 3) brings her personal story to interrogate the patriarchal view that priesthood is strictly men's business. After ordination and having served the church for many years, and though she and her husband are equally qualified, she does not receive the same recognition that he does. The reasons given to justify this are based on biblical passages that have been misinterpreted and misused. Devadason decolonizes this tradition and its manifestation in modern churches in the belittling and rejection of women from the priesthood.

Decolonizing a text goes beyond critiquing all forms of power. A decolonizing reading critiques the biblical text and re-centres the people whom the text marginalizes. So when we tell the biblical story of the priesthood, it is necessary to ask why a particular group of men dominated religious affairs and why they were in control of the temple and its activities. Recognizing this helps us understand how biblical history understood the priesthood and equips us to decolonize those histories in order that we may rewrite the role of women in religious activities.

The decolonizing reading process does not stop at asking the right questions and exposing the patriarchal and colonial legacies of texts: it goes further to reconstruct the voice of the marginalized. Choosing a different starting point, focusing on a different set of characters and retelling a biblical story in a different way are critical steps in decolonizing reading. To reconstruct the role of women in religious functions, Devadason retells the story of female characters who played major roles in biblical history – Miriam, Deborah and the unnamed wise woman of Tekoa.

Third, Angelica Tostes and Delana Corazza (Chapter 4) present a women-of-the-land hermeneutics based on the experiences of the evangelical women who belong to Brazil's Landless Workers Movement (Movimento dos Trabalhadores Rurais Sem Terra – MST). The MST is a social movement formed by rural workers and their comrades who fight for land reform and against injustice and social inequality in rural areas.

One of the important positions that Tostes and Corazza present from their interviews with MST members is that land is not a commodity to be possessed and milked for profit, and it is not for making slaves – through labour and profit-making. Rather, land is for liberation – especially that of landless rural women workers. The inspiration for the liberating stance of the MST women comes from the Bible, especially the stories of peasant women who survived and succeeded: one of the Brazilian peasant women explained that, like 'the peasant women in the Bible, I can do it too'.

Fourth, Anna Kasafi Perkins (Chapter 5) offers a critique of the March 2022 visit of the British Royals to Jamaica appealing to the idea of emancipation (the Caribbean word for liberation). Perkins foregrounds the idea of forgiveness and its socio-political expression via a call for reparations, using the tagline of the Jamaican protests led by the Advocates Network – 'Seh Yuh Sorry!' (Say you are sorry!). Perkins argues that liberation-emancipation remains a contemporary 'already-not yet', which cannot be ignored in religious spaces.

Perkins calls for a decolonial stance (to borrow Devadason's term) towards the British Empire, walking in the footsteps of De La Torre's decolonizing of hope in a God who saves (Chapter 2). In between these framing chapters are the decolonizing of patriarchy (Chapter 3) and of the arms of capitalism in Brazil (Chapter 4) and beyond. The *release* for which this first cluster of chapters call is the platform for the second cluster of chapters.

(re)*lease*

The second cluster of chapters look to the other side of *release* and ask: How do we facilitate the (re)*lease* of, and into, alternative realities? The five chapters circle around three agents of (re)*lease*: praxis, work(ers) and trauma.

First, liberation as praxis. Sithembiso S. Zwane (Chapter 6) shifts the focus to praxis, one of the fundamental pedagogical contributions of Paulo Freire in the field of education. Praxis as a concept underscores the critical role of reflection and action within the community. It is inconceivable to contemplate deep liberation without critical reflection and action in the communities affected by structural poverty. The re-emergence of what the Kairos Document (1985) called 'Church Theology' in South Africa has compromised the work of public 'Prophetic Theology' as appropriated in the postcolonial dispensation.

Praxis is appropriated by the Ujamaa Centre, at the University of KwaZulu-Natal (UKZN), as a collaboration between trained readers of the Bible and 'organic' intellectuals who work in the community. This collaboration creates a conducive environment for Participatory Community Development (PCD).

Zwane promotes PCD with three arguments: first, Zwane uses *denunciation* as a frame for the rejection of structural poverty as a systemic problem that undermines the gains of liberation in post-apartheid South Africa. Second, he argues for *annunciation* in advocating for public prophetic theology that takes into consideration marginalized black Africans as primary interlocutors. Third, he proposes *transformation* as a tool for social change through the mobilization of social movements to embark on campaigns that facilitate liberation and PCD. Release/liberation from structural poverty through public prophetic theology must include the working-class poor as interlocutors to prevent 'liberation as praxis' from being paternalistic or tokenism.

Second, work(ers): Zwane's PCD and call for engaging the working-class poor are the subject of the next two chapters. Chapters 7 and 8 address the struggles of workers (see also Chapter 5), in different contexts but the same predicament, Covid-19.

Lilian Cheelo Siwila (Chapter 7) engages church women's groups. These groups occupy the majority of the pews in the church. Their work is not only vivid in the church but in the society also, as well as in their homes. Some are single parents or widowed while others are married, but they all are caregivers in their homes. Although some of these women are educated and hold good jobs, most of them also run small businesses. The study focuses on church women who are also street vendors or who sell products at local markets for income to help them feed and take care of their families.

Siwila interviewed some of these groups concerning their operations during the Covid-19 lockdowns. How did they, many of whom survive on their everyday sales, continue their operations despite the lockdown restrictions? What kind of theologies did these women embody in the time of the Covid-19 outbreak as caregivers and as church members?

Caught between the lockdown mandate and the need to feed their families, these women had no choice but to go out and trade their goods, and sometimes their bodies. They had to work because they are trapped in the 'shitstems' of capitalism and structural poverty.

Dong Hyeon Jeong (Chapter 8) presents the struggle of another group of workers – the Filipinx Overseas Foreign Workers (OFW). During the Covid-19 pandemic, Jeong argues that OFWs are among the maltreated and unseen, the twenty-first-century minjung. Their stories echo and resonate with the plight of the Markan *ochlos* in Mark 6.30–44, the 'Feeding of the 5,000' narrative. Both the *ochlos* and the OFWs left their homes to find 'salvation'. Both of them 'worked' for their food. And after receiving their sustenance, they both had leftovers or remittances to bring home to their family and communities.

Ahn Byung-Mu's reading of the Markan *ochlos* as the poor and oppressed people of South Korea during the 1970s and 80s endures and still speaks volumes in the Covid time. It endures because, for Ahn, the minjung are not just Koreans. When confronted by a scholar about the applicability of minjung theology in Germany, Ahn points out that the minjung of Germany are the foreign workers who are maltreated and unseen in German society.

Jeong reads Mark 6.30–44 with an OFW perspective because their plight needs to be seen and heard not just in our global society (where they are abused and maltreated) but also in our workplaces. The OFWs are the ones who clear the trash bins and clean the rooms where we pontificate about how much we care about the oppressed. And yet seldom have we seen and uplifted their presence and conditions – in our meeting rooms. The OFWs liberate us from complacency and indifference towards those who are unseen and even maltreated.

The struggles of church women groups (Siwila, see also Tostes and Corazza) and of OFWs (Jeong) require the *release* of the working poor (and other slaves of the capitalist shitstem) and their (re)*lease* into meaningful praxis. This (re)*lease* is possible through managing their stress and trauma – the focus of the next two chapters.

Third, trauma. The final two chapters in this cluster revisit (read: re-lease) trauma in the context of Liberation Theologies.

Trauma studies as a discipline grew out of European and American research in the nineteenth and twentieth centuries, and the models of trauma in those days were combat trauma and trauma due to sexual assault. As a result, individual trauma has traditionally been seen as a response to a single, catastrophic event and characterized by dissociation and the inability to form a narrative about the event.

Diana Paulding (Chapter 9) looks at cultural trauma, understood to be sociological rather than psychological, which is formed by narratives that shape group identity and cohesion. Individual trauma has been described as the 'failure of narrative', while cultural trauma is the construction of narrative. For the biblical scholar David Janzen, this means that individual sufferers will always be silenced by social narratives about their trauma.

Paulding argues that the silencing of individuals is not an inevitability. Writers on the decolonization of trauma studies have recognized that an event-based model of individual trauma does not reflect all experiences and that trauma can be insidious and ongoing, particularly when individuals live under the shadow of colonialism, racism, oppressive regimes and constant threats of violence.

Narrative is not an impossibility but rather an integral part of the trauma process that plays a vital role in changing the circumstances that cause ongoing trauma. By recognizing that individual trauma is inseparable from its social context, and something essentially different, we can construct a model of trauma that allows individuals to speak about their experiences, influence the collective narratives that are formed, and liberate social groups from the causes of trauma.

Thandi Soko-de Jong (Chapter 10) interrogates Liberation Theologies and Liberation Hermeneutics that do not pay attention to the struggles that people face after being emancipated. Liberation Theologies and Liberation Hermeneutics stop accompanying people after their release (post-liberation). This leaves a theological void for helping people who continue to seek spiritual meaning in their post-liberation struggles. To account for this void, Soko-de Jong turns to the 'pastoral spiral' of *see, judge, act*. The pastoral spiral can help us examine an observable struggle in post-independence southern African countries. In particular, the pastoral spiral helps us observe mental health challenges – stress, trauma – which communities that have been politically emancipated continue to face.

Soko-de Jong reflects on the mental health and postcolonization challenges in Tsitsi Dangarembga's post-independence Zimbabwe novel, *Nervous Conditions* (1988). This novel opens up conversation around three critical observations:

- Rising suicide rates, particularly among young (male) celebrities in Southern Africa.
- Increasing references in popular music and social media to depression, anxiety and suicidal ideation/attempts.
- Proliferation of calls for action by young people, who seek life and spiritual guidance post-struggle.

The (re)*lease* into alternative realities has a better chance of taking place for people post-release, Soko-de Jong suggests, if liturgies were infused with story-telling methods. This would create a space for theologies that acknowledge (and attend to) the impacts of 'post-liberation stress'.

This second cluster of chapters affirm that it is not enough to only work for *release*. It is also necessary to accompany those (the released) who are trapped in the struggles to survive (like the working-class poor); and to care for they who have been released, in other words, to find (re)*lease* for they whose daily bread is stress and trauma.

(rel)*ease*

For *release* and (re)*lease* to endure, (rel)*ease* is necessary. The chapters on trauma (9 and 10) indicate that this is not always the case, 'post-liberation'. Hence this third cluster of chapters invite shifting to alternative frames and platforms for doing Liberation Theologies – budget, beauty, dance, being.

First, budget: Sheryl Johnson (Chapter 11) asserts that what we say we believe and what our actions show we prioritize are both important to consider. She based this assertion on her interviews with ministers in the United Church of Christ – a Christian denomination in the United States that has a long history of working for social justice; it has issued many official statements that articulate this commitment. However, living into those commitments in all aspects of church life is a challenge, and financial practices are a particular topic that make this challenge apparent. How does the church budget reflect the social, political, ethical and theological commitments of the church?

The pressures of the 'Church Industrial Complex' often sway churches towards prioritizing profit, self-perpetuation, growth and risk-avoidance, among other business-related practices. In-depth interviews with ten California-based UCC ministers who are themselves strongly committed to justice reveal the many barriers that exist to imbuing church financial practices with justice-rooted values, even with the support of both a denomination and ministerial leaders who hold these commitments. Understanding how these challenges are manifest on a local level through the perspectives of these ministers provides valuable insight into the nuances of these issues as well as possible avenues for addressing them and resisting the Church Industrial Complex.

Second, beauty: S. Lily Mendoza (Chapter 12) asks: in a world full of grief and trauma, unmetabolized and metastasizing into cancer-like growth that is wreaking havoc on the Earth's ecosystems and auguring the end of life as we know it, what is left for us to do? 'We make beauty anyway' is the fierce and stubborn reply of original peoples who still carry a measure of intactness in their lives amid our modern culture's unrelenting assault. This moment not being their first holocaust – fighting the corporate giants that would dam their waters, clearcut their forests, pave over their farmlands, bulldoze their sacred places for real estate development and so on – their call is not just to fight but to keep the seeds of real culture alive through the hard lesson of learning to suffer with grace, beauty and dignity.

Mendoza explores such a witness, beginning with her own mid-30s encounter with indigenous magnificence in an ethnomusicology classroom at the University of the Philippines that spoke profoundly to her body before her head could comprehend – a sensual 'conversion' away from civilization's hollow trappings into an ever-deepening embrace of land-taught wisdom and grace by original peoples both in the USA, where she now resides (and teaches), and in the homeland to which she returns with regularity. In the mix, Mendoza traces the way liberation has become an adventure out of the grip of our species' delirium of supremacy (gone hyper in colonialism's development conceits and mainstream Christianity's convictions of universalism) and into a 'small ordinariness' shot through with the grand potency of a seed.

Third, dance: Ángel F. Méndez-Montoya (Chapter 13) appeals to the work of the German postmodern choreographer Pina Bausch (1940–2009), who destabilized many conventions in the language of dance and the performing arts, incorporating novel intimations regarding the complexity of the body, and the queer motion of desire. At the heart of

Bausch's artistic impulse we find her profound fascination for letting the depths of desire move the body, thus allowing the flux of a performing corporeality engage in a truly 'incarnational dance'.

Méndez-Montoya proposes to let theology *be moved* by Bausch's choreographic provocations, searching for theological expression to emerge. How could glimpses of the emergence of theological impulse be found, intimating an extravagant pulsation that non-identically resonates with the perpetual motion of the gift of divine desire? How to be deeply moved to incarnate a theology of such queer desire? Even more subversively, how to encounter divine desire inscribed in the flesh of those who are rejected because of the colour of their skin, their ethnicity, gender, sexuality, migration/residence status and other supposed 'indecencies'?

Méndez-Montoya presents theological alternatives to counter the conditions of extreme violence, which is systematically implemented by the ongoing iteration of heteronormative, patriarchal and abusive/destructive desire. Against such a sinister backdrop, we can envision another choreography emerging from the pulsations of an extravagant divine desire that disrupts the flux of hegemonic violence and rejection, re-signifying human desire with transcendental and ever-inclusive love.

Fourth, being: Iljoon Park (Chapter 14) also reflects on the impacts of the Covid-19 pandemic. When the pandemic swept through the planet, one realizes that the liberation required for today needs to include material beings. It is symbolic that the virus is an agent at the edge between living and non-living beings. Climate change and the ecological crises that we face globally disclose that the living is already always entangled with the non-living. The climate system is not a living being but it works like a living being, influencing all being on the planet. Here, one can capture the agential power of things. Material beings are not dead and passive but active and agential. The great Pacific garbage patch called the Pacific trash vortex is the aggregation of trashes floating over the ocean, and it is growing.

We don't have a perspective to see material agency so far, because we understand being and agency mainly from the human-centred and organism-centred perspectives. However, 'being' is already always an entanglement of the living and the non-living, and the non-living is not dead and passive.

So far theology has talked about salvation only from our human perspective, and theologies of liberation have talked about the liberation of people. However, human liberation would not be thinkable unless we speculate the liberation of networked beings with us. Then salvation is not a personal matter but that of the collective, in which all forms of being, including the living and the non-living, the natural and the artificial, can enjoy an exuberance of liberation together.

unending

Michael N. Jagessar (Chapter 15) provides the closing frame for the collection, calling attention to re(l)ease as an unending (ongoing) process. The end (goal, purpose) of liberation remains open – it refuses seizure.

Freedom is for freeing! Freedom does not stop (end) re(l)ease. Rather, freedom is a step towards freeing – of others, of ourselves and of other kinds.

uproot

This collection has a simple agenda: to stir up the doing of Liberation Theologies, mindful of the dynamics of re(l)ease and struggles that have recently invaded our world, our mind, our neighbours and our being. It comes with a prayer that Liberation Theologies do not end (stop, expire) – as well as an invitation that Liberation Theologies stir up re(l)ease on the ground and not just in the classrooms and the meeting rooms.

In closing, i return to *Papuan Woman* with this open invitation: what might Liberation Theologies that uproot invasive and enslaving powers from our minds and faiths, schools and churches, fields and markets, (is)lands and seas, look like?

Notes

1 Abraham, Isaac and Jacob also had descendants who were 'diselected' (R. Christopher Heard), including Ishmael, Zimran, Jokshan, Medan, Midian, Ishbak and Shuah (of Abraham); Esau (of Isaac); and Dinah (of Jacob).

2 Pasifika (is)lands under occupation include Kanaky (New Caledonia) and Maohi Nui (French Polynesia) under France; Hawai'i and Tutuila (American Samoa), and the bombed (is)lands and waters of the groups now known as Marshall and Mariana, under the USA; and Rapa Nui (Easter Island) under Chile.

Our islands are occupied by nations that value independence and democracy, similar to the invaders of Ukraine (2022) and Gaza (2023). Go figure.

release

2

What Do You Do When the God of Liberation Fails to Liberate?

MIGUEL A. DE LA TORRE

By the beginning of April 2024, about 7.7 million people had died of Covid-19.[1] In a world of plenty, where enough food exists to feed the entire population of the planet, about 25% (2.3 billion) face moderate or severe difficulty in obtaining food,[2] with eleven people dying of hunger every minute.[3] Among so-called civilized European nations, almost a quarter of a million people had perished by 2023 during the savage Russia–Ukraine war (Enerio, 2023). And here in the USA, the land of the free, the struggle continues in an invisible deadly gun battle. Since 2020, there have been almost two mass shootings a day.[4] One can hear the anguished cry of those perishing – 'My God, my God, why have you forsaken me?' The world's wretched cry out fervent prayers begging for succour only to hear a silent reply as the innocent continue to be led to the slaughter. And as horrific as these contemporary examples are, the trepidation humanity faces is amplified when we consider a history of world wars, crusades, inquisitions, holocausts, savage capitalism, genocide and slavery.

Advocates of a God who liberates, a God ever present in solidarity with the world's oppressed, must ask where this God is as the least among us are being crucified on the crosses of racism, patriarchy, colonialism and neoliberalism. This Father God who we claim has knowledge of every sparrow that falls to the ground appears blind to the plight of the world's disenfranchised. It is as if God's children are crying out for bread and are being given a stone, or hunger for a fish and are instead given a snake. Claims of faithfulness require us to wrestle with the theological perspectives of the dominant eurochristian culture and its incongruency with reality. We must ask what is one to do when the God of Liberation Theology fails to liberate?

All too often we develop theologies designed to save God from God.

We anticipate that with the second coming of Jesus, we would finally understand all the unjust trials and tribulations of history. Until then, we comfort ourselves with a Christian concept of hope, reminding ourselves 'All things work for the good of those who love God, and who has been called according to God's purpose' (Rom. 8.28; author's rendering). And yet our daily witness demonstrates that bad things happen to good people, and often. Claiming hope, believing it will all work for good at the end, is at best naïve, at worse self-delusional. There is nothing 'good' about the death-dealing reality of pandemics, wars and famines that humanity faces daily. And if any 'good' does arise, it surely was not worth the broken lives required in payment. Such events remain beyond the realm of comprehension. Martin Luther King Jr. might encourage us to believe that 'the arc of the moral universe is long, but it bends towards justice' (1986, p. 52); but history seems to dictate that the moral universe doesn't give a damn as to which way it bends. In fact, it is more likely to bend towards injustices than towards justice. And if we want the future to be one based on justice, then it is we who need to do the bending.

If the past and present experiences of the world's colonized are any guide, then the existence of some moral universal arc is an assumed faith statement void of any empirical proof. What hope accomplishes is to provide an excuse for the middle class not to deal with the reality of injustices or offer any practical resistance to oppressive structures. Regardless of any hope professed, the reality for those struggling to survive is more than likely to be destitution and death on the margins of eurochristianity. Our daily newspapers attest that for those minoritized by eurocentrism, there really is no hope of life, or life abundantly. Waiting for liberation often leads to nothingness.

Those intimately familiar with or who grew up within marginalized spaces are accustomed to desperation. The world's disenfranchised occupy the space of Holy Saturday, the day after Good Friday's crucifixion, and the not yet Easter Sunday of resurrection. This is a space where a faint anticipation of Sunday's Good News is suffocated by the realities and consequences of Friday's viciousness, violence and carnage. This is a space where hopelessness becomes the companion of used and abused people. The class privilege of hope provides a barrier from the realities of Friday, or the opium thrust upon the marginalized to numb this same reality until Sunday. Regardless of the hope professed, those subjugated, their children and their children's children, will more than likely continue to live in an ever-expanding poverty and oppression. Sunday never seems to come. Waiting becomes tiresome as the situation remains hopeless.

For those who read 'hope' in English, a connotation exists where one is expecting all things to work for good. But those of us who read 'hope' in Spanish, we arrive at a very different understanding. In Spanish the word for 'hope' is *esperanza*, derived from the word *esperar*, which is translated to 'wait'. To say 'hope' in Spanish is to connote *esperar* (according to the Velázquez dictionary), a waiting in apprehension of either good or evil. To read 'hope' in Spanish signifies a gloomier, more complex meaning that implies fear of what is awaited. Waiting does not always end happily, especially when the waiting drags out for centuries as in the case of Hebrew slaves in Egypt or African slaves in the belly of the Empire.

Although I have no problem with a hope in a deity, I do find it problematic to hope that all things will work out for good. History and personal experience demonstrate this seldom occurs. Good hopeful Christians, like non-Christians, die in global conflicts, experience death by Covid, and lose all they hold dear. With the world's marginalized I can relate to the words of King David, who proclaimed: 'We are foreigners and strangers before the eyes of God, just as were all our ancestors. Our days on earth are like a shadow, without hope' (1 Chron. 29.15; author's rendering). And with Job, and all who unjustly suffer, I am forced to cry out to an apparent silent Heaven, 'Where then is my hope and who can perceive any hope for me?' (Job 17.15; author's rendering).

Maybe if we reduce hope to the personal, we might be able to speak of hope's eventual triumph through some future utopia-based justice. Maybe the hope is in a history that progresses towards ultimate salvation for humanity. Salvation history becomes the theological concept that ensures an eventual Sunday, hence justifying hope because in the end, it all does work for good. Christians believe history has an end (eschatology) when all of humanity – the living and the dead – stands before the throne of Jesus to be judged, with some cast to their eternal damnation while others enter the utopian kingdom prepared for them since the foundation of time. This ideology of salvation history is not limited to religion. Even non-Christians can hope all things work for good, that a moral arc does bend towards justice when they embrace the Hegelian philosophical concept of a 'salvation' history.

The modernity project believes history is comprehensible when its fullness is achieved. Accepting a linear dialectical movement of time, G. W. F. Hegel proposed that humanity is progressing towards a secular utopia (1820, p. 23). Even our economic social structures embrace a salvation history as capitalism (a rising tide will raise all ships) or communism (the eventual withering away of the state) – twins at birth – are based on a progressive linear movement. Hope in a utopian future that will be more forward thinking and egalitarian than the past will exist thanks to some deity or science or human ingenuity. Hope, a product of salvation history (either metaphysical or material dialectic), can be optimistically embraced if we accept that the arc of history does indeed bend towards justice. And yet the claim of a benevolent bending arc is not based on any rigorous or scientific examination. Instead, it is a faith statement, pure and simple, which is assumed as true without proof.

But what if there is no arc, no such thing as salvation history? What if the concept of the linear movement of time is but a philosophical construct designed to provide order to the disorder of time so as to soothe the anxiety of those unable to control their fate? Hope that 'all things work for the good' can be professed only within the security of a dialectical progressive movement that leads to a material utopia based on enlightenment and reason or a metaphysical utopia based on some heavenly paradise. But what if how we create history and remember the past simply seeks to justify the values and social power of those who get to write history, those who literally write their white privileged space into the national epic?

When Walter Benjamin gazed upon Paul Klee's famous 1920 painting *Angelus Novus* depicting the angel of history, he saw 'an angel looking as though he is about to move away from something he is fixedly contemplating. His eyes are staring, his mouth is open, his wings are spread.' For Benjamin, who purchased the painting in 1921 for 1,000 marks from the artist, 'This is how one pictures the angel of history. His face is turned toward the past. Where we perceive a chain of events, he sees one single catastrophe which keeps piling wreckage upon wreckage and hurls it in front of his feet' (1940, p. 257). For Benjamin, there is no lineal progression of time, nothing inevitable about its passage. There is no teleology to history, just random chance. There is no eschatology. What we call history is nothing but chaos, with no rhyme or reason. An event at any point in the passage of time is not necessarily connected to another event for they are as unrelated, unpredictable and contradictive as humans. Historians of the dominant culture hold the power to link incongruent events to create (as did Hegel) a type of progressive dialectical march towards a better human existence to justify the present so that the future can be shaped.

Premodernity (history made by God) and modernity (history made by the human subject) are both social constructions designed to privilege some at the expense of the many. The historical dialectic of philosophical and theological imagination that supposedly moves history in an upward progression is an optimistic theory which is forced on a very select rendition of historical events. For Benjamin, a storm is blowing from Paradise, so ferocious that it violently pinned the angel of history's wings so they could no longer close them. 'The storm irresistibly propels him into the future to which his back is turned, while the pile of debris before him grows skywards. This storm is what we call progress' (1940, p. 257). Dark ages of ignorance can just as easily follow periods of enlightenment creating at times downward spirals, at other times upward spirals may form, yet at other times unrelated and unconnected events can move past each other in opposite directions. What we have is a nonlinear, non-dialectical, disjointed, multidimensional passage of time that is not tied to any reason or mission.

History does not exist as an internal and necessary unfolding dialectic flow moving linearly as per Hegel. History is a kaleidoscope comprised of contradictory and complex untold stories and struggles belonging to the unnamed marginalized, pregnant with accounts of evil overpowering good, inhumanity suppressing harmony. We live in a world where the situation of the global disinherited seems to be getting worse as the wealth gap widens to the detriment of those located in the global South. Billions must be born into poverty and die to its consequences so that a few can enjoy the privileges of First World status. The global dispossessed offer up their lives as living sacrifices so that an elite can be saved and live well. 'Vanity of vanities', says the teacher (Eccles. 1.2). 'Absolute futility. Everything is meaningless', as one might render it.

Rather than examining the reasons for global poverty and oppression, rather than standing in solidarity with the world's minoritized, Western churches provide an intangible dosage of hope. But hope, as a middle-class privilege, becomes an excuse not to deal with the reality of injustices. As long as all things work for good, as long as a rising tide raises all boats, the privileged of the world can wash their hands from any responsibility and leave the fate of the world's disinherited in the hand of either God or the virtues of economic forces. Guilt of hoarding the world's resources is mediated by religious spokespersons from the so-called First World who peddle hope. Jürgen Moltmann – the prophet of hope – has argued for a hope based in a God who keeps promises, a God who is a step ahead of humanity making all things new. But what do you do when God's promises fall short, as they so often do for those on the underside of history? A theology must be created by those possessing unearned power, privilege and profits that limits who is destined for liberation and, by extension, those who will fall short of salvation. This theology of hope based on a God who keeps promises becomes an exclusive theology.

Kept promises by God are solely for God's chosen. Maybe once upon a time God made an original promise of chosenness to the Jews, but it seems as if God changed God's mind as salvation history now belongs to a new chosen people: eurochristians. Originally, God's promises to the Hebrews were achieved through the genocide of the indigenous people of Canaan, massacring everything drawing breath – men, women, children and even animals (Josh. 6.21). Because – per the antisemitic argument – the Jews rejected and murdered Jesus, they ceased being God's chosen, as they were replaced by eurochristians. God promised God's new chosen their own promised land. Euroamericans, since the foundation of the United States, have written themselves into the historical narrative as 'the New Jerusalem' or the 'New Israel'. Following Joshua's lead, Manifest Destiny required the genocide of native people of the Western hemisphere. The indigenous people of both Canaan and the USA were outside of salvation history and thus their eradication was God's will for God's chosen. So when God's previous chosen (Jews) face persecution and death through pogroms, inquisitions and holocausts at the hands of God's newest chosen (Christians), the latter simply become a weapon of divine retribution.

For Moltmann:

> [through] faith in the gospel, [human beings] see themselves as children of God the Father. But in prayer they talk to God as they talk to their friends. ... Wherever a person prays in Jesus' name, God is being claimed as a friend, and the request is urgently made in the name of that friendship. (2016, p. 124)

The problem with the Jews (or any other group who reject the Jesus of salvation history), whose prayers might originate in death camps, is that they are not heard by 'God the Father' because their prayers are not being uttered in Jesus' name. The confidence of heard prayers can lead Moltmann to exclaim that the 'world is full of jubilation, for God is in this world' (2016, p. 200). But if this is true, then God stands condemned for being blind and mute to the cries of those disenfranchised by eurocentric white supremacy, those who do not pray in the name of Jesus.

To protect God from failing to keep God's original promise to the Jews, because God replaced them with the Christians, requires those victimized by antisemitism to bear responsibility for their predicament.

They stand before God guilty for their own slaughter. Moltmann's reasoning absolves eurochristians from their complicity not only with the Holocaust, but with all colonial massacres, gaslighting the Jews and the colonized for not praying in Jesus' name. If God keeps God's promises to act, then we can rely on hope. But if the Hebrews' entire identity is rooted in the promises of God, then we must question if God indeed – as Moltmann claims – keeps promises. The terror of concentration camps bears terrible witness concerning the failure of such promises.

Moltmann's God of promises as the answer to the theodicy question works if the promise made by God is continuously delayed. We can almost hear Martin Luther King Jr. rebuke that justice delayed is justice denied. What good is a promise if it fails to materialize during one's existential reality? Delayed promises by God become unfulfilled promises. God would be perceived as being more just if delayed promises were never made in the first place. Linking an eschatology to ethics allows for any commitment to justice-based praxis to be ignored as the focus remains on some futuristic utopian hope for which the victims of eurochristianity are told to wait. Hope in some pie-in-the-sky in some by-and-by secures the grip of oppressive powers in sustaining and maintaining a reality beneficial to the dominant eurochristian culture at the expense of those on their margins.

To rely on eurochristian hope, like Moltmann, is to suffer from the curse of a eurocentric privilege that leads to an over-acceptance of the present. But what happens when life for the disinherited is cut short? When their lives are relegated to genocidal oppression, deprivation and hopelessness? Because the abundant life promised by Jesus (John 10.10) is denied, hope in an abundant life is problematic for those falling short of the eurocentric ideal as they face genocide by those relying on the divine forgiveness of their complicity with death-dealing oppression. The possibilities for a future not seen but believed might work for the eurochristian centre, but it holds little hope for those on Moltmann's margins. What is usually expressed as hope by the dominant eurochristian culture has often led to acceptance of the present, but not in accepting future possibilities. Any hope proclaimed, for it to have meaning, must be tied to a space and to the now. Because too many of the bodies of the innocent have piled up to the heavens, hope of future promises has become obscured by the tang of rotting flesh ensnared in the nostrils of God and all who are repulsed by eurocentric futuristic fantasies based on a religious ideology constructed to provide peace amid massacres through unanswerable answers. I reject Moltmann's hope crying out, with so many, 'I can't breathe'.

'Christian hope is resurrection hope', Moltmann argues (1967, p. 18). This hope is based on an eschatology which anxiously awaits the:

> return of Christ in universal glory, the judgment of the world and the consummation of the kingdom, the general resurrection of the dead and the new creation of all things ... eschatology means the doctrine of Christian hope, which embraces both the object hoped for and also the hope inspired by it. (1967, p. 15)

Such a hope makes God the foundation for all universal human rights as human dignity emerges throughout the course of God's redemptive history (1984, p. 17). And here is the flaw of Moltmann's thinking, so detrimental to those on his margins. By grounding human rights in the historical expression of a particular religion – Christianity – instead of universalizing human rights, the religious expression is what becomes universalized. If human rights arise from God's redemptive history, then are those excluded from salvation history also peripheral to human rights? This may not be what Moltmann advocated; nevertheless, when viewing the plight of the world's colonized as they encountered European conquerors, capitalists and missionaries, this surely became the case. When we are reminded that the fate of the unfaithful is a lake of fire (Rev. 20.10–15), a certain sadistic brutality to the eurochristian eschaton becomes obvious.

By making God the divine author of history, human responsibility for history is eliminated. The oppressed are given hope instead of justice to pacify their feelings of hopelessness with platitudes concerning a God who keeps God's promises. Regardless of the hopelessness of the now felt, they are evangelized to believe that God's promises will eventually be realized. Moltmann promotes a modified Marxist Hegelianism – an all-knowing, all-powerful God who does nothing about those facing global colonial oppression. 'As the Creator of the world, God also respects this world's space, time, and autonomous movements. The limitation of God's unending power is an act of God's power over Godself. Only God can limit God' (2016, p. 45).

Moltmann, like so many before him, seeks order in the chaos of the passage of time. His faith forces false connections because, as he admits 'Future history loses its attraction if there is no transcendent future for history as a whole' (2016, p. 180). His hope in hope betrays the privilege of his social location where a future is a given. But what about those throughout the world without a future, where early death due to hunger and poverty is a given? Eschatological visions of utopias create an apathy that steers the global disenfranchised away from rebelling and creating new possibilities and realities. Think of the sign that adorns the top of the entrance gates to Auschwitz: *Arbeit macht frei* – work will set you free. These words elicit a violent hope offered to those already condemned to death, encouraging a self-discipline that does not rebel against their slaughter. Giving hope to those being victimized leads to self-policing. If one can keep their head down, avoid eye contact and do their work, they might survive, even as those around them are slain by the millions.

To sit in the reality of (Black) Saturday, that liminal space between (Good) Friday's torture and possibility of (Easter) Sunday's resurrection, is to discover that the semblance of hope becomes an obstacle when it serves as a mechanism that maintains rather than challenges the prevailing social structures. Hope of surviving and fear of losing the only thing one has left – their life – muzzles insurgency. Recognizing the truth that no amount of work would ever set you free is an embrace of hopelessness, probably a more merciful and liberating prospect. When one realizes that they have nothing to lose they are more apt to engage in disruptive praxis, maybe even creating the space for possible survival opportunities to arise. Or not. The end may still be death and not liberation. But at the very least, hopelessness may lead to a chance for liberation.

All too often the advocacy of hope gets in the way of listening and learning from the oppressed. To sit in the reality of Saturday is to discover that the semblance of hope becomes an obstacle when it serves as a mechanism that maintains rather than challenges the prevailing social structures. Hopelessness is never an excuse to do nothing. It may be Saturday, but that's no justification to passively wait for Sunday. The hopeless are cognizant that there might not be a resurrected utopia. Does it matter if there is or is not when it comes to acting? Do I choose to live my life based on some promised heavenly reward, an extra ruby in my crown? Or can my existence have meaning for the short span of years I have on this earth? Maybe 'nothing lives long, only the earth and the mountains'? I'm not necessarily rejecting some afterlife; I simply do not care if the afterlife exists. This present age has too much oppression to be distracted by visions of kingdoms not yet seen. The choice to live a life committed to the gospel message of liberation (salvation) can never be based on some transactional exchange where the reward becomes some future hereafter. One lives by faith according to the meaning and purpose that praxis towards liberation gives to life in the here and now. We are called to follow the example of Jesus's ultimate act of solidarity with the least of these, demonstrated by picking up a cross and following them towards their crucifixion on the crosses of oppression.

I advocate a hopelessness that rejects quick and easy fixes. I reject a hope that may temporarily ease the conscience of the privileged but remains no substitute for bringing about a more just social structure. This hopelessness is not disabling; but rather a methodology that propels towards praxis. To embrace hopelessness becomes the means by which we work out our liberation (salvation) in fear and trembling. This liberation/salvation is not some egocentric project seeking personal saviours or exclusive heavens. What is being worked out is how we stand in solidarity with the hopeless who are struggling for their own liberation/salvation. Embracing hopelessness is never an excuse to do nothing. It may be Saturday, but that's no justification to passively wait for Sunday. To stand in solidarity with those facing genocide, pauperization and unmitigated hatred prevents any simplistic platitudes on hope. Hearts that weep and bleed require brokenness and realism. To stand in solidarity with the minoritized of the world is to share in their hopelessness. We embrace hopelessness when we embrace the sufferers of the world, and in embracing them we discover our own humanity, our own salvation. This discovery provides the impetus for our own justice-based praxis making hopelessness the precursor to revolutionary resistance.

But if it is truly hopeless, why bother? Why continue the struggle for justice? We struggle for justice not because we hope that at the end we will win; we struggle for justice for the sake of justice, regardless of the outcome. And we certainly do not struggle for justice in anticipation of some heavenly reward. Hopelessness is not resignation, nor inertia, nor being in despair or melancholy. Those on the margins have shown how those who are hopeless, having nothing to lose, are propelled towards radical praxis. For many, hopelessness may very well be the realization that the end may be crucifixion. But this realization can never be relegated as the sin of faithlessness lest we blame the victims for the violence that befalls them. Hopelessness is not despair; rather it's perseverance, even while cognizant that the end is so near. Yes, winter is coming. Darkness may very well defeat or even consume us; nonetheless, hopelessness refuses to silently go into the night.

To embrace hopelessness becomes an attempt to figure out how to remain faithful while walking under the shadow of death. To be hopeless is neither ideological nor depressing, because the inevitable is accepted. To be hopeless is to be emboldened, knowing that a different result is not dependent on us for we are not the Saviour. Those who have experienced the consequences of eurocentrism have no option but to continue their struggle for justice regardless of the odds against them. They continue the struggle, if not for themselves, for their progeny. We thus continue the struggle for justice not because we hope it will all turn out good in the end (it probably won't); nor is it an exchange where our praxis leads to some heavenly bliss. We fight for justice because it not only defines the faith we claim to possess, but more importantly, it defines our humanity.

With Jesus at Gethsemane, those who are hopeless drink fully from the cup they desperately pray would be taken away by God (Luke 22.42). On the rim of the cosmic void, God might make God's presence felt. But even if this God remains deaf and dumb, even if we share the forsakenness felt by Jesus while hanging on the cross, our angst makes our presence felt by God. Maybe this is what Job meant when he cried out: 'Though God may slay me, I have no other hope' (13.15; author's rendering). The faith of the hopeless cries out to an absent God, choosing to remain faithful amid abandonment for my decision to have faith was never based on some transactional arrangement of what I would get from the deal. I continue to pray and seek the face of a God who may not even exist, not because I crave a magician who will rescue me from the causes of my hopelessness. I pray and seek the face of God to define who I am, to participate in communion with divinity, to converse with what remains beyond my understanding. I pursue a Messiah in the urgency of the now, a God who claims Emmanuel even though we may not feel God is with us. I hound the Divine so when I walk through the valley of the shadow of death, I would fear no evil.

Notes

1 World Health Organization, https://covid19.who.int/ (accessed 02.04.2024).

2 Associated Press, 'Record Number of People Worldwide are Moving Toward Starvation, UN Warns', *National Public Radio*, 7 July 2022.

3 About 7,750 to 15,345 a day (5 to 11 per minute); Oxfam Media Briefing, 'The Hunger Virus Multiplies: Deadly Recipe of Conflict, COVID-19, and Climate Accelerate World Hunger', 2021, p. 3.

4 Mass shootings were at 610 in 2020, 690 in 2021 and 647 in 2022; Janie Boshma, Curt Merrill and John Murphy-Teixidor, 'Mass Shootings in the US Fast Facts', *CNN*, 26 January 2023.

References

Benjamin, Walter, 1968 [1940], 'Thesis on the Philosophy of History', in *Illuminations*, trans. Harry Zohn, ed. Hannah Arendt, New York: Schocken.
Enerio, Dane, 2023, 'Russian Soldier Death Toll in Ukraine War Hits 115,000', *International Business Times* (January 15).
Hegel, Georg Wilhelm Friedrich, 1991 [1820], *Elements of the Philosophy of Right*, trans. H. B. Nisbet, ed. Allen W. Wood, Cambridge: Cambridge University Press.
King Jr., Martin Luther, 1986, *A Testament of Hope: The Essential Writings and Speeches of Martin Luther King*, New York: HarperCollins.
Moltmann, Jürgen, 1967, *Theology of Hope: On the Ground and the Implications of a Christian Eschatology*, trans. James W. Leitch, New York: Harper & Row.
———, 1984, *On Human Dignity: Political Theology and Ethics*, trans. M. Douglas Meeks, Philadelphia, PA: Fortress.
———, 2016, *The Living God and the Fullness of Life*, trans. Margaret Kohl, Geneva: World Council of Churches.

3

Decolonizing Priesthood: Affirming the Priestly Role of Women in the Hebrew Bible

JASMINE DEVADASON

My journey into ordained ministry was not straightforward. While I now live in the UK, where women are accepted in ordained ministry, my origins lie in India, where some dioceses deny us ordination; as such I cannot take my leadership role in the church for granted. When I first explored my call to be a priest, the main resistance came from my own family. I pursued my ministerial training in the midst of this opposition, only for the diocese to tell me at the end that they did not ordain women, not even if we had completed our training. The only options for me were to become a religious education teacher in a school or to become a community worker. It was not possible for me to carry any responsibility within the church's ministry. And even now, after ordination and having served the church for many years in different capacities, just as qualified as my husband, it is very much evident that I do not receive the same recognition he does among the Asian communities we serve. Only if the men priests are not available will I be approached to lead anything.

The reasons given to justify male-orientated leadership in the church are based on biblical passages that have been misinterpreted and misused. We either fail to find female leaders in active religious duty in the Bible, or passages are quoted that speak against the leadership of women. Despite many studies into the subject of women leadership, discrimination against women in leadership roles continues.

Being a student of the Bible, I would decolonize the idea of biblical priesthood that is the basis for supporting or speaking against women's priesthood in today's context. For this, I find the decolonial approach useful, since it is a reading of resistance, used to criticize all forms of hegemonic power. It challenges political, social, economic and ideological hierarchies, and reconstructs the role of priesthood based on women's experiences and call.

Decolonizing a text, however, goes beyond critiquing all forms of power. A decolonial reading critiques the biblical text and re-centres the people whom the text marginalizes. We need to acknowledge that biblical narratives are constructed and are confined to the limits of the people who constructed them. A decolonial reading therefore deconstructs the colonial reading of a text and reconstructs the story/narrative from the perspective of marginalized voices.

In a decolonial reading, we need to question who the story is about and who is telling the story. Within this process, these questions are important: Whose story is this? Who benefits in this story? Who holds the power? Whose voice is heard? These questions will determine our starting point for reading the text, and help us decide whose voice should be included in our decolonial reading of the text.

When we tell the history of priesthood in the Bible, it is important to see why a particular group of men dominated religious affairs and why they were in control of the temple and its activities. Recognizing this will help us understand how biblical history has dealt with the concept of priesthood and decolonize those histories so we can rewrite the role of women in religious activities.

While I say that we need to decolonize the history of priesthood, which is written by men, I am conscious that the role model we have in that history suits men. I would therefore decolonize the role of priesthood itself and establish alternative priesthood, which is inclusive, without hierarchical structures and beyond the temple structure.

Decolonization does not stop at asking the right questions nor at recognizing the answers. It also challenges the traditional narrative of the text with the purpose of recovering the biblical story from the patriarchal/colonial influences and reconstructing it from the voice of the marginalized. Choosing a different starting point, focusing on a different set of characters, and retelling a biblical story in a different way are how we create a decolonial reading. To reconstruct the role of women in religious functions (which will help us shape our theology to accept women in church leadership), I would retell the story of female characters who are given minimal attention in the Bible but played a major role in history, like Miriam, Deborah and the wise women in Samuel.

First, my approach to biblical priesthood is to acknowledge the fact that the Bible was written by men in favour of men. To decolonize the text, it is essential to become aware of the world view of these men, so that we can make the hidden colonizing strategies visible for the reader and find a way to confront the marginalization of women in religious affairs.

Second, what is the role of a priest? Who defined the role of priest? How can we deconstruct the role description of the priest in order to reconstruct and redeem it from the male-orientated world view? This would help us to expand the priestly role to include women.

Origin and development of priesthood

Biblical priesthood is often associated with legal materials in the book of Leviticus. The development of high priesthood is a later entity, but equating men with religious duties started early in biblical history. Often the temple was connected to the ruling class of the time. The empire and colonial power controlled the temple's affairs. In the post-exilic period, high priests were in charge of the civil system along with the religious system, which led high priests to become rulers in the later period. Since religious affairs were controlled by a certain group of men and often affiliated with the empire, women were excluded from both religious and civil affairs.

The origin and development, together with the relationship of priests and Levites, constitute one of the major problems in OT scholarship, since the relevant information about the priesthood of the earlier period was written in later centuries after the events. For instance, the priestly code, which has full information about the priesthood, is the latest of the chief documents in the Hexateuch.

In the earlier period of Hebrew history, the priesthood was wider than the Levitical priesthood, and this wider priesthood was narrowed down during the seventh century BCE the priesthood of that time was exclusively a Levitical priesthood.

The earliest traditions of the Hebrew Bible presuppose that there was no regular priesthood. In the time of the ancestors there was no official priesthood. The head of the family performed the acts of public worship. The ancestors themselves offered their sacrifices in the sanctuaries. The priesthood in the earlier period consisted primarily in the guardianship of a shrine and its sacred contents (Peters, 1932, p. 135). There is no mention of priests in the book of Genesis except in reference to foreign nations (Gen. 41.45; 14.18). Therefore, the priesthood probably did not appear until the social organization of the community had been developed (de Vaux, 1961, p. 345).

In the earliest period we have two representations. According to one, Moses, for a period, was the sole priest in Israel. He exercised the priestly functions only for a short time and one of his first acts was to consecrate his brother Aaron (Gray, 1925, p. 216). From Aaron, the later Jerusalem priesthood traced its descent.

We have another tradition, which assigned this position to Joshua. In Exodus 33.11, we have the form of tradition current in Ephraimite northern Israel. According to this, while the priesthood was still vested in Moses, it was given to a subordinate person in his own household. We do not have any clear evidence to show that the priesthoods of different traditions were related to one another. In the earlier time there must have been a priesthood of some kind, to tend the shrines and its contents, to regulate the human approach to YHWH and to interpret the will of God to the people. Originally this priesthood was in some way connected with Moses and the people vested in him all the functions of a leader, civil and ecclesiastical. In the beginning Israel recognized priesthood as a divine leadership even though it was communicated through a human intermediary.

Since the primitive priests were seers, or oracle men, Moses seems to have accepted these functions. The centre of religious worship was the ark, the representation of the deity. It was the function of the priest to guard this ark. But this is not the only function of the priest. According to the earliest historical documents, after the occupation of Canaan, the ark was placed in a sanctuary at Shiloh. It continued until the time of Solomon. After the settlement in Canaan, Eli and his sons, descendants of Phinehas, the sons of Aaron, were the guardian priests of the ark (1 Sam. 1; Peters, 1932, p. 135).

After the settlement of the people of Israel all the tribes were allotted a portion of land except the Levites. In the period of Judges, not all of the priests were Levites. Micah, a man of Ephraim, appointed his own son as a priest (Judges 17.5). Samuel too was an Ephraimite (1 Sam. 1.1). During the period of the Judges, the Levites were already recognized as interpreters of the will of God.

We have evidence that in the pre-monarchic period, the priestly office was occasionally hereditary. The house of Eli constituted a priestly family at Shiloh (1 Sam. 1—4). The priesthood in the pre-monarchic period was not Levitical as such. There were priests from other tribes; and sometimes it was hereditary.

The appearance of the monarchy did not at once affect the priesthood. Generally, it served to strengthen the authority of the priests. The importance of the priests at the royal sanctuaries was enhanced by the growth of the temples and their connection with the king. The king eventually took over the management of the priesthood, at least in Jerusalem. And the organization of the priesthood became more inflexible (Peters, 1932, p. 160).

Since the temple at Jerusalem was a royal chapel, the priests naturally were royal officials. They were appointed and removed by the king (1 Kings 2.27, 35). Sometimes the king even intervened in the priestly administration of the temple (2 Kings 12.5; 16.10; 22.3). We also find that the head of the Jerusalem priesthood was simply called 'the priest' (1 Kings 4.2; 2 Kings 11.9f.; 16.10f.; 22.12, 14; 1 Sam. 8.2). Only in 2 Kings 25.18 is he called the 'chief priest'. There are evidences for the title 'high priest' but according to Ringgren those are probably a later addition to the accounts of monarchy (2 Kings 12.11; 22.4, 8; 23.4; Ringgren, 1962, p. 211).

In the time of the monarchy the temple in Jerusalem became an important place. It was a state sanctuary, and the king appointed its civil servants. The head or chief of the clergy was mentioned among the king's officials (1 Kings 4.2). They were appointed and dismissed by the king (1 Kings 2.27, 35). The king issued all the orders regarding the duties in the sanctuary. For example, 2 Kings 16.10–16 tells of the order of King Ahaz to Uriyyah to build a new altar, and the priest obeyed the order of the king (de Vaux, 1961, p. 376).

The priesthood under the monarchy served in the state sanctuary, Jerusalem. The priesthood of this period worked under the guidance of the king. Since the temple at Jerusalem became the main worshipping place, the priests at Jerusalem were also given importance. This may be one of the reasons for the hierarchy among priests in the later period.[1] Power struggle and hierarchical structure developed in the later period.

In the development of the priesthood in Israel's history, we have complex information about which order of priesthood they followed or came from, whether Levite, Moses, Aaron or Zadok. Notwithstanding, the exclusion of women from any cultic function or role is unequivocal. As Phyllis Bird stated:

> The question about the place of women in the Israelite cultus exposes a defect in traditional historiography – beginning already in Israelite times. It is a question about a forgotten or neglected element in trad-

itional conceptions and presentations of Israelite region, which typically focus on the activities and offices of males. Where women appear at all in the standard works, it is in incidental references, as exceptional figures, or in limited discussion of practices or customs relating especially to women. (Bird, 1997, p. 83)

Even in the midst of a male-dominated religious system, despite the deliberate decision to exclude any role played by women in religious roles, the Hebrew Bible tells us that women did serve in a limited role at the tabernacle (Exod. 38.8; 1 Sam. 2.22). And while women could serve as prophets (though not many did), communicating God's will, the priestly role was reserved for men. Though the history and development of the priesthood do not include women, the role and function of women in various capacities served the temple and society.

In the next section, I give examples of women who played religious leadership roles but were not recognized by patriarchal society. Since the role and function of the priesthood in the Hebrew Bible were based on what men of their society did and could do, such as sacrificing animals and other work that men normally do in society, so the role description of a priest needs to be reconstructed by female leadership.

Reconstructing the priestly role of women

We have no record of women in the Bible being called priests. However, in Ancient Near Eastern countries, priestesses were poets, prophets and participants in religious rituals. If priestly rituals are to maintain the relationship between humans and God, then women performed those duties in ANE countries. In the Bible, we do have evidence that women performed religious duties equivalent to priesthood, which the world of men did not recognize or record in biblical books. We can identify the call and vocation of women in religious and pastoral affairs in Miriam, Deborah and the wise woman in 2 Samuel 14.

The question for us is whether to identify women who performed religious duties as male priests did and bring them to light in order to reclaim their priestly role, or whether the duties of priests must be reconstructed in order to affirm the female role in priestly function. I will attempt to do both by using examples from the Hebrew Bible.

Reclaiming the role of Miriam

Miriam is traditionally accepted as a prophetess, but she also performed religious functions as a priest did. She is a Levite by birth, as she is described in Exodus 15.20 as Aaron's sister. Miriam led women in choral song and performed a dance at the Sea of Reeds with a timbrel, which is often considered to be one of the traditional ritual instruments of ANE priestesses. In Numbers 12, she appears by the side of the high priest.

Numbers 12 is a multi-faceted text. As Eryl Davies (Davies, 2017, p. 27) rightly points out, feminist biblical scholars deal with the patriarchal bias in this text while postcolonial scholars highlight the racial overtone within the text. And the postcolonial writers try to bring the unnamed Cushite wife of Moses to the forefront. While I see the importance of the postcolonial lens to bring out the silenced and discriminated Cushite wife, I would also identify the importance of Miriam's leadership struggle in the patriarchal world in this text. There are two problems that have been combined in this text, but which we need to acknowledge and look at differently. The first part of the complaint is against the Cushite wife and the second part is on leadership. Numbers 12 presents Miriam joining her brother Aaron to complain against Moses' Cushite wife, which is the first part, and then they claimed their call into the role by asserting, 'for God has also spoken through us'. The complaint is against Moses for not sharing the leadership role with Miriam and Aaron in the second part.

I am not ignoring the issue of racial discrimination here; my purpose is to see whether Miriam had any religious leadership role that's been sidelined. The author of the text very nicely mixed up the racial and leadership issues so that the matter related to women could be bypassed. I would like to explore the second part of the complaint, which is about the role of mediation.

In this passage, the whole reason behind the complaint is suppressed by highlighting her leprosy as punishment for her rebellious attitude. If Miriam was punished for her complaint, why not Aaron? Aaron wasn't punished because of his gender, or had Miriam been discriminated against by the male-dominated leadership so that she does not reclaim her leadership? Or was Miriam's leprosy not punishment for her complaint, but rather the male-dominated leadership covered her leadership by portraying her illness as a punishment?

Rabbi Jill Hammer points out that the ritual that Miriam undertook to re-enter the camp (Num. 12) is similar to the ordination rite of priests in Leviticus 8 (Hammer, 2013). The story of Miriam is not a story of a rebellious character who had been punished for her sin, but rather the story of a priestess who fought for her leadership role in the midst of strong male leadership and patriarchal society.

Miriam was an excellent leader who was rooted in her ancestors' struggle, resilience and cultural life – as was Moses. She was a dancer, singer, poet and a mediator between God and human beings. In her people's struggles, Miriam led by example of love and solidarity. Even though she was kept outside the camp for seven days, the community accepted her leadership and demonstrated their loyalty and solidarity with her (Num. 12.14–15). Moses didn't give the leadership role to Miriam but the community did by waiting for, and standing with her when she was excluded from the community.

Renaming the role of Deborah

Deborah, Lapidot's wife, was a prophetess who presided over Israel's judicial system in the book of Judges. The Israelites used to approach her for judgement while she was seated under a palm tree on the highlands of Ephraim, halfway between Ramah and Beth El.

Accepting Deborah as a judge and a prophet was not a problem for the biblical world or modern readers. Deborah's strong leadership is undeniable. But when it is suggested that Deborah's role could be a priestly one, a problem arises.

Deborah was chosen by God to be Israel's leader and judge. She had authority over males, elders, generals and tribal heads after being ordained to the office of Judge (Judg. 4.5). Her authority was respected by both men and women. Deborah's advice and presence on the battlefield were important to Barak, the military leader. He waited for her order before fighting and immediately obeyed when she gave it. She was a prophet who spread God's word. Everyone in Israel was aware of who the 'judge' was. Her ministry was public and not private.

Jill Hammer suggests a few reasons why Deborah could be a priest: first, the palm tree under which Deborah sits could be a shrine or a pilgrimage location where people regularly go (Hammer, 2013, p. 103). During the time of judges, there were many shrines or worship spaces and this could be one. Since the author is very specific about the tree under which Deborah sat as a judge, it might be one of the local shrines where she delivered oracles for the people. Second, the name Deborah means 'bee', and the Hebrew word for 'bee' (*dbrh*) is related to 'shrine' (*devir*) and 'word' (*davar*) – and her name suggests a priestly role. Moreover, there is no mention of goddesses in the story, but the palm tree is often considered a sacred place. More than all these, teaching or communicating God's words, and mediating between God and humans, are priestly functions, and accordingly Deborah was one of the priests during the Judges period.

Redefining the role of the wise woman of Tekoa

2 Samuel 14 is about a situation that arose for King David, and a woman from Tekoa played an important role in resolving it. The plot revolves around King David and his three children, Amnon, Absalom and Tamar. Tamar and Absalom were born by the same mother, but Amnon was born by a different mother. Amnon raped Tamar, and Tamar's other brother, Absalom, exacted revenge by killing Amnon and fleeing to avoid punishment (2 Sam. 13.10–39).

When David's mourning for his son Amnon ended, he learned that Absalom was still alive and longed to see his estranged son. David was hesitant to bring him back because of the legal ramifications of having killed his brother. Not being able to bring him home fuelled David's longing for his son. David, the famous king of Israel, was in a crisis that he did not know how to handle and no one in the palace could solve. Joab, David's chief general, realized that he couldn't solve the problem on his own and decided to enlist the assistance of another person who possessed a skill that could help.

Joab looked for someone who could not be easily recognized but who could perform the chosen task, and the unnamed woman of Tekoa was suitable for this role. Although we are not familiar with the services of 'wise women' from the Bible, Joab was aware of their existence. The task for the wise woman was, as Joab explained: 'If you please, pretend to be a mourner. Wear garments of mourning and do not anoint yourself with oil; be like this for many days as a woman mourning over a dead person. Then come before the king and speak these words to him ... And Joab put the words into her mouth' (2 Sam. 14.2–3; author's rendering).

The instruction to the woman and her act afterwards suggest that Joab explained the situation and what needed to be done in detail, and left it to her to deal with the situation as she saw wise. Taking on her role like a skilled actor, she presented herself as a woman in mourning in front of the King. It looked like Joab fully trusted the wise woman to handle the task well and the outcome of her intervention confirmed that she was extremely courageous and wise.

The woman of Tekoa appeared as a mourner before David. She shared a made-up story to explain her situation, which resembled David's situation with Absalom and Amnon; a tactic similar to how Jesus conveyed messages through parables. The woman expected to get her point across to David and encouraged him to assess his own situation and relieve his depression by bringing back his son Absalom.

Absalom's anger had grown so much that he was a threat to Israel. The woman of Tekoa, an outsider, confronted David with the consequences of not initiating reconciliation. She had the courage and the skills needed to make him see sense when his closest aide was not able to. What were those skills?

First, the crisis demanded a person who was a good actor and not recognizable by the King. Joab could not convey his message himself. Maybe he had already tried to convince David without success, and it had become clear that only a person who was new and from outside of the King's palace had a chance of breaking through the King's inertia. Joab identified the need, found the right person outside of the familiar system and completed the task of being heard.

Second, Kind David was in need of psychological support or counselling to change his mind, which the wise woman provided. David's crisis was not only political but also very personal. David was unable to make a decision because the issue related to himself, and it affected him mentally. So the task required a skilful person who was experienced in life and could provide pastoral support. The woman from Tekoa had this skill and hence was able to help David find a way out of the situation.

Third, the woman played the role of mediator between David and Absalom. David as the father, king and chief judge of Israel had a responsibility to initiate reconciliation and to do it without bias. But David might not have succeeded because of his acrimonious relationship with his son and Absalom's rebellious character. The wisdom of the woman from Tekoa urged David towards reconciliation with his son: 'David, we all die and then the opportunity for reconciliation is over. Do it now.' When David thought there was no way for reconciliation, the woman made it possible.

Fourth, the wise woman was bold and courageous enough to bring what was right and just for this crisis in front of the king. Wisdom is the ability to employ one's God-given skills for good. This holds true for the wise woman from Tekoa, who managed a difficult situation with astonishing skill and sensitivity. More than what she said, her courage and boldness to stand before the king were the achievement. Her strength came from being brave enough to surpass fear and stand before the king, which she saw as a right thing to do. At the end the wise woman took pastoral responsibility and made David reconcile with his son.

Women priests

Priestly roles in the Hebrew Bible were written by and for male priests. Recognizing the historicity of this is a first step towards seeing that priesthood extends beyond male leadership. Looking at the origins and development of the priesthood in the Hebrew Bible reveals that any religious duty is contextually developed, and the practice of priests is time-limited. Perhaps religious leadership emerged during a time of spiritual crisis. This emerging leadership can be seen in Deborah, just as it can be seen in Moses, who emerged in the context of oppression.

Priestly roles were defined to fit the work done by male religious leadership. The historical significance of a male-dominated priesthood calls us to reclaim the roles of women in the Hebrew Bible. In the process of decolonizing the priesthood, we recognize that the priestly role extends beyond temple sacrifice and rituals to include people who are involved in the priestly role in the wider community.

While women's voices were silenced, Miriam played an important role in Exodus, demonstrating courageous leadership in a world dominated by male power. Deborah's role was not only that of a judge and a prophetess; she also served as a mediator between God and humans, through her advice and guidance during war and battles, which modelled priestly leadership in the context of a national crisis. The wise woman of Tekoa is a model for bringing peace and reconciliation in a time of personal crisis.

As a result, the role description of a priest must be rewritten in light of the needs and skills of those who offer their gifts to perform religious duties in order to meet the needs of the community. The traditional male-dominated priestly role description must be reimagined so that all who have served the community are recognized and valued.

Moving to the time of Jesus: as a high priest, Jesus did not follow the Aaronic priesthood, nor was he recognized as a priest from the Zadokite order. Rather, he was recognized as a high priest from the order of Melchizedek, whose name means 'king' for 'justice'. This demonstrates that he was not like the priesthood that the people in Jesus' time were familiar with, and his role is embedded in the name itself, which is justice-orientated. The priesthood must be discerned in every context. We are called to discern the call and vocation regardless of gender or any other bias, so that God's ministry is carried out.

Conclusion

The stories above demonstrate that God can call anyone to accomplish the task, and gender is not a barrier for women to fulfil their vocation as priests. And it is calling us to recognize the priestly role of women in the church and in the larger context. The congregation must be taught to accept women's roles as equally important as men's.

The priesthood is a call from God to anyone, regardless of gender, to have a relationship with God and with the people. We, as humans, have no say in who God calls. Priesthood is a call to serve the people, and the role is not limited to the priestly function within the church and its activities related to rites. A priest is someone who brings and works for peace and reconciliation in society, as well as establishes justice in the world, all of which are essential components of establishing God's kingdom in this world. None of these roles are exclusive to men. Wherever there is discrimination against women in the priesthood, the values of God's kingdom are not fully established and experienced.

Note

1 We do not have detailed information about the priesthood during the exile but there is some evidence; for example, the prophet Ezekiel was also a priest by education.

References

Bird, Phyllis A., 1997, *Missing Persons and Mistaken Identities*, Minneapolis, MN: Fortress Press.
Davies, Eryl W., 2017, *Numbers: An Introduction and Study Guide: The road to freedom*, London: Bloomsbury.
de Vaux, Roland, 1961, *Ancient Israel its Life and Institutions*, London: Darton, Longman & Todd.

Gray, G. Buchanan, 1925, *Sacrifice in the Old Testament*, Oxford: Clarendon Press.
Hammer, Jill, 2013, 'Priestess, Bibliomancy, and the Anointing of Miriam', https://rabbijillhammer.com/2013/11/25/priestesses-bibliomancy-and-the-anointing-of-miriam/ (accessed 02.04.2024).
Peters, John P., 1932, *The Religion of the Hebrews*, Cambridge, MA: Harvard University Press.
Ringgren, Helmer, 1962, *Israelite Religion*, Philadelphia, PA: Fortress Press.

4

Hermeneutics of the Land: Evangelical Women and the Landless Workers Movement in Brazil

ANGELICA TOSTES AND DELANA CORAZZA

Conhecer Deus é conhecer a terra![1]
(Nancy Cardoso, 2019b, p. 129)

This chapter reflects on the perspectives of 15 evangelical women, members of the Landless Workers Movement (MST) in Brazil, who attended the first National Meeting of Landless Women held in Brasilia in 2020, attended by over 3,500 women from different parts of the country. The purpose of this chapter is to comprehend the feminist interpretation of the land from the evangelical women of the movement, drawing on theological and methodological contributions from Latin American Liberation Theology and Feminist Theology, with thinkers such as Nancy Cardoso, Ivone Gebara and Milton Schwantes. The aim is to shed light on the possibility of the evangelical faith and popular movements coming together in the struggle for land, justice and dignity, despite potential contradictions. Additionally, four interviews with movement leaders from various regions of the country were conducted to gain a deeper understanding of the relationship between gender, religion and the MST.

In these reflections, we aim to avoid stereotyping or making conclusions about what an evangelical woman in the MST is, but rather to consider the possibilities for dialogue between faith and struggle, which are so prevalent in Latin American history and the history of the Landless Workers Movement. The reflections reveal a diverse range of gods and a pluralistic faith that drives the struggle. We see internal negotiations between spirituality and the social movement, seeking to unify them into a single entity, and a willingness to re-evaluate concepts such as gender and land through contact with the MST.

Knowing the rhythm of the MST

The Landless Workers Movement (MST) in Brazil is the largest popular movement in Latin America that works to bring hope every day. It emerged at the beginning of the 1980s, quickly transforming the peasant struggle into a means to challenge authoritarianism during the military dictatorship that ruled Brazil at the time. Its actions, which go beyond just the struggle for land, include the pursuit of agrarian reform to democratize access to land, produce healthy foods and fight for social justice. Currently, around 500,000 households in rural areas are members of the MST. Some of them live in encampments while they fight for access to unused land, while others live in settlements, having won land ownership through struggle. These families continue to organize themselves in a participatory, democratic and inclusive manner at local, regional, state and national levels.

The struggle and popular faith are intertwined in the foundation of the MST and the development of Liberation Theology, a religious movement that emerged in Latin America as a response to various popular organizations formed during a period of growing industrialization, in which the peasant masses became proletarianized, exacerbating the structural social inequalities in the region. The 1970s solidified this new theology, which became the support for popular organizations by interpreting the historical Jesus and using it to guide their practices in the fight against injustices and for the liberation of the poor and oppressed.

The Pastoral Land Commission (CPT) was established in 1975 in the city of Goiânia, with the goal of organizing rural struggles and advocating for the rights of the poor. The CPT takes a political and popular approach to reading the Bible, and its actions are guided by the principles of justice, love and freedom. The CPT's work in the southern region of Brazil was instrumental in the formation of the Landless Workers' Movement.

Women of faith: evangelical movement in Brazil

The dominance of Christianity in Brazil is undeniable and, as noted by the sociologist Antônio Flávio Pierucci, the most common religious transition in recent decades has been from Catholicism to Protestantism (Pierucci, 1997). A 2016 Datafolha poll supports this observation by revealing that 44% of evangelicals were previously Catholic. According to IBGE data, Catholic membership has declined over the years, from 83.3% in 1991 to 64.6% in 2010. During the same period, the evangelical movement grew from 9% to 22.2% (IBGE, 2010 demographic census). This growth of evangelicalism in Brazil can be attributed to the spread of Pentecostalism, and as of the last census, with the decrease in members of traditional Protestant churches, they now make up 60% of evangelicals (Machado and Burity, 2014).

In January 2020, Datafolha released the results of a survey conducted between 5 and 6 December 2019. The survey was conducted with 2,948 people from 176 cities across the country and focused on the evangelical faith. Despite the media portrayal of the evangelical movement as being dominated by angry, fundamentalist, cis-heterosexual white men, the survey results showed a different picture. The face of evangelicalism was revealed to be that of a black woman, with 58% of evangelicals being women, of whom 43% identify as brown and 16% as black.[2]

It is not possible to ignore the experiences of women in Latin America who turn to religion in search of gender justice, as the theologian Nancy Cardoso highlights. Women find comfort and support in their faith to overcome life's difficulties. Although Christianity has imposed layers of oppression on women's bodies for centuries, women have a God that is intertwined with their everyday lives.

> Countless times, Christianity (including Catholics, Protestants, and various waves of Pentecostals) has been an instrument of oppression against women in society. The idea of women as being of lesser value can be traced back to the theological writings of the 'fathers of the church', making it a fundamental thought of Christianity. Historically, religions have not been driving forces behind social change in overcoming the notion of female subordination. (de Souza, 2007, p. 19)

> The strong female presence in religious communities is a result of the weakening of women in the highly disruptive capitalist system. Many women seek immediate comfort through religion in order to face the challenges of everyday life. However, this comfort often reinforces the stereotype of women's domestic role and perpetuates male domination, whether through the domination of pastors or priests. (Gebara and Rosado-Nunes, 2006, p. 306)

According to Magali Cunha (2020), the strongest flag in Latin America is anti-gender and anti-sexuality. The defence of moral guidelines based on a fundamentalist reading of the Bible is a significant banner in Brazilian and Latin American fundamentalism, which manifests itself in the executive and judicial branches of power. This was also discussed in a dossier of the Tricontinental Institute for Social Research (2022), which explores the relationship between fundamentalism and imperialism and how it impacts the daily life of the urban and rural working class.

'Land is not for making slaves, it is for liberation!': agrarian reform in Brazil

Brazil is known for having one of the greatest areas of land in the world, as well as the largest latifundia. This has had disastrous consequences for the poor working class, who have suffered from unjust land confiscation since the colonial period. The legacy of colonialism, which Anibal Quijano refers to as coloniality, involves the exploitation of both land and enslaved people and the private ownership of land. This legacy is difficult to overcome in Brazil, where the elites still hold power, leading to continued social inequality and structural racism. The country has a history of struggle, resistance, bloodshed, and genocide against parts of the population that resisted massacres carried out by the Brazilian elites. Therefore, addressing the struggle for land is essential in order to achieve social equality.

We are not only discussing history but also the current reality, which shows how colonial roots still shape Brazilians' access to land. The latest Agricultural Census (IBGE, 2017) shows that only 1% of landowners control 50% of the country's agricultural land. This unbalanced ownership of land has taken on a new form, the expansion of agribusiness, which gained strength in the 2000s. As Nancy Cardoso points out:

> Latin America has a long history of exploitative extractive ventures dating back to the colonial period and continues today. In Latin America, human and environmental rights activists are criminalized because they challenge the extractivist ideology. Even the popular governments that emerged from 2000 to 2015 were unable to break away from the extractivist model (such as the exploitation of crops, water, minerals, energy, etc.). (Cardoso, 2019b)

The extractive practices of large estates and monoculture are a legacy of colonialism and take on new forms with agribusiness. They have transformed land into a capitalist enterprise that relies on pesticides and agrochemicals. This is facilitated by a toxic agribusiness policy promoted by a political group in Brazil known as the BBB: bullet, Bible and bull. The health of Brazilians is endangered by multinational companies that use countries in the Global South as test subjects for the harmful effects of exposure to excessive pesticides used in food production.

Furthermore, they have further enclosed the land, turning seeds, a common resource and essential for the production and reproduction of life, into private property. The result of agribusiness is the exacerbation of exploitation of rural workers, who are unable to compete with the technology of large capitalist landowners and become overworked salaried employees, with their traditional knowledge being obliterated. From an environmental perspective, monoculture and toxins destroy the land and biodiversity and conflict with the needs of the people due to the persistent and destructive pursuit of profit.

> Capitalism is an economic fundamentalism against the land, treating it merely as a 'means of production' and source of income and accumulation. In Brazil, calls for agrarian reform and a different agricultural model are stymied by the fundamental principles of capitalism. Interpretation is paralyzed, and the media asks the landless majority to passively accept and comply with the unchanging truths of private property. (Cardoso, 2017)

Parallel to this reality, 70% of the food consumed daily by the Brazilian population is produced by small-scale family farmers (IBGE, 2017). The majority of these family farmers are women, who are also responsible for producing and reproducing life through their main role in domestic work, both in rural and urban areas. The organization of women against agribusiness and for life is crucial for saving the planet.

According to Ceres Hadich (2021), a settler in agrarian reform and a militant of the MST, male decision-making and power relations are visibly and socially hierarchized as more important, but it is actually women who have the power to deepen the dialectic between historical and ancestral knowledge and scientific advancement by reclaiming their traditions. This task must not be romanticized; *just as the struggle for land is historical, so is the invisibility of women's struggle*. Peasant women have always been on the forefront, and their participation was crucial in the 1980s in the fight for many rights that were won later. The existence of women as rural workers was a major step in the recognition of these women as a crucial part of the struggle for land.

Given the nature of agribusiness in Brazil, agrarian reform is not only about democratizing land but also about fighting against the destructive and deadly model of dominant agriculture. A new model of agriculture must also be linked to a new model of gender relations, recognizing the crucial role of women and transforming the way life is produced and reproduced, breaking away from the logic of violence and patriarchy. This new model must also be deeply rooted in traditional knowledge, where women play a significant role: 'They embody an economy of life. One that connects the backyard, the kitchen, the forest, the animals, the celebration of life, the diverse needs of the family, and the land. Peasant women have a deep connection with the land' (Cardoso, 2019c).

Feminist hermeneutics: 'reading the Bible is different'

The profile of women interviewed at the first Meeting of Women of the MST: they are aged between 28 and 50 years; 60% attend the Assemblies of God Church, 13% attend the Universal Church of the Kingdom of God and 27% attend small local churches (all Pentecostal or neo-pentecostal) or have no church affiliation. These women have multiple identities, including being mothers, daughters, evangelical, landless, black, brown, white, movement leaders and leaders in faith communities. Their bodies are spaces of creative power and new opportunities, bodies that experience the world and are part of it.

For Rubem Alves, the body is the cornerstone of all things, as it is through our bodies that we experience and are impacted by the world. Alves often poses the question, 'Is the body not the absolute center of everything, the sun around which our world revolves?' (Alves, 1985). The theologian Ivone Gebara answers this by stating that the body is 'the center of all relationships, the starting point of all problems and the solution to which all solutions tend to converge' (Gebara, 2016, p. 90). Feminist biblical hermeneutics begins with the body, one that is intertwined with daily life and finds the sacred in the everyday:

> Feminist theology always begins with lived experiences in the present. This leads to a rejection of abstract language in relation to life and the things that deeply impact human relationships. As a result, there is a growing effort to 'deconstruct' traditional theological concepts to uncover the underlying vital realities they represent. Vital realities are the

starting point for a more structured theological exploration. (Gebara, 1986, p. 11)

According to Gebara, women's theological work involves reclaiming existential realities and giving them a voice. It starts with life and reality and then connects it with any existing tradition. The purpose of a feminist liberation biblical interpretation is to search for and uncover stories and memories of women within their socio-historical context. According to Ivoni Richter Reimer, there are important considerations for a Latin American feminist interpretation of the Bible:

(i) Critique androcentric-patriarchal discourse and norms regarding the roles of minority groups;
(ii) Examine the historical impact of the text on the formation of our identities and relationships;
(iii) Break the silence surrounding experiences of oppression and liberation/resistance in gender relations;
(iv) Recognize that sacred texts are reflections of faith lived in specific historical-cultural contexts;
(v) Discover and reconstruct images of God that aid in the process of deconstruction and reconstruction. (Reimer, 2010, pp. 45–6)

One aspect of Latin American feminist theology is that it is not limited to academic circles but rather is rooted in the lived experiences of people of faith. What does the Bible mean for an evangelical Pentecostal woman within a social and popular movement fighting for land rights? Here are some responses from our interviewees:

> I turn to the Bible and pray if I have any doubts. I used to do this before making any decision. Joyce invited me to participate in the meeting, but I sought guidance from the Word of God. I prayed and asked the Lord if it was meant for me to attend. I used to be part of a cult and was in a worship service when the Holy Spirit spoke to me, telling me that I was free to choose what He had decided. This is how I was allowed to come. Everyone interprets it differently. (Luzia, Assemblies of God, São Paulo)

> I have been studying about the MST, Che Guevara, Paulo Freire, and various other books to gain a deeper understanding. Although I read several books, the Bible is the one I read the most. Reading the Bible is

different from reading books about the MST. While the MST focuses on the rights of workers, the Bible deals with more spiritual matters related to God. (Elisangela, Assemblies of God, Goiás)

The hermeneutics, or interpretation, of the women interviewed is focused on practical, everyday issues rather than dogmatic aspects, while still demonstrating a strong spiritual connection to the Bible. The questions they raise blend their religious beliefs with their activism, with one member of the movement seeing the Bible as supporting the fight for land rights. This member, Rosana, says she has learned from both the Bible and the movement to not accept everything, but instead to fight for what is right. She shares this perspective with other members of the movement:

We are fighting to conquer the lot. And I believe that, in the name of Jesus, we will succeed, because if God spoke, it's spoken. In one assembly, I told the people, I will only leave here when God says it's time for me to leave, because I think when God determined something, it's not for us to fail, it's for us to have hope. This time we are going through now is a time already predicted in many prophecies, so, within the Church, it's not just me speaking, but many other prophecies, that there would be a very big change and people can't grasp that, but within that I believe it's being a learning experience for all of us today and when this changes, many doors will open, you know? Many good things will happen. (Rosana, Assemblies of God, Santa Catarina)

The evangelical women interviewed bring the word 'struggle' into their vocabulary. And with this word, they dance in their biblical interpretations, finding in the text of thousands of years ago, with countless marks of physical and symbolic violence against women, the silenced voices of women in the biblical context, women who possibly also had the word 'struggle' in their daily lives. This identification is almost immediate, and it is what further promotes the taste and empowerment of these women through faith, because the rescue of 'the history of women' includes rescuing the 'history of women's oppression by men' as well as 'the historical act of women and their struggles against subordination and oppression' (Santos, 2010, p. 40).

'The LAND is the LORD's and the fullness thereof': *terra* is biblical

The struggle for land remains a unifying banner that more directly and unquestionably links faith and struggle for the women we interviewed, unlike more complicated and disputed issues with conflicting and negotiated narratives, such as gender or sexuality. Progressive sections of the Catholic and Protestant Churches have been part of the history of the struggle for land and the birth of the MST, as we discussed in the first part of our text. Within the MST, Rosa Maria, a black woman and an evangelical from the Assemblies of God, understands the land as a fundamental space for the production and reproduction of the lives of workers, as well as for their liberation: 'Land is not to enslave anyone, it is to free! There must be freedom to work, to be happy, to create a family, to see one's children grow, to become what they want to be'. She continues:

> I always sought God's guidance on the land issue. Because there was already a struggle for land at that time, and I found in the Bible that the political issue was already present. In their era, in the time of the Romans, everything was a political matter in order to survive. But now, it continues, even in our present day. So I searched for this question about the land, and I knew that what we were doing was right. I found the answer in the Bible, and there it is! (Rosa Maria, Assemblies of God, São Paulo)

The most quoted sacred text in the interviews concerns the Land. A psalm. A prayer that carries within it the feelings of the daily life of the people of God. The liberation biblist Milton Schwantes said that, 'Psalms are not just prayers, they are also wise and practical guides for life'. The most cited psalm among our interviewees is Psalm 24.1 – 'The earth is the LORD's, and the fulness thereof; the world, and they that dwell therein.' In Portuguese this verse is: *Do SENHOR é a **terra** e a sua plenitude, o mundo e aqueles que nele habitam.*

Psalm 24 is a text attributed to David and is a unique liturgical text. Schwantes points out four parts in its structure, which structurally resemble other psalms in the biblical text, but Psalm 24 has its own peculiarities. The text cited by the evangelical women of the MST has a poetics inspired by the Jerusalem sanctuary, which breathes a Jerusalem theology and liturgy, with examples of terms such as 'Yahweh's mountain', 'blessing', 'the king of glory' among others. The responsorial liturgy contained in

Psalm 24 connects to the 'festive liturgical ceremony of the procession of the Ark in front of the gates of the temple courtyard' (Schwantes, 1982, p. 298), especially in verses 3–6. We will not focus on the entire psalm, but on verses 1–2, most cited in the interviews conducted.

The opening verses of this hymn point to a creator YHWH, not a God of history; the verses celebrate a liturgy of the God of Creation. The first verse, which was on the lips of our interviewees, is commonly understood as an affirmation of God's lordship over the Earth, a God-owner, owner of everything and everyone. But it is worth going to the text, as Schwantes points out that the most accurate translation/interpretation would not be of a God who claims possession, but rather one who directs: 'The statement that heads our psalm does not so much emphasize ownership, but rather the direction of the earth to God. It is land of belonging to the extent that it is turned to him in praise (Schwantes, 1982, pp. 292–3).

However, for the interviewed women this verse is about a possessive God, a creator God who created the earth and everything in it, and therefore is the owner of all things. This interpretation sets this understanding of a powerful God against those who claim to be the owners/proprietors of the land, who commercialize and exploit the land:

> I believe that God helped me, through MST, to conquer my land. Because the land is biblical. And God says this, it is ... Psalm 24: the earth and all its fullness belongs to the Lord, and the Lord gives the land to those who fight. God gives the land to those who are fighting. Now the state and capital are the ones who have tangled everything up. ... Then they think we want land to sell and spend the money. The land is for survival, to plant food for the family. (Rosa Maria, Assemblies of God, São Paulo)

To better understand this dimension of the earth/*terra*, we need to understand that *terra* in Portuguese is not just land. *Terra* is a simultaneous and multiple word, as Nancy Cardoso (2019c) puts it: 'For us, *Terra* is at the same time: *terra, terra, terra*.'

- *Terra* is where we cultivate crops and harvest fruits, where water flows and the forest grows along with animals, flowers, and birds. It is the ground we walk on, it is the dust from which we will return. It is where daily life, art and creation arise.
- *Terra* is the name of our planet, the pale blue dot in the middle of the universe, where all living beings live, where gases, water cycles and minerals reside.

Cardoso points out that from the Latin American perspective, *Pacha-Mama/MadreTierra* is a simultaneity of cosmic earth and daily earth.

The understanding that *terra* and its fullness belongs to God goes beyond the earth world for the women interviewed: it encompasses the planet earth and its creation, but it is the *terra* of soil cultivation, the earth that feeds its children. Recovering what belongs to the working people appears in the mysticism and concrete needs of our people; faith and struggle are almost umbilically joined on the path of agrarian and urban reform, which is today the task of the countryside and the city, and for many women a divine task. For the evangelical women of the MST, the struggle for the land is not something material but spiritual, as comrade Rosa Maria points out:

> That's why I tell you, there is a land struggle, it's not just a material struggle, it's a spiritual struggle. Because it has been since the time of the Lord, and this struggle does not end. It will be a constant struggle. Let's suppose, even if that government doesn't release those lands now, but a government that can understand and release the land will come in, because it's biblical! The struggle for land! Because there have already been those biblical struggles, I mean it like this: people who struggled to conquer their lands, and today we continue the struggle to conquer more land, our land. (Rosa Maria, Assemblies of God, São Paulo)

The interviewees, even though they attend traditionalist churches that use fundamentalist language, find, or rather rediscover, a popular faith and religiosity that seeks a dignified life. For them, this God is not far away but close, a complicit God who is by their side in the struggle. The common understanding among women of the verse from Psalm 24 is that the earth is from God, not from the owners or capital but rather God gave it to the people! Maria das Graças points out:

> The struggle for land is good because God didn't leave the land to the landowners, to the president, when he made the world, he left the land for us to plant and harvest, so it wasn't for them to take control and leave us without, so this part, we are right, the people who are fighting are right, they are wrong because they take control of all the lands, how will the poor work? He had to work, he has to feed his children, he has to take care of the land, not let everything be destroyed. How are we going to live from now on without water, without land, without anything? Our time is here, Jesus is coming, it's a lesson he gives us every

day, he gives us a sign every day, it's just a matter of believing in our eternal father. (Maria das Graças, Assemblies of God, Maranhão)

The evangelical women of the MST are creating their own views about faith and political struggle, often through mytho-religious language, seeking biblical solutions to everyday problems. When we talk to the women interviewed, we find not only participants in the MST but militants, leaders, educators, women engaged not only in small churches and their ministries but also with concrete tasks and articulating the MST's struggle in their territories.

From this journey, we observe in the women's reflections visions of how faith is a matter of the earth, how faith and reading the Bible are an inspiration for the struggle for land. When women act, whether in the Church or in MST, things change, they take on different rhythms, different textures. Helena, from the Assemblies of God and camping in Goiás, says: 'I think, like this, that the person is in faith for a purpose, which is Agrarian Reform to have their land, so that each one has their piece of land. And I think that including this together with faith is easier to achieve' (Helena, Assemblies of God, Goiás).

Final considerations

The MST is a large and influential popular movement in Brazil working towards social justice and access to land, food and other resources. The struggle for land is intertwined with the development of Liberation Theology, a religious movement that emerged in response to growing social inequalities in Latin America. The Pastoral Land Commission, established in 1975, also advocates for the rights of the poor and inspired the MST's actions through a political and popular interpretation of the Bible, based on principles of justice, love and freedom.

Christianity is the dominant religion in Brazil, with Catholicism on the decline and Protestantism, specifically Pentecostalism, growing. A recent survey showed that the face of evangelicalism in Brazil is that of a poor woman, of whom a significant portion identify as black or brown. Although Christianity has been used as a tool of oppression against women, many women find comfort and support in their faith to cope with life's difficulties. The strongest sign of fundamentalism in Latin America is anti-gender and anti-sexuality, with a moral defence based on a fundamentalist reading of the Bible impacting the executive and judicial branches of power. Fundamentalism has a significant impact on the daily life of the urban and rural working class and is the subject of ongoing research and resistance.

Brazil has a long history of land concentration and exploitation, dating back to colonialism. This legacy has had negative consequences for the poor working class, leading to continued social inequality and structural racism. The expansion of agribusiness has resulted in the exploitation of rural workers and the destruction of the environment. The majority of food in Brazil is produced by small-scale family farmers, with women playing a crucial role. Agrarian reform is necessary to address the current situation, but it must also be linked to a new model of gender relations and traditional knowledge. Women, who embody an economy of life, must play a significant role in the transformation of the way life is produced and reproduced.

The women interviewed have multiple identities and see their bodies as spaces of creative power. Feminist theology begins with lived experiences, leading to a rejection of abstract language and the uncovering of vital realities, as seen in the work of Ivone Gebara. Latin American feminist theology is rooted in the lived experiences of people of faith and focuses on critique of androcentric-patriarchal norms and the examination of the historical impact of texts. The women interviewed blend their religious beliefs with activism and focus on practical, everyday issues in their interpretation of the Bible. They bring the word 'struggle' into their vocabulary and find in the text support for their fight for land rights.

The struggle for land is a key issue that connects faith and struggle for the women interviewed in this study. They see the land as a crucial space for the liberation and survival of workers. The most quoted text among the interviewees is Psalm 24.1, which affirms that the earth belongs to God and is not just a matter of possession but also of direction. The interviewed women understand God as a powerful and possessive creator who gives land to those who fight for it. For them, *terra* is a multi-faceted term encompassing daily life, art, creation and the environment. They see the struggle for land as a fight against those who exploit and commercialize it.

The MST is the result of rural workers who, expelled from their lands, organized themselves to build a movement that would guarantee not only their rights but also their dignity. These workers bring not only the peasant identity in their stories but their faith also. With the changes and religious transitions in our country, currently many MST base militants are Evangelicals. The women interviewed were able to show how much faith and struggle are connected in their identities, although not free from contradictions. These two small words – faith and struggle – walk together, hand in hand, cross and feed back into an effort to transform not only their lives but all of society.

Notes

1 English translation: 'Getting to know God is getting to know the *terra* (earth/land).'
2 Available at https://www1.folha.uol.com.br/poder/2020/01/cara-tipica-do-evangelico-brasileiro-e-feminina-e-negra-aponta-datafolha.shtml (accessed 16.01.2023).

References

Alves, Rubem, 1985, *Variações sobre a Vida e a Morte: o feitiço erótico-erótico da teologia*, 2nd edn, São Paulo: Ed. Paulinas.
Cardoso, Nancy, 2017, *Duas. Uma. Nenhuma mulher?!* CEBI: https://cebi.org.br/noticias/duas-uma-nenhuma-mulher-nancy-cardoso/ (accessed 07.02.2023).
———, 2019a, 'A América Latina feminista que queremos não será possível sem as mulheres pobres, que hoje encontram refúgio na religião', http://www.ihu.unisinos.br/78-noticias/591255-a-america-latina-feminista-que-queremos-nao-sera-possivel-sem-as-mulheres-pobres-que-hoje-encontram-refugio-na-religiao-avalia-a-teologa-nancy-cardoso (accessed 04.09.2020).
———, 2019b, 'Conhecer os desejos da terra profecias de Gomer no livro de Oséias', *Ribla* 80.2, pp. 125–44.
———, 2019c, 'Pachamama corpo e território: ancestralidades ressurgidas, reinventadas e rebeldes', in Márcia Alves da Silva, Graziela Rinaldi da Rosa, *Pedagogias populares e epistemologias feministas latino-americanas*, Curitiba: Editora Brazil.
Cunha, Magali do Nascimento, 2020, 'Fundamentalisms, the crisis of democracy and the threat to human rights in South America: trends and challenges for action', Salvador: Koinonia, https://kn.org.br/wp-content/uploads/2020/10/FundamentalismsIN.pdf (accessed 02.04.2024).
Datafolha, 2020, 'A cara típica do evangélico brasileiro é feminina e negra', https://www1.folha.uol.com.br/poder/2020/01/cara-tipica-do-evangelico-brasileiro-e-feminina-e-negra-aponta-datafolha.shtml (accessed 20.09.2020).
De Souza, Sandra Duarte, 2007, 'Violência de gênero e religião: alguns questionamentos que podem orientar a discussão sobre a elaboração de políticas públicas', *Mandrágora* 13.13, pp. 15–21.
Gebara, Ivone, 1986, 'A Mulher Faz Teologia – Um ensaio para Reflexão', *Revista Eclesiástica Brasileira. Petrópolis* 46, pp. 5–14.
———, 2016, 'Corpo, novo ponto de partida da teologia', in Cláudio Ribeiro (ed), *Rasgando o Verbo: Teologia Feminista em foco*, São Paulo: Fonte Editorial.

———, and Maria José Rosado-Nunes, 2006, 'Teologia feminista e a crítica da razão religiosa patriarcal: entrevista com Ivone Gebara', *Revista Estudos Feministas* 14.1, pp. 294–304.

Hadich, Ceres, 2021, 'As Mulheres e a Agroecologia. Disponível em', https://mst.org.br/2021/10/08/as-mulheres-e-a-agroecologia/ (accessed 23.01.2023).

Instito Brasileiro de Geografia e Estatística (IBGE), *Censo Agropecuário 2017*, https://www.ibge.gov.br/estatisticas/economicas/agricultura-e-pecuaria/21814-2017-censo-agropecuario.html?=&t=resultados (accessed 23.01.2023).

Instituto Tricontinental de Pesquisa Social, 2020, 'Dossiê 27 – Reforma Agrária Popular e a luta pela terra no Brasil' (06 de Abril de 2020), https://www.thetricontinental.org/pt-pt/dossie-27-terra/ (accessed 15.03.2021).

———, 2022, 'Dossier 59 – Religious Fundamentalism and Imperialism in Latin America: Action and Resistance', https://thetricontinental.org/wp-content/uploads/2022/12/20221213_D59_EN_Web.pdf (accessed 02.04.2024).

Machado, Maria das Dores Campos and Joanildo Burity, 2014, 'A Ascensão Política dos Pentecostais no Brasil na Avaliação de Líderes Religiosos', *Dados, Rio de Janeiro* 57.3, pp. 601–31.

Pierucci, Antônio Flávio, 1997, 'Reencantamento e dessecularização: a propósito do auto-engano em sociologia da religião', *Novos Estudos Cebrap* 49, pp. 99–117.

Reimer, Ivoni Richter, 2010, 'Para memora delas! Textos e interpretações na (re)construção de cristianismos originários', *Revistas Estudos Teológicos São Leopoldo* 50.1, pp. 41–53.

Santos, Odja Barros, 2010, *Uma hermenêutica bíblica popular e feminista na perspectiva da mulher nordestina: um relato de experiência*, Dissertação de mestrado, Faculdades EST.

Schwantes, Milton, 1982, 'Salmo 24: uma liturgia singula', *Estudos Teológicos* 22.3, pp. 283–304.

5

'Seh Yuh Sorry!': Jamaica Talks Back to the British Empire

ANNA KASAFI PERKINS

When this chapter was conceptualized, the Queen of England was celebrating her Platinum Jubilee to much global acclaim; she was being represented across the realm by younger royals such as Prince William and Kate Middleton, the Duke and Duchess of Windsor, on a so-called 'Charm Tour'. By the time this fuller narrative was penned a lot had happened – Queen Elizabeth II, the longest-reigning monarch in British history, had died.[1] The reins had passed to King Charles III and Queen Consort Camilla. William was elevated to Prince of Wales, first in line to the throne. Harry and Meghan had renounced royal duties and were living abroad. The world was all abuzz, questioning what all that meant, especially for constitutional monarchies like Jamaica for whom the British monarch remained head of state. Of much consequence was Barbados, which, four months earlier, had renounced the monarchy, becoming the world's newest republic, even as they remained in the British-led Commonwealth.

Charles and Camilla's coronation in May 2023 added an urgent dimension to my critique of the March 2022 visit of the royals to Jamaica. I deploy the idea of emancipation, which according to the Antiguan theologian Kortright Davis (2008) is the Caribbean word for 'liberation', to question the meaning and impact of the visit. My critique foregrounds the idea of asking for forgiveness and its socio-political expression via a call for an apology and reparations, using the tagline of the local protests led by a Jamaican group, the Advocates Network (AN) – 'Seh Yuh Sorry!' (Say you are sorry!). It weaves into the conversation relevant visual representations, including the AN poster – depicting a sign tied to the gates of Buckingham Palace – as well as descriptions of various images of the royal visit and resulting protests. Poetic responses also add texture to the discussion.

In so doing, I argue that liberation-emancipation remains a contemporary 'already-not yet', which cannot be ignored in religious spaces in the Caribbean. At the same time, I maintain the importance of engaging theological and religious reflection on the ideas and discussions of social movements, even those that consider theology and religion a large part of the problem (Boodoo, 2019). This is but a small contribution to the theological enterprise in the Caribbean, which is 'a postcolonial and decolonial discourse ... chiefly concerned with a new theological paradigm grounded in the Caribbean landscape towards the radical transformation and liberation of Caribbean societies and the betterment of Caribbean people' (Joseph, 2018, p. 3). I conclude that Caribbean theology has not sufficiently wrestled with the question of forgiveness in its socio-political dimension (Perkins, 1996), much less the concreteness of reparations (James, 2017).

A brief background

When the then Duke and Duchess of Windsor landed in Kingston, Jamaica, in March 2022, as part of that now infamous 70th anniversary celebratory tour across the Caribbean, they were met with full-throated opposition and protests from a wider cross-section of Jamaican society than normal. This time the usual suspects, members of the Rastafarian community, who vehemently oppose the British monarchy, were joined by Jamaicans from all walks of life (see https://www.facebook.com/Advocatesnetworkja/). Protests against the 'Charm Tour' had started in Belize, where the Royals first touched down in the region (Sanchez, 2022). After Jamaica, they toured the Bahamas, where they were also met with protests and calls for reparations. Indeed, across the Caribbean, people voiced their rejection of the Royals loudly and clearly. For example, the head of the Ethiopia Africa Black International Congress, a Rastafari mansion in the Bahamas, The Most Right Honourable High Priest Rithmond McKinney, penned a letter to the Royals ahead of their visit, in which he declaimed, 'Our system is based upon Westminster's style of government; it seems this country is not serious about our liberation – we say we're an independent nation but swearing allegiance to the monarchy. It's a lie!' (in White, 2022a).

Similarly, Priest Marcus of the House of Rastafari in the Bahamas protested, 'Bahamas is still under colonial rule and the Westminster system but we, as Rastas, don't serve the system or the Queen. We can never forget slavery or the atrocities done to my people from the royal family ... We're looking forward to an official apology and reparations – many Bahamians feel the same way. 400 years of slavery can't be forgotten easily just like that; the damage has to be repaired' (in White, 2022b). Calls for reparations were vehement: 'They hunted us down, they kidnapped us, they stole us, they worked us. They owe us and they must now pay us' (Jomo Thomas, a former chair of the St Vincent and the Grenadines National Reparations Committee, in Chance and Das, 2022).

Not only did the visit cause offence but so did activities during the visit. William and Kate's visit to a cacao farm in Belize was scuttled because they had not obtained permission to land their helicopter on communal lands of the Maya Village, Indian Creek, and there were already tensions with Flora and Fauna International (FFI), a conservation group that lists Prince William as a patron, concerning encroachment on the land (Sanchez, 2022). In Jamaica, they were allowed to beat Nyabinghi drums on a visit to Trench Town, the inner-city community renowned for fostering Bob Marley's prodigious talent. The Trench Town Culture Yard had been developed as a significant tourism product, attracting visitors from all over the world. Showing off the Rastafari drumming tradition was particularly fraught in this instance given that White Royals were beating the very instruments of their doom. This drew much condemnation from the Rastafari community as far as the Bahamas. High Priest McKinney spoke out indignantly:

> Watching Prince William & Kate playing Nyabinghi drums in Trench Town, Jamaica was a slap in our face as Rastafarians of the Bobo Shanti House. ... There's no way they're supposed to be beating Nyabinghi drums which is part of our defence as Black people. ... You can't say Nyabinghi against the world of Babylon then you get the Babylon people, who represent white supremacy, beating our drums. That's our tool. (White, 2022a)

The contradictions inherent in the secularization and commodification of Rastafari, especially as a tourist product, was at the root of this misstep.

A month later, William and Kate were followed by other Royals – the Wessexes, Prince Edward and Duchess Sophie – who were as tone deaf in their interactions with Caribbean people. The Wessexes were condemned for their gift of a photo of themselves to the PM of St Lucia. 'Some commentators have condemned the Wessexes' gesture as "narcissistic," "tone-deaf" and "insulting" with claims that their present would "make a lovely ash tray"' (White, 2022a). The PM's expression showed he was less than impressed with the gift. Edward and Sophie visited only St Lucia, St Vincent and the Grenadines, and Antigua and Barbuda,[2] having been forced to make a last-minute cancellation of their visit to Grenada, due to protests.[3] The Prime Minister of Antigua and Barbuda indicated that they would one day seek republican status, although it was not currently a priority. He, however, asked the Wessexes to use their influence to obtain 'restorative justice' for the people of Antigua and Barbuda, whose ancestors suffered under slavery. Furthermore, PM Brown said:

> They [the British] left us and deprived us of modern institutions, such as universities and medical facilities, said Brown about the European country's departure from the region without having first built the basic infrastructure. (Braga, 2022)

His words echoed much of what had been said by protestors in Jamaica.

The Jamaica tour

In Jamaica, protesters demanded not only an apology for the horrors of the transatlantic trade of Africans, but reparations. Many among these were members of a group known as the Advocates Network (AN), a group that emerged in April 2021 in response to the alleged physical abuse of his female partner by a sitting member of parliament MP captured on widely circulated video. Insisting that 'Wi Nah Ease Up!' (We Won't Ease Up), the AN has persisted in demanding higher standards of behaviour from Jamaica's elected officials and other leaders in the society. The group acknowledges the underlying structural issues of inequality, injustice, discrimination, abuse and violence that continue to shape Jamaican society. These and other issues have persisted from our history of slavery/colonization and contribute to human rights abuse and poor governance in Jamaica today. AN is committed to addressing these structural legacies of inequality and other human rights abuses that were exacerbated during and linger after the Covid pandemic.

Seh sorry!

The Advocates Network designed a campaign around the words 'Seh yuh sorry!' (Jamaican for 'Say you're sorry!' and 'Apologize!'), emblazoned on an evocative poster, which was shared widely on social media, along with press releases and other tools of communication. They generated a groundswell of response and reflection from persons across the Jamaican society, some of whom did not necessarily agree with their demands. Among the various activities of the campaign was an open letter to the Royals noting the coincidence of the Queen's 70th Anniversary and the 60th Anniversary of Jamaica's Independence from Britain, which was signed by over one hundred persons.[4]

In that letter, the Advocates Network charged that the Queen had done nothing to redress or atone for the suffering of our ancestors that took place during her reign or during the entire period of British trafficking in Africans, enslavement, indentureship and colonization. The letter was accompanied by 60 Reasons for Britain and the Royals to apologize and pay reparations to the Jamaican people (McGowan, 2022).[5] The 60 reasons were carefully chosen, one for each year of independence from British rule; independence which is in many ways meaningless with the Queen (as she was then) – represented by a Governor General – as the island's head of state.

On the day the official visit began, dozens of protesters gathered in front of the British High Commission in Kingston demanding not only an apology for the horrors of the transatlantic slave trade, but reparations. The signage at the protest bore the words of the campaign tagline or variations thereof: 'Apologise and Pay Reparations'; 'Reparations Due'; 'Apologise now!' One girl child held up a placard stating, 'Kings and Queens belong in fairytales not in Jamaica!' Protesters used loudspeakers to read the '60 Reasons' over and over, eventually presenting a copy of the letter to a representative of the British High Commission. The Advocates Network made their case on numerous local and international media and via social media efforts. There were also discussions with protestors from Belize to the Bahamas as solidarity in the commonality of cause was expressed. As Roselea Hamilton, one of the founders of the AN, argued, '[A]n apology is the best Jubilee gift that the Queen can give us. It's the first step in a long process of reparatory justice' (*Jamaica Gleaner*, 2022a).

Despite this, in a formal speech at the state dinner given in their honour, Prince William said, among other fatuous things: 'I strongly agree with my father, The Prince of Wales, who said in Barbados last year [2021] that the appalling atrocity of slavery forever stains our history. I want to express my profound sorrow. Slavery was abhorrent. And it should never have happened. While the pain runs deep, Jamaica continues to forge its future with determination, courage and fortitude' (*Jamaica Gleaner*, 2022a).

His words, which referenced those of his father King Charles at Barbados' official republican ceremony, caused much affront and continue to echo. The Jamaican Roman Catholic theologian and priest Donald Chambers penned a response to the visit in his blog (Chambers, 2022). It reads in part:

> No apologies.
> No reparation.
> No remorse.
> Only diplomatic smiles, charm, and words ...
> Protest.
> Advocacy.
> Challenge.
> Rebellion.
> Dialogue.
> Prayer.
> These are the new oceans pounding, persevering, and persisting against the stubborn and hard heart of post-modern European imperialism disguised,
> Even in non-European fashion.[6]

Chambers alerts us to the imperial agenda disguised in the charm offensive and the vociferous response of the Jamaican people, ranging from protest to advocacy to prayer. So too does the persona in the Dominican poet Celia Sorhaindo's poem call out those 'herds of elephant ghosts', who are terrified by what are arguably no longer 'reparation whispers', having exploited the nations and peoples of the region for the benefit of colonizers/abusers/elephant ghosts:

> Now waking our abusers with death rattle
> reparation whispers; we are terrifying
> herds of elephant ghosts, tormenting
> the dreams of our colonisers,
> who played ping-pong with countries,
> and traded us, their bastard babies, for
> dollar bills and bases. (Sorhaindo, 2018)

Arguably, the tenets of diplomacy circumscribed the Prince's response. Major-Campbell (2022b) maintains that the response 'actually says, "Your ancestors are not deserving of an apology, you are not worthy of an apology, and you are not even intelligent enough to understand what this statement is doing."' Such expressions of regret do not acknowledge culpability and are a sign of refusal to take responsibility. 'The lack of remorse and a formal apology is an insult to the Caricom Reparatory Justice Programme. Who knew that we would have gotten a response that is so crude?' (Major-Campbell, 2022b). Yet a political system and political leadership must come to terms 'with the legacy of hurt which it has engendered and which it has inherited' (Perkins, 1996, p. 50). The Royals have been the beneficiaries of their ancestors' trade in African bodies, 'their bastard babies, for dollar bills and bases'. While they do not inherit guilt for the sins of their ancestors, they inherit a debt (Perkins, 1996).

The Advocates Network continue to press the Jamaican government for a timeline for the referendum on becoming a republic, which the Prime Minister promised in his response to the Prince: 'We're moving on and we intend to attain in short order ... to fulfil our true ambitions as an independent, developed and prosperous country' (*Jamaica Gleaner*, 2022b). This would be part of the way to emancipation-liberation, which Barbados recently undertook.

Emancipation-liberation in Caribbean theology

Emancipation-liberation and decolonization are two interrelated imperatives that thread through Caribbean theology, as is evident in the work of people like Idris Hamid, Noel Erskine and Kortright Davis (2008). Indeed, the imperative to decolonize Caribbean life and emancipate Caribbean people from neocolonialism is central to Caribbean theological discourse (Joseph, 2018). Davis (2008), who is noted for the claim that 'emancipation is the Caribbean word for liberation', maintains that the emancipatory imperative calls for action within the theological sphere. Theological self-reliance, rejecting dependence on and imitation of theologies from the metropoles, is central to this call. Theological paradigms in the Caribbean must draw on local sources such as Caribbean folk wisdom and cultural world views. It should draw on Caribbean poetics and philosophies such as those expressed by Chambers and the persona in Sorhaindo's poem. The spiritual energies and cultural powers of indigenous and Afro-Caribbean religions such as Rastafari and

Spiritual Baptists should be drawn upon. Furthermore, this theological enterprise needs to be very practically focused to respond effectively to the needs of Caribbean people, including their 'economic life, political distresses, and socio-historical circumstances' (Joseph, 2018, p. 11). This should lead to praxis that contributes to a life shaped by anti- and decolonial practices as the work of Advocates Network prioritizes.

The lives of ordinary people, especially the poor and vulnerable, are to be central to this theologizing. Importantly, Davis called for women to be allowed full participation in the ecclesial, educational and theological enterprise. True emancipation requires a process of decolonization to remove the yoke of dependence and cultural and theological imperialism. Importantly, the Churches need to be fully engaged in regional developmental efforts and efforts to reclaim political sovereignty, cultural renewal, economic independence and Caribbean unity (Joseph, 2018).

No engagement with reparations

Such calls for emancipation and decolonization, however, tend to be localized and do not contemplate the kind of engagement towards reparation, which has become part of more recent human rights discourse in the Caribbean, as the response to the Royals' visit demonstrated. Indeed, such reparation discourse is a miniscule and very recent thread among Caribbean theologians and churches, perhaps because of how implicated they were in enslavement and colonization. Even Davis, who is perhaps best known for his classic theological reflection, *Emancipation Still Comin'*, does not call for reparations in so many words even as he is clear about the need for repair.

The Grenadian Baptist pastor Vonnie James (2017) is an exception; he attempts to craft a reparations theology, making the biblical case drawing on Numbers 5.5–7. James calls out the lack of reparations theology in the region, where the Church is to be a prophetic voice, but has remained suspiciously silent on this pressing issue. James makes the biblical case to support the work of the Caribbean Reparations Commission. According to James, biblical and theological responsibility begins first with public acknowledgement of the wrong committed, followed by full restitution plus one fifth. At the same time, James is critical of statements of sorrow (such as the one made by Prince William). Such statements are condemned from a theological perspective, since refusing to take responsibility for and make reparations for transatlantic trade is not only 'unethical, immoral, illegal and irresponsible, but more so it is an affront on the very image of God' in whose image all are made (James, 2017). Furthermore, James denounces such a statement as 'an affront to the very [biblical] foundation' that these colonial nations claim to believe in and build on. Most importantly, he denounces the perspective as corporate sin and biblical distortion.

Garnett Roper, a Jamaican evangelical theologian, would argue in this regard that the Church has failed to fully develop Caribbean theology as a public theology operating in the public sphere to bring God's grace, power and wisdom in working for justice and equality 'in a manner that seeks to approximate the eschatological ideal' (Roper, 2012, p. 172). Approximating the 'eschatological ideal' – the already-not-yet dimension of our existence – requires the Church to engage in advocacy and protest, especially on behalf of the vulnerable. The Church is called upon to collaborate with others to advocate and protest. This is especially important as the Church can bring important insights into the meaning of apology-forgiveness-emancipation. Indeed, that forgiveness can and must take shape within the political sphere.

In addition, the work of individual pastors and theologians such as Sean Major-Campbell, Anglican priest, social justice advocate and member of the Advocates Network, in his public calls for an apology from the Royals for their family's history of enslavement, is an example of such advocacy. Major-Campbell makes his claims in the public square often based on human rights without any explicit grounding in the theological, perhaps given his awareness of the many interlocutors who consider the Church a large part of the problem and, therefore, not able to genuinely contribute to the solution (Boodoo, 2019).

In a newspaper article on forgiveness, Major-Campbell is forthright about ways of understanding forgiveness supported by the actions of the Church that may be damaging to persons and the process. Regarding reparations, he questions, 'Might perfunctory forgiveness be an opiate to silence the descendants of the transatlantic slave trade, the victims of white supremacy and racism, and the calls for reparatory justice?' He suggests, therefore, that to avoid this, '[f]orgiveness with its theological import must, therefore, be subjected to the lens of human rights concerns and the process of psychological engagement' (Major-Campbell, 2022a).

Conclusion

It is unsurprising that the clamour for reparations and republican status from Jamaica and other constitutional monarchies has grown louder since the Queen's death. Arguably, the passing of Queen Elizabeth II resurfaces the concerns with her role as monarch working to present a benign face to the Empire and the missed opportunities for apology and repair. The advocacy of groups such as the Advocates Network in our call on the British Monarchy to 'Seh Sorry' continues to be amplified in the local, regional, and international media; the commitment to reparations and republican status has not eased but has grown in momentum.

Nor has the moment for theological reflection on apology and reparations passed. It has likewise deepened. Indeed, 'the modern Church' (should) have a keen interest in restorative justice. In this regard, 'the cause for reparation and restorative justice must form a wholesome part of religious teaching' (Roberts, 2018). Therefore, as the Jamaica Bicentenary Committee argues, 'sorry is never enough' as an apology calls for concrete reparatory action (Shepherd et al., 2012, p. 97), for regional development and efforts to reclaim political sovereignty, cultural renewal, economic independence and Caribbean unity, in which the Churches need to be fully engaged.

Notes

1 Elizabeth II died at 15:10 BST on Thursday 8 September 2022; she reigned for 70 years, having acceded to the throne in 1952.

2 Reports are that Antigua and Barbuda was the only country where there were no protests.

3 Protests were also held outside of the Caribbean. Toronto residents with ties to the Caribbean, for example, sympathized with the protests. 'One hundred individuals and organizations issued an open letter demanding that Britain apologize and award reparations to its former colony for forcing hundreds of thousands of slaves to toil in dire conditions' (https://www.cbc.ca/news/canada/toronto/toronto-residents-support-protests-british-monarchy-jamaica-1.6395646, accessed 03.04.2024).

4 The full letter is available online: https://our.today/advocates-network-dear-william-and-kate-why-not-just-say-you-are-sorry/ (accessed 03.04.2024).

5 The 60 reasons are available online: https://petchary.wordpress.com/2022/03/21/60-reasons-for-apologies-and-reparations-from-britain-and-the-royal-family/ (accessed 03.04.2024).

6 I thank Fr Don for his powerful words and permission to share them.

References

Boodoo, Gerald, 2019, 'Spaces of Possibility: Contributions of Local Theologies', *CTSA Proceedings* 74, pp. 46–61.

Braga, Bruno, 2022, 'The Earl And Countess of Wessex Received With Protest During Royal Trip to The Caribbean Region', *Travelnoire*, 27 April, https://travelnoire.com/the-earl-and-countess-of-wessex-received-with-protests-during-the-royal-trip-to-the-caribbean-region (accessed 03.04.2024).

Chambers, Donald, 2022, 'Reflection on the Visit to the Caribbean of the Descendants of the English Oppressors – William and Kate', Blog (26 March).

Chance, Kenton, and Shanti Das, 2022, 'Slavery protesters target royal tour in St Vincent', *The Guardian* (23 April), https://www.theguardian.com/world/2022/apr/23/slavery-protesters-target-royal-tour-in-st-vincent (accessed 03.04.2024).

Davis, Kortright, 2008, *Emancipation Still Comin': Explorations in Caribbean Emancipatory Theology*, Eugene, OR: Wipf & Stock.

Deyoung, Kevin, 2021, 'Reparations: A Critical Theological Review', *The Critical Gospel Review* (April), https://www.thegospelcoalition.org/blogs/kevin-deyoung/reparations-a-critical-theological-review/ (accessed 03.04.2024).

Jamaica Gleaner, 2022a, 'Advocacy and reparation, conversation with Rosalea Hamilton', *Sunday Gleaner* (12 June), https://jamaica-gleaner.com/article/focus/20220612/advocacy-and-reparation-conversation-rosalea-hamilton (accessed 03.04.2024).

Jamaica Gleaner, 2022b, 'We're moving on ... Holness says Jamaica intent on removing Queen as head of State', *Jamaica Gleaner* (23 March), https://jamaica-gleaner.com/article/news/20220323/royal-visit-were-moving-holness-says-jamaica-intent-removing-queen-head-state (accessed 19.04.2024).

James, Vonnie, 2017, 'Reparation Theology, Reconciliation and Empire System', Available at researchgatenet.com.

Joseph, Celucien L., 2018, 'Towards a Caribbean Political Theology of Emancipation and Decolonization: A Comparative Analysis of Four Caribbean Theologians', *Black Theology* 16.2, pp. 1–33, DOI: 10.1080/14769948.2018.1460553.

Major-Campbell, Sean, 2022a, 'Letter of the Day – Royals should apologise for crimes against humanity', *Daily Gleaner* (22 March), https://jamaica-gleaner.com/article/letters/20220322/letter-day-royals-should-apologise-crimes-against-humanity (accessed 19.04.2024).

Major-Campbell, Sean, 2022b, 'The many layers of forgiveness', *Jamaica Gleaner* (14 August), https://jamaica-gleaner.com/article/news/20220814/many-layers-forgiveness (accessed 03.04.2024).

McGowan, Casey, 2022, 'Jamaicans demand apology and reparations from British Royals', *The Jurist* (23 March), https://www.jurist.org/news/2022/03/jamaicans-demand-an-apology-and-reparations-from-british-royals/ (accessed 03.04.2024).

Perkins, Anna Kasafi, 1996, *The Political Dimension of Forgiveness in the Light of the Proceedings of the Third Conference of the Latin American Episcopate, Puebla, 1979*, Phil thesis, University of Cambridge, UK, May 1996.

Roberts, Danny, 2018, 'Church, reparation and healing', *Jamaica Gleaner* (25 February), https://www.pressreader.com/jamaica/jamaica-gleaner/20180225/282321090492871 (accessed 03.04.2024).

Roper, Garnett, 2012, *Caribbean Theology as Public Theology*, Kingston, Jamaica: Xpress Litho.

Sanchez, Jose, 2022, 'Start of British royals' Caribbean tour marred by Belize protest', Reuters (19 March), https://www.reuters.com/world/start-british-royals-caribbean-tour-marred-by-belize-protest-2022-03-19/ (accessed 03.04.2024).

Shepherd, Verene, Ahmed Reid, Cavell Francis and Kameika Murphy, 2012, *Jamaica and the Debate over Reparation for Slavery: Discussion Paper Prepared by the Jamaica National Bicentenary Committee*, Kingston, Jamaica: Pelican.

Sorhaindo, Celia, 2018, 'Caribbean Elephants' (17 May), http://www.celiasorhaindo.com/caribbean-elephants/ (accessed 03.04.2024), quoted with the author's permission.

White, Nadine, 2022a, 'Prince Edward and Sophie mocked for "tone-deaf" gift of a signed photo to St Lucia leader', *The Independent* (25 April), https://www.independent.co.uk/world/prince-edward-sophie-st-lucia-b2064754.html (accessed 03.04.2024).

White, Nadine, 2022b, 'Prince William and Kate face more protests in Bahamas Exclusive: "I want the royal couple to report back to the Queen – 400 years can't be forgotten" a priest from The House of Rastafari said', *The Independent* (24 March), https://www.independent.co.uk/world/kate-william-bahamas-jamaica-protests-slavery-b2042771.html (accessed 19.04.2024).

(re)*lease*

6

Liberation as Praxis: Structural Poverty and Public Prophetic Theology

SITHEMBISO S. ZWANE

The South African context of struggle has evolved over the last three decades. The standard of living has changed drastically with a persistent energy crisis that has plunged the country into darkness. In the process, poverty has escalated because of chronic unemployment that has been exacerbated by the Covid-19 pandemic.

In the context of escalating poverty, this chapter addresses three concerns: first, *denunciation* of structural poverty as a rejection of the reformist approach to neoliberalism which manufactures structural poverty and chronic unemployment. Second, *annunciation* through sharpening of forms of progressive and redemptive public prophetic theologies as sacrosanct in challenging structural poverty in the public realm. Third, *transformation* is the envisaged utopia for the majority of the working class affected by structural poverty. These concerns intersect in the context of liberation as praxis.

Liberation as praxis

Liberation is a contested terrain, given how people have experienced it in different contexts. The process of reflection and action has the potential to oppress or to liberate. The ultimate goal of liberation praxis is to facilitate reflection and action that lead to social transformation. Paulo Freire provided the basis for thinking about liberation through the concept of praxis. Freire's praxis is premised on the notion of transformation through action and reflection (Freire, 1970, p. 36). Gustavo Gutiérrez published his seminal work on liberation theology (Gutiérrez, 1973) building on Freire's liberation praxis of action and reflection. So how is praxis defined in the context of liberation?

According to Mario and Osorio, praxis is a 'principle of transformation and synthesis produced when the theoretical-practical contraction is solved' (Mario and Osorio, 2009, p. 14). The movement of theory to practice is central to praxis as a process rather than as an event. The cycle of theory and practice finds expression through ideology and dialogue that facilitates transformation. Furthermore, Mario and Osorio argue that 'praxis as transforming principle transcends the theory and practice contradiction and fosters interactions between action and reflection' (Mario and Osorio, 2009, p. 14). Part of this contradiction is the difference between theory and the lived reality of the people. Praxis attempts to engage with this contradiction through dialogue between theory, in the form of methodologies and frameworks on one side, and practice through the experience of the lived reality of the people on the other. The collaboration between the practitioners (activists) and academics (scholars) is one of the examples of the productive use of praxis (West, 2013, pp. 43–8).

Praxis as a transforming tool is subjected to and also subjects the transforming experience to an interpretative process (Mario and Osorio, 2009, p. 14). It is a movement from abstraction of ideas in the form of conceptual processes in theory to practicality as an expression of thinking. So praxis takes the shape of a process. The people are the subjects of praxis and not objects in the realm of theory with no relevance to a lived reality of human existence that is characterized by marginalization, oppression and exclusion of the poor. Ronald Glass argues that 'the praxis that defines human existence is marked by historical and cultural contexts that shape and set limits on activity' (Glass, 2001, p. 16). These marked historical and cultural contexts are contested spaces that can curtail human existence and activity. This has the propensity to undermine liberation as a praxis and lead to dehumanization. Liberation as a process of praxis involves producing resources for dialogue.

Tom Moylan (1991) and Linden West (2021) offer conceptual resources for liberation praxis. Both Moylan and West use the concepts of denunciation and annunciation to discuss praxis in the context of liberation. Moylan describes denunciation as a non-reformist but revolutionary praxis that has the potential to reject the hegemonic systems of oppression within a particular world order. Furthermore, Moylan defines annunciation as an alternative reformist praxis that seeks to redeem the system order of things (Moylan, 1991, p. 26).

West on the other side used these concepts to amplify Freire's concept of liberation as praxis. West states that 'by annunciation, I mean the role of love, affirmation and potentially profound, agentic encounters with otherness in existentially significant forms of learning; by denunciation, a spirit of critique and fundamental questioning of the established order of things' (2021, p. 422). West uses these concepts as an affirmation of others in inclusive spaces and also as a tool to critique oppressive and exclusive spaces that undermines the recognition of others.

In this chapter, I use these concepts of denunciation and annunciation to reflect on structural poverty and public prophetic liberation theology. In addition, I argue that campaigns form the basis for movement building and fostering participatory community development. Furthermore, these concepts provide the framework for rejecting systems of exclusion and oppression (Denunciation: structural poverty) and the facilitation of alternative systems of inclusion and liberation (Annunciation: Prophetic African liberation theology) that ultimately lead to social change (Transformation: Movements and Participatory Community Development).

Denunciation: structural poverty

Structural poverty is a form of 'invited space' (Zwane, 2020a) that necessitates the process of denunciation. The ushering of the new dawn in South Africa in 1994 came with hope after many years of racial segregation and apartheid capitalist system that subjected the majority of black people to economic slavery in their own country. Consequently, the African National Congress (ANC) in their election manifesto promised South Africans a 'Better Life for All' (Kroth, Larcinese and Wehner, 2016, p. 774). The promise came in the midst of despair because of high levels of poverty in the community. Fast-forward 28 years and the question remains: has the ANC delivered a 'Better life for all' in South Africa or has the problem of poverty worsened since 1994?

Jeremy Seabrook argued that 'poverty is not a form of "illness" that demonstrates the malfunctioning of capitalism and can be "cured." On the contrary, poverty is proof of the "good health" of the capitalist system' (cited in Rist, 2007, p. 489). Seabrook locates the capitalist system at the centre of the problems of structural poverty in South Africa and the globe. The glaring economic inequalities and class polarization are evident in the community. The high levels of unemployment among the youth has contributed to extreme poverty and huge inequalities. According to David Francis and Edward Webster, 'the capitalist system in contemporary South Africa continues to reproduce inequality across all areas of social and economic life, despite the demise of the apartheid' (Francis and Webster, 2019, p. 793). Political expediency and nepotism have decimated the public service, paving the way for the corrupt forces to loot with impunity. The majority of South Africans continue to live in poverty and it is unlikely that this will change any time soon.

The energy crisis in South Africa has exacerbated the problem of poverty, especially among the poorest of the poor in rural areas. South Africa's energy crisis is severely compromised. The unreliability of energy has obliterated informal small business and increased the unemployment problem. The electricity (load-shedding) crisis undermines economic growth projections and reverses the gains made in past years. This energy crisis tends to affect mostly the rural communities, who are forced to use alternative energy sources to survive in areas that have limited resources. The rural communities rely on the use of woods from the forest to make fire for cooking and heating. In this case, the women bear the brunt of producing these alternative sources of energy when they travel to the forests to collect wood for the household. This brings to bear the reality of the feminization of poverty in rural areas.

According to Cheteni, Khamfula and Mah, 'gender plays a huge role in the household-decision making process, as a result, it can determine whether the household falls into poverty trap or falls out of poverty' (2019, p. 4). The decision-making process, especially in rural households, is premised on hierarchical and patriarchal structures that often undermine the 'voice' of women. Furthermore, 'Customary laws contribute to poverty because they allow males to have polygamous families [resulting in] large number of children' (2019, pp. 5–6). In most cases these children have limited opportunities in accessing quality education because of the challenges within the polygamous marriages. Women have no power to change this practice in a male-dominated context that is protected by patriarchy. What does this mean for understanding liberation in the community?

A focus group discussion was organized and facilitated by the Ujamaa Centre with organized groups from the community on the meaning of liberation. The groups reflected on liberation in the context of poverty, education, oppression and safety in South Africa. The responses from the groups supported the dominant narrative that the communities have lost trust in the liberation movement, which resulted in the ANC underperforming in many municipalities during the 2021 local government elections (ANC, 2022, p. 4).

The four study groups who participated in the discussion on the meaning of liberation in the community asked the following questions:

- What is your understanding of liberation in South Africa?
- Who needs to be liberated and from what?
- What role should the church play in the liberation of South Africans?

The Myezane group[1] that was interviewed (on 3 October 2022) about liberation argued:

> When it comes to liberation in South Africa, it's just the word freedom, there isn't any. There is only oppression felt by people, they don't have clean water, no electricity, suffering from hunger and it seems to be getting worse. The price of petrol keeps going up which contributes to high food prices. All this affects our children and the future we are trying to build for them, this is very bad because people were promised a 'better life' when freedom came. Black people need to be liberated from poverty. Everything that happens affects them first, there is water shortage in our community and the persisting electricity problems are not attended to with the urgency that is required. If the other races (whites and Indians) complain, their cries get a quicker response then that of black people. We are forever told that the country has no money, but the looting taught us that there is money. The places that were affected by the looting were fixed and they received assistance to rebuild. There were many foreign nationals who were part of the looting, but only South Africans were arrested. In the church married get preferential treatment which is a form of discrimination. Class still matters in church and how you look influences the treatment. They need to treat everyone equal in order for oppression to end. The judgemental attitude of believers is something that the church must change in order for it to be regarded as playing a role in liberation.

The Myezane group consists of unemployed young graduates and is apprehensive about the concept of liberation and how it is being used in South Africa's discourse. The term does not reflect the reality of the people since 1994: the lack of basic services like access to clean water, reliable energy (without continual blackouts because of load-shedding), the triple challenge of unemployment, poverty and inequality. All these social ills are an opposite of what was promised to South Africans; 'A better life for all' has become a 'A better life for a few politicians'. The education system has been compromised by political decisions aimed at achieving political expediency. The quality of education is compromised by the lack of resources for quality teaching and learning.

The Sakhingomuso[2] group concur with the Myezane group on liberation, suggesting that it means different things to different people. They argued (on 3 October 2022) that:

> Liberation is a mixed bag in South Africa. Free education for people as a basic need is good, but the[re is also] realisation that after basic education we receive a piece of paper that has no meaning without skills and experience. The job market is still oppressive, it doesn't allow the unemployed youth to access employment to end poverty and inequality. Young people cannot gain experience after leaving tertiary institutions because they do not have adequate experience for the available jobs in the market. The community as a whole need to be liberated from the culture of entitlement. Grants like the Social Relief Distress (SRD) which started during Covid-19 was supposed to be a relief but some people have a sense of entitlement and no longer looking for work. Protection for women and children in the community is important because women are still oppressed because of Gender-Based Violence (GBV) and femicide that is rampant in South Africa. So, we are liberated on paper but not in reality. The church must serve as an institution that facilitates liberation rather than the oppression of women.

The Sakhingomuso group consists of unemployed young people who have had experience in the job market and have been retrenched. These young people have education, but lack the required experience to enter the job market permanently. The system has failed these young people by not recognizing the skills they already have that need a platform to gain the required experience. The system is impatient with the poor and marginalized working-class youth.

The Masibheke Phambili[3] focused on the opportunities that have been created by the transition from apartheid to democracy. They stated (on 3 October 2022) that:

> We are now free as a country to vote, to live where we want depending on affordability, jobs are opened to everyone, but are limited and corruption is a major problem. The young people born after 1994 were born to freedom, but the reality is that life is really tough. Although children have been given rights, they have also caused a big disadvantage to the parents. Children and youth are very arrogant, they can

drink and smoke at 18 years which is the legal age but they are not matured at that age to make their own decisions. Teachers are also suffering because of these children that are disrespectful because of rights. We also have a huge drug problem in the townships, that on its own is problematic. The black mind needs to be liberated to begin to think more openly or broadly about the meaning of liberation. Black people need to be liberated to gain access to the economy so that they can see how to create job opportunities to alleviate poverty in their families. Land is the economy and access to land will open more opportunities for the poor to address the challenges of poverty. The church can help in reducing poverty using its own resources and land for gardening that can provide food for poor families. It shouldn't just take money from people but not find a way to give back to the community. The church should play an active role in contributing to change, the church members can collect food and help to support poor families in the area. At times people in the church are the ones who play a role in disrupting church programmes.

Freedom means the right to vote for most South Africans who were deprived of this important democratic principle. This is the greatest achievement of the postcolonial dispensation and should be respected and appreciated. The issues raised by the Masibheke Phambili group are pertinent to the South African contextual reality. However, the continual reference to apartheid whenever the lack of service delivery is raised undermines the gains that have been achieved through human rights that are enshrined in the Constitution, which includes the right to vote.

The Silwela Inguquko[4] group stated (on 3 October 2022):

In terms of oppressive laws then yes, we are free. No more pass laws, freedom of association and sexual orientation. Although we say we are free, we are not completely free, those who have money experience it better than those who do not have money. Marginalised groups still not completely free like the LGBTIQA+ as they face a lot of discrimination from family and their community. There is a need to engage parents of LGBTIQA+ children so that they better understand their children. The issue that is a concern is safety which means there is no liberation for the vulnerable groups in South Africa. Men, women, children and LGBTIQA+ need to be liberated from the abuse they face in their daily lives. Racial discrimination still happens in schools which means teachers and children need to be liberated from racial abuse. The judgemental nature of the church needs to change in order for the church to be effective in the liberation of the oppressed.

The Silwela Inguquko group is comprised of young people from the LGBTIQA+ community who are discriminated against because of homophobia and hate crime in the church and community. They have embraced the laws enshrined in the Constitution that are meant to protect them from nefarious criminal acts. Unfortunately, some families and communities still discriminate and are hostile towards the LGBTIQA+ community despite the progressive Constitution in South Africa. The experiences of the members of these groups indicate a degree of frustration among the communities of the poor in South Africa.

This is where a public prophetic African liberation theology remains relevant after 1994. A shift from what the South African Kairos Document (1985) calls 'church Theology' and 'State Theology' to a public prophetic liberation theology is an alternative (Ramalho, 2020). It is inconceivable that the God of liberation can also be the God of oppression. Therefore, public prophetic African liberation theology is the affirmation of the God who is concerned about the suffering of the poor and the oppressed. The God who is a liberator is an alternative to economic and political hegemony.

Annunciation: public prophetic theology

Annunciation is a form of 'invigorated space' that contends with the 'invited space' (Zwane, 2020a). Invigorated space facilitates an alternative understanding of God in the context of oppression and marginalization. According to Olehile Buffel, 'God is the God who expresses a divine concern for the underdogs' (Buffel, 2010, p. 2).

Buffel's use of the term 'underdogs' in reference to the poor and marginalized, the working class and the predominantly black people in the South African context is ideological and contextual. The underdogs shape the ideo-theological landscape through their lived and embodied reality of structural poverty. For Buffel, God is not oblivious to the situation of the underdogs but expresses concern for the poor and the oppressed. Public prophetic liberation theology praxis as an alternative should take into consideration the underdogs – that is, black masses who are poor and oppressed – as the primary interlocutors in the formulation and appropriation of the public prophetic liberation theology.

According to Kanayo Nwadialor and Charles Nweke:

> The African theologians are now confronted with the problem of finding out whether the God of Moses who liberated the Israelites from Egyptian bondage and the God of Jesus of Nazareth who came to set the captives free created the blacks to remain in perpetual captivity and dehumanization. (Nwadialor and Nweke, 2014, p. 81)

Nine years later, African theologians are still grappling with the perpetual economic captivity and dehumanization of black people and the pertinent question about whether the God of Jesus of Nazareth created blacks to remain in perpetual captivity and dehumanization still remain.

The discussion about the God of Moses who liberates has to begin with the reality of blacks as the underdogs in dialogue with scripture as an alternative theology for the liberation of the underdogs. This process lays the foundation for praxis that facilitates prophetic African liberation theology. For Nwadialor and Nweke, 'the contemporary task of African liberation theology is to abolish the current unjust situation and build a different society freer and more human' (2014, p. 81).

A credible public prophetic African liberation theology must engage critically with its socio-economic and political landscape. This black liberation theology (Zwane, 2020b) should consider the socio-economic conditions of black working-class communities. This theology must be concerned with practices that undermine the liberation of African people from systems of oppression and marginalization. A paradigm shift from socio-historical to contemporary context is critical in the formulation and location of any theology.

According to Nwadialor and Nweke, 'African Christian Theology is one rooted, as it were, in African culture; that is to say this theology arises in response to the problems inherent in or peculiar to African culture' (2014, p. 81). This assertion is important, but not without challenges. First, it is important because it is a reminder that theology is intricately linked to its cultural context. It has to take into cognizance the emerging cultural challenges and issues in order for it to be genuinely contextual in its approach. Second, the challenge with this is that it often presupposes that culture is static and not dynamic. In this instance, theology like culture cannot afford to be static but must evolve when the issues change in the cultural context. This means critical reflection and analysis of the cultural context becomes sacrosanct.

Nwadialor and Nweke argue that 'African liberation theology ... in a nutshell could be seen as a critical reflection on the experiences of the African people ... down through the ages and a total commitment to the process of development and the building of a new social order, all in the light of the gospel' (2014, p. 83). What is evident from this argument is that central to African liberation theology is the experiences of African people as interlocutors. African theology should be premised on the notion of liberation from all forms of oppression and injustice.

Buffel argues that 'liberation theology insists on the preferential option for the oppressed and marginalized' (Buffel, 2010, p. 2). Furthermore, liberation theology emerged from the experiences of black struggle in the South African context (Mosala, 1989; West, 2013; Maluleke, 2000). According to liberation theologians, God is not neutral but is on the side of the poor and the oppressed. This assertion is based on the existential reality of the oppression of blacks by the whites through economic and political systems during the apartheid period in South Africa.

Similarly, the Israelites did not only struggle with their spirituality in the foreign land in Egypt but had to grapple with the hard facts of their socio-economic and political realities that confronted them through slavery (Nwadialor and Nweke, 2014, p. 84). Economic marginalization remains the reality in South Africa post-independence. It has been over 28 years since independence, but a section of the black population is yet to be liberated economically from racial segregation. Economic marginalization of the poor is not good news.

Okolo states that, 'Christ preached the good news, proclaimed release to the captives, gave sight to the blind and set the oppressed free (Lk 4: 18–21)' (Okolo, 1985, p. 96). The good news of Jesus Christ provides the basis for a prophetic African liberation theology that is not only concerned with the spiritual realm but engages robustly with the socio-economic and political hegemonic systems that marginalize and oppress the people.

'Any theologian worth the name is thus challenged to make an option for the poor with the view to liberating them (the people) from unjust structures that shackle them. Such an option becomes an imperative for the theologian because it is God's own option' (Odey, 1996, p. 12). Odey's argument is important especially in the context of socio-economic injustice that most people are experiencing in Third World countries. Public prophetic theologians are called to speak with the poor and the oppressed because they represent God's project of liberation. This is an obligation and not optional for the theologians. An alternative public theology ought to be overtly ideological and address pertinent socio-economic challenges. This is a struggle that most poor and marginalized communities in Africa are grappling with on a daily basis. The socio-economic struggle is the basis from which a prophetic African liberation theology can be developed as an instrument of transformation, that can be used by social movements to facilitate Participatory Community Development (PCD).

Transformation: movements and Participatory Community Development (PCD)

Transformation is a form of 'invented space' that is premised on the concept of 'participation' and change in the community. The works by Robert Chambers (1994a, 1994b, 1995) provide a theoretical basis for understanding the concept of 'participation' in community development. For Chambers, there are three areas in which the concept of 'participation' is used.

First, it is used cosmetically to define and justify anything that is proposed as relevant and good. Second, it is utilized to describe a co-opting practice that mobilizes local labour to reduce costs by communities contributing their time and effort. Third, it describes an empowering process that empowers the local people to do their own contextual analysis, to take command, to gain in confidence and to define their own destiny as citizens. The latter is a progressive realization of the notion of participation that contributes to movement building and participatory community development. This is what Chambers attempted to create through his work on participation. Chambers' work is complemented by the seminal contribution by John McKnight (2017) and John Kretzmann and John P. McKnight (1996) on mapping community-based assets as a form of participation in community development.

The Ujamaa Centre's contribution in the community of community assets used Chambers' concept of 'participation' together with McKnight and Kretzmann's concept of asset-based community development. These processes produced the concept of 'Participatory Community Development' as the foundation for social movements to effect transformation. This foundational concept has been used by the Ujamaa Centre to capacitate social movements through social action in the form of campaigns. The social movements' socio-economic analysis is already pregnant with religious images drawn primarily from the Bible (West, 2013, p. 84). These important campaigns have been used to advocate for a public prophetic African liberation theology premised on resilience and resistance in the communities of KwaZulu-Natal.

Campaigns for transformation

The campaigns in the South African context are a form of protest against established structural and oppressive systems. The campaigns are a platform for lobbying and advocacy aimed at challenging the hegemonic forces. The landmark campaign by women took place on 27 October 1955 against the pass laws in South Africa and laid the foundation for women's agency against all forms of marginalization and oppression. The Ujamaa Centre's Tamar Campaign created spaces of reflection, analysis and liberation. I will reflect on the campaigns that contributed to challenging the oppressive patriarchal gendered culture and economic injustice in our communities.

First, the Tamar Campaign began in 1996 as a response to the call by women who attended the 'Bible and violence in South Africa' workshop (West, 2016b, pp. 135–47; West and Zondi-Mabizela, 2004). The primary focus and emphasis of the Tamar Campaign is the elevation and privileging of the 'voices' of the marginalized women affected by Gender-Based Violence (GBV). These 'voices' participated in building and nurturing resilience. From the established praxis of Contextual Bible Study (CBS), both resilience and resistance forged a path towards a theology of resistance. The Tamar Campaign has received international recognition as an important tool for the deconstruction of patriarchal and systemic oppression of women. Oppressive systems have one common element: domination and oppression. The Campaign has empowered women because they are no longer silenced. Furthermore, the campaign has incorporated elements of HIV and AIDS that have affected the majority of women.

Second, the Worker Sunday Campaign started in 2003 and is part of the Mzwandile R. Nunes Week lecture series, which is a response to the neoliberal capitalist economic system oppressing and marginalizing the working-class communities. This campaign was established by the Industrial Mission of South Africa (IMSA) Network, which included the Institute for the Study of the Bible and Worker Ministry (ISB-WM), Pietermaritzburg Agency for Community Awareness and Social Change (PACSA), Ecumenical Socio-Economic Transformation (ESSET), and a Catholic Church and Work programme. The primary objective of the campaign is to develop critical reflection on socio-economic justice. This reflection included the call for a Basic Income Grant (BIG), challenging the government through lobbying and advocacy. This call was justified by the impact of Covid-19 on communities and churches (Zwane, 2021).

Each of these campaigns has been used by social and ecumenical movements in the community to champion transformation on GBV, femicide and socio-economic justice. The Ujamaa Centre's Body Theology and Bread Theology are actively engaging with these issues in the community supported by organized social movements led by activist groups.

Conclusion

The impact of the neoliberal capitalist economy is evident in structural poverty that affects most black working-class communities in Africa. This structural poverty requires an alternative prophetic theological reflection to take into consideration the experiences of the black working-class African communities subjected to socio-economic injustices as interlocutors. These interlocutors are organic activist intellectuals in the social and ecumenical movements. Our public prophetic theology should reflect contextual socio-economic realities of the working-class poor in our society for it to be transformative. The social and ecumenical movements are a starting point for social change that ultimately leads to Participatory Community Development.

Notes

1 The name means 'excellence' or 'awards' – the name promotes excellence and awards for innovation among unemployed young people.

2 'Building the Future' – the name of the group is futurist and hoping to build the future of unemployed young people with a focus on entrepreneurship.

3 'Let us look forward' – the name of the group postulates a shift from backward looking to futurist hope for a new South Africa that is better than yesterday.

4 'Fighting for Change' – the name of the group implies the existence of oppression that requires a need for change to facilitate liberation.

References

African National Congress (ANC), 2022, 'January 8th Statement', *The Year of Unity and Renewal to Defend and Advance South Africa's Democratic Gains*, ANC: https://www.anc1912.org.za/wp-content/uploads/2022/01/January-8th-Statement-2022.pdf (accessed 06.04.2024), pp. 1-31.

Buffel, Olehile, 2010, 'Preferential option for the poor in the current context of poverty in South Africa: doing liberation theology in the footsteps', *Globethics*, https://uir.unisa.ac.za/handle/10500/4593 (accessed 10.04.2024).

Chambers, Robert, 1994a, 'Paradigm shifts and the practice of participatory research and development', in Nici Nelson and Susan Wright (eds), *Power and Participatory Development: Theory and Practice*, London: IT, pp. 30-42.

———, 1994b, 'The origins and practice of participatory rural appraisal', *World Development* 22 (7), pp. 953-69.

———, 1995, 'Poverty and livelihoods: whose reality counts?', *Environment and urbanization* 7 (1), pp. 173-204.

Cheteni, Privilege, Yohane Khamfula and Gisele Mah, 2019, 'Gender and poverty in South African rural areas', *Cogent Social Sciences* 5 (1), https://www.tandfonline.com/doi/full/10.1080/23311886.2019.1586080 (accessed 06.04.2024).

Francis, D. and E. Webster, 2019, 'Poverty and inequality in South Africa: critical reflections', *Development Southern Africa* 36 (6), pp. 788-802.

Freire, Paulo, 1970, *Pedagogy of the Oppressed*, New York: Continuum.

Glass, R. D., 2001, 'On Paulo Freire's philosophy of praxis and the foundations of liberation education', *Educational Researcher* 30 (2), pp. 15-25.

Gutiérrez, Gustavo, 1973, *A Theology of Liberation*, New York: Orbis Books.

Kretzmann, J. and J. P. McKnight, 1996, 'Assets-based community development', *National Civic Review* 85 (4), pp. 23-30.

Kroth, V., V. Larcinese and J. Wehner, 2016, '"A better life for all?" Democratization and electrification in post-apartheid South Africa', *Journal of Politics* 78 (3), pp. 774-91.

Maluleke, Tinyiko S., 2000, 'Black and African theology after apartheid and after the Cold War – an emerging paradigm', *Exchange*, 29 (3), pp. 193-212.

Mario, J. and F. Osorio, 2009, 'Praxis and liberation in the context of Latin American theory', in Christopher C. Sonn and Maritza Montero (eds), *Psychology of Liberation*, New York: Springer, pp. 11-36.

McKnight, J., 2017, 'Asset-based community development: the essentials', Chicago: Asset-Based Community Development Institute, https://resources.depaul.edu/abcd-institute/publications/publications-by-topic/Documents/ABCD-%20The%20Essentials%20-2.pdf (accessed 06.04.2024).

Mosala, Itumeleng J., 1989, *Biblical Hermeneutics and Black Theology in South Africa*, Grand Rapids, MI: Eerdmans.

Moylan, T., 1991, 'Denunciation/annunciation: the radical methodology of liberation theology', *Cultural Critique* (20), pp. 33-64.

Nwadialor K. L., and C. C. Nweke, 2014, 'The relevance of the church in oppressive situations: the praxis of liberation theology in Africa', *OGIRISI a New Journal of African Studies* 10 (1), pp. 79-96.

Odey, J. O., 1996, *Africa, the Agony of a Continent Can Liberation Theology Offer Any Solution?* Enugu: Snaap.

Okolo, C. B., 1985, 'The Igbo church and liberation motive', in C. B. Okolo (ed.), *The Igbo Church and the Quest for God*, Obosi: Pacific College, pp. 89–113.

Ramalho, W., 2020, 'Historical time between Chronos and Kairos: on the historicity of The Kairos Document manifesto, South Africa, 1985', *Rethinking History* 24 (3–4), pp. 465–80.

Rist, G., 2007, 'Development as a buzzword', *Development in Practice* 17 (4–5), pp. 485–91.

West, Gerald O., 2013, 'People's theology, prophetic theology, and public theology in post-liberation South Africa', unpublished paper.

——, 2016a, *The Stolen Bible: From tool of imperialism to African icon*, Leiden: Brill.

——, 2016b, 'Recovering the biblical story of Tamar: training for transformation, doing development', in Robert Oden (ed.), *For Better or Worse: The Role of Religion in Development Cooperation*, Halmstad: Swedish Mission Council, pp. 135–47.

——, 2017, 'The co-optation of the Bible by "Church Theology" in post-liberation South Africa: returning to the Bible as a "site of struggle"', *Journal of Theology for Southern Africa* 157, pp. 185–98.

West, Gerald and Phumzile Zondi-Mabizela, 2004, 'The Bible story that became a campaign: the Tamar campaign South Africa (and beyond)', *Ministerial Formation*, Geneva: WCC, pp. 2–12.

West, Linden, 2021, 'Annunciation and denunciation in Paulo Freire's dialogical popular education', *Australian Journal of Adult Learning* 61(3), pp. 421–41.

Zwane, Sithembiso S., 2020a, 'Invited, invigorated and invented spaces: trans-development approach', in Jin Young Choi and Joerg Rieger (eds), *Faith, Class and Labor: Intersectional Approaches in a Global Context*, Eugene, OR: Wipf & Stock, pp. 1–24.

——, 2020b, 'Transition, reflection, rethinking and re-imagining: the relevance of Black Liberation Theology (BLT) in South Africa post 1994 – A tribute to Vuyani Vellem', *HTS Teologiese Studies/Theological Studies* 76 (3), pp. 99–106.

——, 2021, 'Solidarity assurance: reality, faith and action', in Jione Havea (ed.), *Doing Theology in the New Normal: Global Perspectives*, London: SCM Press, pp. 159–73.

7

'We Can't Stay Home, Our Children Must Eat': African Women, Street Markets and Survival during Covid-19

LILIAN CHEELO SIWILA

The various waves of the Covid-19 pandemic impacted the well-being of people – socially, economically and spiritually – across the globe. In most parts of the world, the pandemic restricted movements and gatherings, leading to lockdowns in all sectors of life. For many people, life came to a standstill. This included any form of business that attracted physical contact. These restrictions affected people's lives negatively to the extent that they also brought about fear and anxiety about the future. Since Covid-19, some people have failed to go back to their old ways of life, be it socially, economically or spiritually.

The motivation for this chapter is twofold: first is my ongoing research on the experiences of women to Covid-19. This chapter focuses on how the lockdown restrictions are experienced by church women who are street vendors and those who sell in marketplaces as income providers for their families. The study was conducted with ten women aged between 45 and 70 years who sell in the markets and streets of Kaoma and Chingola districts of Zambia. These women are also members of the Women Christian Fellowship in the United Church of Zambia. The second motivation for this chapter is that women in Zambia are within the population group that is actively involved in economic development of the country. Despite this fact, the world of employment does not seem to recognize women's contribution to the country's economy, because most women involved in business entrepreneurship are dealing with ordinary small-scale businesses such as selling in the markets and street vending. This is very common among women in Zambia, providing the country's basic needs to most of the low-income population. Therefore, talking about these women as working women becomes a challenge for many due to the way the concept of work is viewed in society.

African women and the theology of work

Although there are scholars writing on the theology of work, there hasn't been much scholarship that focuses on women and the theology of work. Amina Mama states that 'studies of women's work have led to major reconceptualization of what we mean by the terms "work" and "economy"' (Mama, 1996, p. 55). This is an important observation especially as it relates to women marketers who in most cases move between domestic work at home and selling in the market. Mama further observes that:

> African research into gender relations and work is particularly fascinating because of the enormous range of activities that African women engage in and the permutations that these have undergone with the changing circumstances of pre-colonial, colonial and post-colonial ... consideration of the activities that these women are involved in subvert many of the dichotomies that have been developed to characterize what women do between formal and informal work, between productive and reproductive work, between household and market work. (Mama, 1996, p. 57)

Despite these challenges, women themselves have been able to creatively find ways of making what they do remarkable and valuable to their families and communities. Selling basic food products that are consumed on a daily basis such as fresh vegetables, fish, bread and other related food products as a way of generating income is also a positive way of demonstrating how these women understand the concept of work. From a theological perspective, work can also be viewed as God's mission for the church. Throughout the Bible we see God's call for humanity to commit to working hard as fundamental to one's faith. As the Psalmist declares: 'You shall eat the fruit of the labour of your hands, you shall be happy, and it shall go well with you' (Ps. 128.2). Another biblical text that can be related to the theology of work is 2 Thessalonians 3.10, where Paul warns of the danger of idleness, saying, 'Anyone unwilling to work should not eat'. A call to hard work is also demonstrated in the very first few chapters of the Bible, where God is a working God who calls for humanity to do the same. David J. Schnall, talking about the theology of work in the Genesis story, comments that:

> this text supports the view 'that the six days of labor hold intrinsic religious value in rough parallel to the spiritual benefits derived from the Sabbath itself'. The creation story in Genesis shows God being pleased after each day of creation with what He (*sic*) has accomplished, demonstrating that even God finds great joy in productive labour. Humankind works to improve the world and make it a better place for everyone. (Schnall, 2001, p. 49)

Schnall here tries to make us aware that work is the art of God, and that God finds pleasure in the work that one does and not so much in the type of work – be it paid work or not. In relation to the understanding of women's work, Mama makes us aware of the way in which society tries to make women's work invisible both in the home and on the economic global market. In most cases women's work such as the one under study is not included in the formal definition of work or labour. Therefore, when a woman marketeer wakes up every day to go and sell her merchandise, in most of our societies where colonialism redefined what work means to us, this is not considered as work. In view of this, Mama argues that in capitalist economies work has been unjustly divided into productive and unproductive labour, with productive being the most preferable as it is referring to tradable economic products with expropriated surplus while reproduction is seen as work associated with unpaid labour that is not included in macroeconomic calculations. This kind of perception of women's work is also confirmed by Lilian Cheelo Siwila (2017) in her discussion of how mine bosses on the Copperbelt defined work of the wives and mistresses of mine workers as reproductive labour that only contributed to the economic output in the copper production through the wives' maintenance of their husbands. And yet their domestic work was also a key asset for copper production. Therefore, a theological reflection on the concept of work should take into consideration the fact that at creation God undertook a project on reproductive labour that had no reward from anyone and yet even after the task was accomplished God handed over the beautiful world to humankind.

Brief history of the development of markets in Zambia

In most Zambian communities, marketplaces are the most common points where one finds women selling their products. These places are mostly located in the city centres or strategic points that are easily accessible to many people in the city. Most of the marketplaces in Zambia are attached to colonial history as trading points either with the colonial masters or with traders from outside the country. Most of the markets in Zambia are the busiest trading points, where one finds millions of people passing through each day to buy a variety of affordable food products – affordable in the sense that food products are sold in smaller portions so they are affordable by those on a low income.

Market trading is one of the oldest stories in the history of humankind. Within the Zambia context, trading between ethnic groups from outside the country can be traced as far back as the fourth century (Siwila, Mwale and Chita, 2020). In the Copperbelt province of Zambia where this study is partly located, women were the first people to introduce the initiative of trading in goods such as vegetables and other farm produce. Women's labour is recorded by scholars such as Chauncey (1981) and Siwila (2017). At the same time, scholars such as Chauncey (1981), Rakodi (1988) and Siwila (2017) further argue that the history of women on the Copperbelt is wide-ranging in that on one side it talks of women who were seen as hindrance to economic progress in the mines while on the other hand they are said to have contributed to improve copper production. Besides the many activities that these women were involved in, such as taking care of the mine workers who happened to be their partners, and beer brewing for the entertainment of these mine workers, they also grew and sold vegetables and other food products within the mine area. Reflecting on the history of women's involvement in agricultural and food production in the Copperbelt mine towns, Chauncey states that:

> The Roan Antelope Mine at Luanshya, which most actively and successfully encouraged the presence of women, established a system of agricultural plots on otherwise unused company land where miners' wives could grow gardens in the early thirties. By 1935 some 2,000 plots were in use, producing groundnuts, maize, beans, and green vegetables to supplement the diets of women and their husbands on the mines. The official plot system was most fully developed at the Roan Antelope during the thirties, and investigators in 1935 received noticeably fewer complaints about the food supply from workers there than from those

at Mufulira and Nkana, where the system was fully developed only later. Management thus expected women to supplement substantially the food rations provided by the companies; and they used women's labour to reduce the expense of the ration program itself even more directly by purchasing large quantities of vegetables for distribution to workers from the women instead of from the more expensive European farmers. (Chauncey, 1981, p. 139)

Following this development, most of the wives of mine workers become more involved in agriculture to the extent that they began to have excess produce after they had supplied the management at the mine. This meant that they needed more buyers for their produce. Chauncey (1981) observes that the exchange of goods was carried on informally or door-to-door. The Lamba women who lived nearby the mines came into the compounds to sell their produce and they also exchanged various items with miners' wives. Chauncey further states that as time went by, 'the management at Roan, followed by that at Nkana, built a marketplace in the early 1930s where women could sell their produce under company supervision during specified hours. These became social as well as economic centers, where women spent hours in conversation and making plans' (Chauncey, 1981, p. 148). It is from this background that we continue to see women today on these marketplaces selling food products. These marketplaces also help them to create their own community of faith and empowerment. A community that welcomes and embraces women marketers provides a strong base for these women to support one another. For most women, marketplaces sometimes act as their second homes where they spend more time than in their own homes.

During the Covid-19 pandemic, this kind of setting became a danger to these women and their families because places such as markets were viewed as super spreaders for the pandemic. Highlighting the significance of the marketplace for women during the colonial era, Chauncey observes that:

The particular form taken by many women's involvement in the market economy of the mining towns had important implications for their social position and relations with men. Their ability to transform their traditional productive roles into means of earning cash enabled them to remain relatively independent of the monopolistic employer to whom most men were subject, to achieve greater control over the form of their relations with individual men. (Chauncey, 1981, p. 152)

The idea of financial independence that Chauncey raised is one of the positive factors that women marketeers benefit from in this business enterprise. This is because most of the women selling in these marketplaces are either single parents, widows or those whose husbands earn a very low income with high poverty levels, therefore being able to gain financial freedom becomes a source of empowerment. This is because poverty alleviation and women empowerment need to be accompanied by financial freedom.

Challenges faced by women marketeers and street vendors

The subject of women marketeers and their role in economic empowerment of their families does not come without challenges. Most of the women involved in this business venture endure several hardships that are mostly not recognized by either their family members or the society. For years some of these women have stood up as sole providers for their families' income while their husbands remain negligent and use their money for personal pleasure. Some of the challenges include the difficulty of accessing products for sale, the stress of managing the roles at home and at the marketplace, and the intensity of the work involved. Access to products also means that these women have to travel several kilometres in unpleasant conditions to buy their merchandise. For those who sell vegetables, some have to travel at dawn to go and order the vegetables in the farms for their day's sale so that they are able to be at the market by sunrise to catch their customers on time. Women's vulnerability to this kind of movement ranges from being robbed to being raped by strangers.

Sex for fish

The other challenges involve the women travelling to other towns to access products such as fish, *mopane* worms or kapenta[1] for sale. Research conducted by scholars such as Merten and Haller (2010) and Camlin, Kwena and Dworkin (2013) all points to the vulnerability and experiences of women who engage in buying fish for sale. Using the term 'sex for fish', the scholars argue that women engage in sex activities with fishermen in order to gain preferential access to fish. This sex-for-fish relationship has been observed worldwide, especially in Africa and in Asia. Camlin argues that:

> In Zambia, women involved in the trade have invoked lumambo, a former customary regulation of extramarital sexual relations among the Ila, to provide legitimacy and a cover of respectability for sex-for-fish exchanges. ... A stigmatization of women involved in the sex-for-fish trade has been perpetuated in the fisheries literature, in which fish-for-sex has been confused with prostitution, and women are discursively placed as victims within the fisheries sector economy. With women viewed 'only as sexual partners, spouse or prostitute', this literature has overlooked the active role that women play as economically productive agents within the sector. (Camlin, Kwena and Dworkin, 2013, p. 218)

The point raised by Camlin et al. clearly demonstrates some of the gender stereotypes on women marketers that has been sustained by society without any hermeneutical analysis of the factors behind women's behaviours in the industry. The pressure to give in to sex in order to put food on the table is one aspect that Njoroge (1996) would call African women's way of carrying their cross to Golgotha at the expense of others. In response to this kind of self-sacrifice, Merten and Haller further argue that:

> The common request 'no deal, no fish' forced many women into sexual activities they did not want. Female traders either had to agree to fish-for-sex deals, or they had to wait, sometimes for days, to purchase fish. In addition, women became increasingly vulnerable to fraud: some female traders tried to book fish by paying in advance, but never received their merchandise. (Merten and Haller, 2010, p. 75)

All these risks that these women face are easily ignored by society; instead, societal constructs will judge them as being wicked and coercing the fishermen into sexual activities. Suffice to say that it is not the aim of this chapter to comment on the wistful desire of some of the women to indulge in this kind of sex affair, but rather to seek to demonstrate the vulnerability of those women who would say, 'If I don't do it what shall my children eat, if I don't concede what happens to my children's education fees? Where will my children sleep?' If these women are accorded an opportunity to tell their stories of how they find themselves in these unpleasant ordeals, it will be surprising to some of us to discover that most of these women are found in such circumstances and do what they do as a survival strategy for their families. Most African women theologians state that in most African societies, women are silenced by culture, religion, society and now – the economy. Mercy Amba Oduyoye

(1995) argues that, in most cases, African women sacrifice their lives to patriarchy in the quest to protect their loved ones.

Discussing further on women's vulnerability in the sex-for-fish trade with fishermen, Merten and Haller (2010) bring out the issue of sexual vulnerability. The authors observe that although female fish traders have internalized key messages of the HIV/AIDS discourse about risk behaviour as moral norms, economic constraints and a lack of alternative income-generating opportunities have forced some to engage in sexual transactions despite the risk of HIV infection and moral sanctions. Therefore, in the name of economic liberation, these women sacrifice their sexual and reproductive health rights to their small business.

Experiences of women marketeers and street vendors from Covid-19

As the title of this chapter indicates, the focus highlights the experiences of these marketeers to the recent pandemic that swept across the globe. As stated in the previous sections, the experiences of these women are varied and mostly negative. Their experience of Covid-19 was an added burden to the already existing pressure in their lives. In this chapter I chose to lift their experience of Covid-19 by listening to their own stories. Women's stories are the starting point for their experience of society and the divine. Listening to their stories is also because the pandemic did not only challenge their everyday life but removed them from the marketplaces, which are the places of their income generation for daily survival. The participants who were interviewed for this study indicated that in their families, they were the primary providers. Out of the ten participants, three were married, four widows and three unmarried single mothers. Each of these women had a responsibility to provide school fees and food to a family of not less than eight people in a home.

When I asked why they started selling in the market or streets, the women gave various reasons, including death of their husbands, retirement of their husbands and single parenting. Respondent #3 explained what prompted her to start a business.

> *I started selling because I had no formal employment but had many children to take care of. My parents also were looking to me for assistance.*

Another point to note is that these women are also active members of the church, holding various positions. Four of them are in the leadership as elders who help in the running of the affairs of the church. During the Covid-19 pandemic it was very hard for these women to spend time with other members of the church and with the women's fellowship groups, since church gatherings were on and off due to lockdown regulations. The lockdown also affected their businesses as they did not have specific times to be at the market; as such, the women feared for the lives of their families due to lack of foods in the homes. This led to a high level of anxiety to the extent that some experienced immense stress.

When asked how they coped with this anxiety, all the women acknowledged that attending church services renewed their faith and hope, especially in the daily struggles of looking for income for their families. 'Being in the presence of God usually gave me hope and guide to life and strength to overcome any challenges life threw at me during this time' (Respondent #2). But it was hard to cope without the daily message of God's love, provision, sustenance and protection. As Respondent #4 lamented:

> Prayer is what I missed most because in our district there are people who were not doing genuine businesses during this time of Covid-19 so the prayers we were deprived during lockdown really help us.

Business experiences during Covid-19 lockdown regulations

With the increasing number of infections, the World Health Organization through the government of Zambia released guidelines of how the people were to safeguard their lives by frequently washing of hands, wearing facemasks, using hand sanitizers, maintaining social distance, restrictions in movements and getting Covid vaccinations. Finn and Zadel (2020, p. 3) point out that, to prevent the spread of Covid-19 and to ensure that measures are put forward to slow the spread of the pandemic, all gatherings that attracted large numbers of people were restricted. The mobility of people was limited, which affected all forms of trading in the markets, including street vending. As this became the new norm, many people started shunning public places such as the markets, church services, weddings, funerals and malls because they were viewed as super spreaders. Respondent #3 had this to say about her experience:

'WE CAN'T STAY HOME, OUR CHILDREN MUST EAT'

It was really a difficult time in that travelling out to order stock was limited as there were restrictions in the movements. It was difficult to even receive those who were coming from other places later on buying from them as everyone was scared of the disease. There was a huge draw-back on our business.

These restrictions contributed to the crumbling of small businesses, making life very difficult for these women. For women who depended on products such as fish that needed to be ordered from another city, they lost some profit because they had to pay local suppliers (for they could not go to the other city, due to restrictions on mobility as stated by Respondent #3). The other challenge stated by these women was related to the decision to either stay home and be safe or come to the market and risk their lives. Most of the women who were interviewed stated that they disobeyed the government orders to stay home because they needed to earn some cash for their continued survival. Their businesses needed to continue running because they depended entirely on daily sales which were not easily sustained because Zambia as a developing country cannot afford to offer social security to such businesses as some of the developed countries did.

These women also argued that selling in the market for daily survival was a God-given gift for their survival and that God was going to protect them through prayer. Respondent #5 from Copperbelt province had this to say:

In the beginning we stayed at home, we were keeping a distance, and sanitizing, but as time went on, we stopped and decided to go back to the market because there was no food in the homes. At the same time, it was difficult for us to be telling a customer to keep a distance each time they came to our shop to buy, when in actual fact we needed money. In fact, even when we were not wearing our masks, some customers too were not wearing masks and we could not chase them or observe social distance. How can I chase a customer who has come to do business with me when I needed the money? I cannot stay home. I need to survive. I need food for my children. I just had to trust God for protection.

Respondent #8 from Copperbelt, talking about the danger of transmission through money exchange, stated:

We were also afraid of the money, they said that Covid-19 is transmitted like that. For instance, one customer who comes to my table has gone

> *round other tables, probably wanting to buy green vegetables, at the same time the same customer will come to my table to buy tomato. In the same process, there is also the handling of money the change from another table. That is how this Covid-19 is transmitted here at our markets. We stay at the market the whole day; we cook and eat here and share food with others and use same pots and plates. We are not safe but what can we do? Only God is keeping us.*

Respondent #5 also had this to say:

> *It was hard for me because I thought to myself how we are going to live if the government closes down the markets because this is our means of survival with my children and family. I thought to myself it is finished now will starve I have my mother and my late sister's children at home and I have no husband to help me.*

From the stories above, it is very clear that these women faced many challenges during the lockdown restrictions. Hence for them it was either one dies of Covid-19 or of hunger. One of the respondents indicated that she got infected with Covid-19 and was very sick while others indicated that although they followed the guidelines well, to the extent of receiving vaccinations, some members of their families tested positive for Covid-19, which they believe could also have been contracted from the market.

Notwithstanding, the significance of the marketplace to women was also supported by Chauncey:

> Market places are places where women share love and nurture one another in times of celebration and bereavement. They share their experiences in marriages, about their children their church, share meals, child support and support for each other's business. It is from this space that women are also able to protect one another from abusive relationships. (Chauncey, 1981, p. 148)

The church's role in supporting women entrepreneurs

The church is known to be a place to where people can run for refuge, spiritual and material help in times of trouble, but during Covid-19 the church was also not spared: it suffered closure of its activities due to the high risk of infections. This made it difficult for the church to offer the necessary support and counselling to its members. Since religion informs and affects every aspect of our lives, people needed the church at this point more than ever; there was need for the church to find a way of ministering to this population group by providing a certain kind of help that would provide them with hope, and be 'less stressful' (Mutemwa et al., 2021, pp. 40–1). Even the women's Christian Fellowship, for example, which meets every Tuesday to visit and encourage members in their homes, was not able to reach out to these women. This meant that they could not benefit from these spiritual enrichments derived from the church. When asked whether they have ever received any support from the church even before the Covid-19 outbreak, all the women expressed their disappointment on the way the church treats these disadvantaged groups of women. They stated that the church does not show interest in their business or struggles to maintain their families. One widow (Respondent #1) said:

The last time the church leadership came to show support was when I lost my husband some years ago. I depend on my sisters in Christ here and a few of them from our women's fellowship.

The first point I derive from this study is that ordinary women's work is not taken seriously by the church. This is despite the fact that these women too are part of the economic ladder that helps to provide the nation's food autonomy. The women also contribute to the church's resources through the offerings and tithes from these very meagre resources. Therefore, there is need for the church to begin conversations around the work that these women do so that a theology of work that is redemptive can be developed. Instead of condemning them when they are found in compromising situations one needs to understand their theology of economic sacrifice for the sake of the children and family.

My own experience of this kind of scenario was when I was serving as a leader in one of the congregations where the pastor's wife was involved in this kind of business and sometimes missed church services because she was away on business. While it seemed right to condemn them then, in my naivety not understanding their struggles, looking back I feel for this woman who had ten children living on a pastor's salary in a developing country. Beyond developing theologies of liberation for these women, the church needs support structures that will be able to provide counselling for these women. A church that has no silver or gold could still give the word of life to these women, and provide space for them to encourage one another. In the interviews, most of them pointed out how they sought divine intervention in times of crisis, which just proves the value of these support structures.

Empowering the church members for Pauline Theologies of caring for the widows and single mothers should be embraced as part of the church's ministry. The church needs to open various social media platforms in order to reach out to these members. Boban states that 'by including "accompanying measures" focused on economic inclusion, human capital ... cash transfers can also help diversify households' livelihoods, further building their resilience' (Paul et al., 2021, p. 19). This is one thing that needed to be done in response to the Covid-19 pandemic so that these women could be reached in their homes or marketplaces. In conclusion of this section, I echo Kanyoro's (1992) call for African women to name their oppression and celebrate their stories of success.

Conclusion

The focus of this chapter was to address the issue of women marketers during Covid-19 and their value as economic assets of the nation. In this chapter I pushed for recognizing the contribution of this population group to both economic development and development of new theologies of liberation. Market theology of liberation as I would call it needs to be celebrated and upheld for its value to our society. The chapter also demonstrates that the qualities that these women bring to African feminism need to be upheld if we are to empower women in our society. These women live out the theology of hard work and entrepreneurship, which is slowly being lost from African communities. At the same time, the chapter calls for a need to protect these women from their vulnerability as they thrive to contribute to economic empowerment of their families. The impact of Covid-19 is still evident in the lives of many people who still need healing from the loss of loved ones, businesses, opportunities and faith.

Note

1 This is a small type of fish that is bred in most of the rivers and lakes in Zambia, especially in Luapula, Northern and Southern provinces. The three provinces are the industrial ports for kapenta and fish. Besides the western province that supplies fish at a commercial level.

References

Camlin, Carol S., Zachary A. Kwena and Shari L. Dworkin, 2013, 'Jaboya vs. Jakambi: Status, Negotiation, and HIV Risks among Female Migrants in the "Sex for Fish" Economy in Nyanza Province, Kenya', *AIDS Education and Prevention* 25(3), pp. 216–31.

Chauncey, George, Jr, 1981, 'The Locus of Reproduction: Women's Labour in the Zambian Copperbelt, 1927–1953', *Journal of Southern African Studies* 7 (2), pp. 135–64.

Finn, Arden and Andrew Zadel, 2020, 'Monitoring COVID-19 Impacts on Households in Zambia: Results from a High-Frequency Phone Survey of Households (English)', Report No. 1, Washington DC: World Bank.

Kanyoro, Musimbi R. A., 'The Power to Name', in Musimbi R. A. Kanyoro and Wendy S. Robins (eds), *The Power We Celebrate: Women's Stories of Faith and Power*, Geneva: WCC, pp. 67–88.

Mama, Amina, 1996, *Women's Studies and Studies of Women in Africa During the 1990s*, Dakar: CODESRIA.

Merten, Sonja and Tobias Haller, 2010, 'Culture, Changing Livelihoods, and HIV/AIDS Discourse: Reframing the Institutionalization of Fish-for-Sex Exchange in the Zambian Kafue Flats', *Culture, Health & Sexuality* 9 (1), pp. 69–83, https://doi.org/10.1080/13691050600965968 (accessed 06.04.2024).

Mutemwa, David, Veronika Zvánovcová, Anna Helová and Daniel D. Novotný, 2021, 'The Role of Religion, Philosophy of Life, Global Health, Traditional Medicine, and Past Experiences in the Covid-19 Pandemic Response: Zambia Case Study, *Caritas et Veritas* 11 (1), pp. 34–49.

Njoroge, Nyambura J., 1996, 'Groaning and Languishing in Labour Pain', in Rachel Angogo Kanyoro and Nyambura J. Njoroge (eds), *Groaning in Faith: African Women in the Household of God*, Nairobi: Acton, pp. 3–15.

Oduyoye, Mercy Amba, 1995, *Daughters of Anowa: African Women and Patriarchy*, Maryknoll, NY: Orbis Books.

Paul, Boban Varghese, Arden Finn, Sarang Chaudhary, Renata Mayer Gukovas and Ramya Sundaram, 2021, *COVID-19, Poverty, and Social Safety Net Response in Zambia*, Policy Research Working Paper 9571, Washington DC: World Bank.

Rakodi, Carole, 1988, 'Urban Agriculture: Research Questions and Zambia', *Journal of Modern African Studies* 26 (3), pp. 495–515.

Schnall, D. J., 2001, *By the Sweat of Your Brow: Reflections on Work and the Workplace in Classic Jewish Thought*, Hoboken, NJ: Ktav/Yeshiva University Press.

Siwila, Lilian Cheelo, 2017, 'Reconstructing the Distorted Image of Women as Reproductive Labour on the Copperbelt Mines in Zambia (1920–1954)', *Journal for the Study of Religion* 30 (2), pp. 75–89, available at https://www.academia.edu/54377857/Reconstructing_the_Distorted_Image_of_Women_as_Reproductive_Labour_on_the_Copperbelt_Mines_in_Zambia_1920_1954_ (accessed 06.04.2024).

———, Nelly Mwale and Chita Joseph Chita, 2020, 'Religion and Economic Justice: Jewish Migrants and the Making of Zambia', in Ezra Chitando, Masiiwa Ragies Gunda and Lovemore Togarasei (eds), *Religion and Development in Africa*, Bamberg: University of Bamberg Press, pp. 203–22.

8

Mark's *Ochlos* as Minjung: An Overseas Foreign Workers' (OFW) Reading

DONG HYEON JEONG

The OFWs as twenty-first-century minjung

The Overseas Foreign Worker (OFW) is an umbrella term for those who seek employment beyond the confines and comfort of their homeland because they have perceived that the income they could earn in certain foreign nations is more lucrative (Mapa, 2022). For this chapter, I will limit the definition/scope of OFWs to the two million contractual and migratory Filipinx[1] workers who are employed by foreign countries and companies. With the higher income that they have earned, they usually send a (large) portion of that income back home, to their families and friends, in the form of remittance. The OFWs work in various industries, such as service (cruise ships, restaurants, hotels, resorts), medical (nurses, physical therapist, medical technicians), domestic (home assistance, care-giving), and trade (seafarers, construction, mining). Their remittances are considered one of the most important sources of Philippine national income and foreign currency. The remittance sent by the OFWs is almost 11% of the GNP of the nation. In 2019, the OFWs sent 33.5 billion US dollars back to the Philippines.

And yet their ubiquity is unseen. They are the backbone of the Philippines and of many nations. They are called *bayani* or heroes by the Philippine government. But when the Covid pandemic struck, the Philippine government's response and assistance to the OFWs was wanting. They were left to fend for themselves in their host nations after they were forcefully terminated from their jobs. Such neglect reminds me of Harrod Suarez's critique of this pseudo-nationalistic tendency to lull the OFWs into docility in the name of extractive globalism and heteropatriarchy

(Suarez, 2015, p. 74). Moreover, many host nations had no qualms about letting the OFWs who are nurses and caretakers get sick and even die from Covid-19 (Constante, 2021; see also Choy, 2003).

I read the New Testament with and through them because the OFWs are my friends. As I grew up in the Philippines, many of my acquaintances are currently and previously OFWs. As a United Methodist Church elder in the Philippines, I had a chance to assist the Board of Church and Society's ministry[2] for the OFWs. But it was not enough. As a biblical scholar, I realized that I need to use my capacity to make their presence visible and voices heard. This chapter is my way of acknowledging, thanking and supporting their cause and labour. Among many possible ways, the pandemic triggered me to rethink the struggle of the OFWs as manifesting the struggle of the minjung (the mass/*ochlos*).

Why minjung again? Also, isn't minjung about Korean labourers?

Yes, Ahn Byung-Mu's minjung theology manifested, emerged out of, his life-changing encounter with Jeon Tae-il's protest (13 November 1970; Kim, 2013, p. 19). Jeon self-immolated himself as an act of protest against South Korea's oppressive labour system in the 1960s and 70s. The stories and struggles of thousands of poor and oppressed Koreans became the foundation of minjung theology.

Also, no. According to his memoir compiled, translated and edited by Hanna In and Wongi Park, Ahn never defines or limits minjung to one group of people. Ahn expresses minjung as sites of struggle where the exploitative systems manifest against the poor and the oppressed (In and Park, 2019, p. 221). In other words, minjung is less a persona or a 'monolithic group' (Yung Suk Kim, 2013, p. 9), more an event, an event that 'transcends' (In and Park, 2019, pp. 19–20) by ironically being experiential. It cannot be limited to a person or group. That is why minjung cannot be limited to the South Korean proletariat (In and Park, 2019, p. 29). Ahn even deconstructs minjung not as a fixed term but a term that is fluid, and even Deleuzian (fluidity of ontology, see Deleuze and Guattari, 1987) in its re-emergence: 'Someone who confesses, "I am the minjung," of their own accord is not true minjung' (In and Park, 2019, p. 220). Rather, like the Jesus event (or the encounter of the Jesus' suffering, death and resurrection), which is happening in various parts of the world throughout the decades, the Jesus/minjung event is emerging wherever the struggle is happening. For example, Nami Kim considers the ongoing revolutionary movements in Hong Kong as an emergence of the minjung spirit (Nami Kim, 2021). This emergence transgresses borders and boundaries, creating ruptures/confluences of various minjung spirits that cannot be defined by one racial/ethnic, political/national group.

The key narrative that buttresses this understanding of the minjung is Ahn Byung-Mu's encounter in Germany. After his lecture in Germany, somebody approached Ahn and argued that minjung theology cannot be applied in Germany. This is a summary of their conversation:

> [This person asked:] 'Who are minjung in Germany? In Germany there is no slum, and laborers there have strong labor unions.' At that moment the laborers from foreign countries crossed my mind. In particular, there are many laborers from Turkey in Germany. So I asked, 'What about the laborers from foreign countries? I am responding with another question rather than an answer.' Then the person who asked the question blushed, for he himself already knew. Germany once invited more than a million foreign laborers for their need to run the factories. But now that they outlived their use, Germany is treating them as a nuisance. For the Turkish people have been the enemy of Germans from the olden days. Now Germans harbor a serious hostility toward the Turks. The person who asked the question blushed perhaps because he himself disliked the Turks. (In and Park, 2019, p. 221)

Minjung are sites of struggle. They are the (re-)emergence of the ever-evolving encounters between the oppressors and the oppressed. Interestingly, the 2021 Netflix TV series called *Squid Games* also tapped into the emergence of minjung by having a character by the name of Ali Abdul (player 199), a Pakistani OFW working in South Korea. Ali represents the thousands of foreign workers who are trying to make a living in South Korea so that they can support their families back home.[3] Ali is also the unfortunate recipient of neocolonial abusive tendencies of his Korean employers. Here, we see that minjung cannot be limited to the Koreans, especially when some Koreans manifest neo-colonization. Yong-Yeon Hwang expounds upon this with the citizen versus non-citizen paradigm (Hwang, 2013, p. 226). As South Korea transitioned into an ultra-capitalist (pseudo-)democratic nation, this paradigm turned the immigrant/foreign workers into non-citizens or dispensable ones who are victims of extractive systems of oppression. Not that there are no Korean citizens who are oppressed and victimized; scholars such as Jiseong J. Kwon (2022), Kang Won-Don (2018, pp. 78–9) and J. B. Banawiratma

(2018, writing on Indonesian OFWs) challenge Korean minjung activists to expand and include into their spheres of concern the global workers who are toiling day and night in South Korea.

OFW as a way of reading and relating

The Philippines is the only Christian nation in Asia; over 90% (approximately 100 million) of Filipinx are Christians – Roman Catholic, Protestant and other identifications (Miller, 2022). And yet the number of publications and readings of the Bible from and with the Philippines is disproportionately low compared to other Asian nations. Such disproportion is perhaps due to the global extractive economy that prevents the Filipinx from having the (financial, temporal, spatial, psychological, physical and even spiritual) luxury of reading and writing convoluted articles and books. Their work hours and conditions, especially of the OFWs, are inhumane. And yet their resilience is seen. We see them on their phones watching and listening to Bible Study podcasts. Their religiosity and active participation in the life of the church is beyond perfunctory. They might be disproportionately unpublished (as expected by the academic elite), but their devotion and desire to keep their faith/religion central in their lives are more than what we can say about certain privileged Christian communities.

The Filipinx have experienced colonization and (forced) migration/diaspora due to land grabbing/annexation and even neo-colonization. The same goes with the New Testament texts. In particular, I follow Jin Young Choi's invitation to read the Gospel of Mark 'around the themes of home, dispersion, and border' (Choi, 2021, p. 107) with Ahn Byung-Mu's minjung theology. By doing so, this intersectionality illuminates the ubiquity of movements, transgressions and settling/unsettling happening in Mark. Moreover, Margaret Aymer, from her 1.5 generation perspective, narrates how the Gospel of Mark (even the entire New Testament) speaks of 'rootlessness, migration, diaspora, contested spaces, and migrant strategies' (Aymer, 2014, pp. 47–8). One detail I would highlight/add is that migrants/itinerants travel to a new place to work/live with the intention of connecting back with the homeland through various means. For Filipinx OFWs, they connect back to their families and communities through various expressions of remittances. The Gospels are remittances because the authors are giving back to their homeland by writing about them and their faith from diaspora. Luuk de Ligt and Laurens A. Tacoma

(2016, p. 17) also highlight that Jewish persons and communities collect funds for a cause regularly during the first century CE (Philo, 1962, pp. 156–7, 291 and 312–16; Josephus, 1963, 16.163–4). In particular, many devout Jewish persons and communities provided funding in the upkeep of the Second Temple of Jerusalem. The New Testament texts echo this practice/occurrence. Paul (and perhaps his followers) has a history of collecting funds for the church of Jerusalem (1 Cor. 16.1–4; 2 Cor. 8.1—9.15; Rom. 15.14–32). Following David J. Downs, the purpose of the collection could be two-pronged. First, the collection is a material relief for the poor of the saints. This relief though, according to Downs, is contrary to the Greco-Roman patronage system that obliges the recipient with inimical conditions. Instead, this material relief acknowledges that God is the patron whose 'generous grace (*charis*) does not require invasive reciprocity' (Downs, 2016, pp. 157–65). Second, the collection is also an ecumenical offering that symbolizes unity among the churches (2016, pp. 131–45). In other words, it is Paul's attempt to unify the Jews and the Gentiles with and through the gospel of Christ Jesus.

Among many possible interpretative approaches in reading with and for the Filipinx community, I chose to uplift the presence of the OFWs because, as Choi argues (2021, pp. 112, 117), writing about minjung should engage those who are marginalized in our current society. There are many marginalized voices in various Filipinx communities. And yet I choose to engage the OFW communities because of their precarious situation especially brought about by the Covid pandemic.

Here I am cautious and admit that I am writing from a privileged position in an elite context. With their permission, I hope to uplift the OFWs' presence in my Filipinx hermeneutical reading of Mark. I also acknowledge the danger of saviourism or messianic complex in my upliftment of the OFWs. I am an ally and a friend who is driven to write this chapter due to survivor's guilt and the commission to care for the other. As Jordan J. Cruz Ryan (forthcoming) invites and challenges persons like me, I hope that this chapter is my expression of *bayanihan* (togetherness as a community) with the Filipinx communities. I hope to co-emerge with them in their struggles.

Reading the feeding narratives (Mark 6.34–44; 8.1–9) with an OFW hermeneutic

The feeding narratives of Mark (6.34–44 and 8.1–9)[4] are appropriate narratives for the OFW hermeneutics. Here I argue for a three-step narrative flow. First, the OFWs travel in order to find help/hope. Second, they engage/work with the host individual/community through work/encounters. Third, they return and/or send the remittance to their home community. I see this narrative flow with the (but not only) *ochlos*/minjung of the feeding narratives.

Please note that the three-step narrative flow of OFW hermeneutics that I propose is not a socio-scientific method that applies to every narrative/encounter found in the Gospel of Mark. My reading is a pastoral response in assisting the OFWs see/read themselves better in the text. I do not think that Mark was written to be a cipher text in which we could find a formula that decodes all narratives. My OFW hermeneutics are not a/the key or some kind of 'formula' in reading Mark. My hope is to speak, write and read Mark in ways that will create a space for the OFWs to connect with the text. The three-step narrative flow of OFW hermeneutics resonates with Suh Nam-Dong's 'echo theology' and his hermeneutical principle of 'convergence of two stories' (see Kang 2018, pp. 15–24).[5] Suh's hermeneutics sees the minjung as both text and context in reading the Bible (Küster, 2010, p. 86). Suh is a fellow first-generation minjung theologian of Ahn Byung-Mu who read the Bible with minjung stories and vice versa. Suh's reading strategy, as Hur Joo-Mee suggests (2018), echoes Edward Said's contrapuntal reading.

Thus, I begin with the first step where I see the 'great crowd' (*polun ochlon*;[6] 6.34) travelling 'from all the towns' (*apo pason ton poleon*; v. 33), like the OFWs travelling from various countries/nations, to meet Jesus and his disciples (host individuals/nations). Such movements, whether short or long, permanent or semi-permanent, are highly attested in Greco-Roman literature. Ligt and Tacoma argue that several publications on migration during the Roman imperial period quote Sallust's *The War with Catiline* 37.7 (Sallust, 2013, pp. 82–3) in order to demonstrate how 'large numbers of poor country-dwellers moved to Rome because they preferred an easy life in the city, supported by private and public grain doles, to hard toil in the country' (Ligt and Tacoma, 2016, p. 3). The crowd of Mark could be a mixture of different groups of persons, such as elites, slaves, soldiers, farmers/peasants, crafts persons and seasonal workers. Zerbini even mentions that seasonal migratory workers include professionals such as athletes, thespians, stone-masons and architects (Zerbini, 2016, pp. 328–9). One aspect that unites these various groups is their decision to 'migrate' or move/travel in order to find help/hope. Here I follow Ligt and Tacoma's definition of migration as 'the movement of humans by which they change their residence from one place to another on a permanent or semi-permanent basis' (2016, p. 4). This semi-permanence though has to be qualified with Greg Woolf's argument that 'most movements are local or regional' (2016, pp. 450–51). Most of the movements/migrations/mobilities are between neighbouring villages and town, with a few travels to distant places. Thus, to describe the *ochlos* as migrants is less on their permanence but more of their intentionality. The OFWs and the *ochlos* of Mark are semi-permanent migrants who are forced to move and find Jesus for various reasons, albeit migration due to economic hardship is usually the most prominent reason during ancient times (Ligt and Tacoma, 2016, pp. 9–10).

One cannot surmise how long the *ochlos* were with Jesus. In any case, following the consensus that the Markan Jesus' ministry only lasted a year, then the *ochlos*' encounters with Jesus were diverse but limited. The distance of their travels and the durations of their encounter with Jesus are unknown; nevertheless, one thing is traceable: their intent is to find assistance from/through Jesus. Of course, the *ochlos* could be local residents who heard about Jesus. They could also be passers-by, busybodies, or other groups of persons who are not seeking Jesus actively for help/hope. In any case, the intentionality of these individuals and groups in seeking Jesus is the reason why I perceive them as closer to those who left their homes in order to find help/hope. I see them as semi-permanent migratory/mobile travellers who sought Jesus for help/hope.

I see the second step when the *ochlos* encounters Jesus. Seeing the crowd, Jesus realizes that the crowd was 'like a sheep without shepherd'[7] (*probata me echonta poimena*; v. 34) who needed compassion and guidance from a teacher. Jesus responded to the crowd by teaching/giving them 'many things' (*autous polla*; v. 34). The second step does not end here. The narrative continues into the night. The hour is now very late; and the crowd (including Jesus and the disciples) are getting hungry and tired. So the disciples encouraged Jesus to send the crowd away. But he answered by taking their five loaves of bread and two pieces of fish, blessing them, breaking them and giving them to the crowd (vv. 35–42). Whether the multiplication of the bread and fish is a miracle or a manifestation of (demythologized) sharing of food as demonstrated and encouraged by Jesus, an OFW hermeneutic would first see this event as a miraculous event because they are 'filled/satisfied' (*echortasthesan*; v. 42) one way or another in their moments of difficulty. This miraculous event is a divine encounter (perhaps even liturgical; see Deut. 8.10) in which the miracle of Elisha (2 Kings 4.42–44) is once again with the people in their hunger, and even perhaps in the midst of their famine (see Aus, 2010, pp. 26–40).

One could argue that the OFWs did not work in the typical sense for Jesus at all. Here one has to redefine 'work' not simply within the confines of labour and wages. For the OFWs, it is an implicit search for hope and a better future for their family and themselves. For those who find listening laborious, one could argue that listening to Jesus for a prolonged period of time is 'work' because the *ochlos* performed the role of audience and/or discipleship for Jesus – a fulfilment of their part in this contractual narrative.

Moreover, in *Migration and Mobility in the Early Roman Empire*, Colin Adams (Oxyrhynchos), Christer Bruun (northern Italy), Paul Erdkamp (Rome), Claire Holleran (Iberian peninsula), Andrea Zerbini (Jerusalem, Palmyra, Antioch) and other scholars marshalled literary texts, inscriptions and epigraphs that prove the existence of seasonal migrants who travelled short and long distances, variegated time periods, in order to find (better) work and/or additional income. Among these seasonal migrants, women and children were also involved (Holleran, pp. 117–19; Bruun; Foubert; and Zerbini, p. 321). Work/jobs could be in construction, port labour, mining and even sex work (Foubert, 2016, p. 300). Interestingly, their pay scales are inconsistent. As Matthew 20.1–16 (the Parable of the Labourers of the Vineyard) attests, the first labourer hired received the same amount of pay as the last person hired. The enforcement of wage equity is hard to come by because of lack of labour laws, corruption and other factors (Holleran, 2016, p. 96). The Roman Empire was a slave society in which wages were 'spasmodic, casual, marginal' (Temin, 2017, p. 115).

Furthermore, one has to question the quid pro quo assumption that people receive certain things because they have paid/worked for them. For example, Rome's *annona/frumentationes* system provides grain dole of five *modii* (approximately 33 kilograms/73 pounds) to its privileged individuals: 'those who were settled and well-integrated in the city, who had a permanent job or profession, a skill or stable employment' (Erdkamp, 2016, p. 47). The number of the recipients are limited and the migrants/outsiders are in a disadvantageous position in obtaining this privilege (Bernard, 2016, p. 65). In other words, this dole system is less about social welfare and more about symbolic privileging of the few (Bernard, 2016, p. 54). Compared to this system, Mark depicts Jesus' magnanimity as more generous than Rome. Jesus gave his bread and fish dole to everyone. Here it seems that Mark is demonstrating that Jesus' empire can provide better stability, security and sustenance to the *ochlos*. If these privileged few receive 'pay' without or barely any work, then Mark provides a counter-cultural narrative in which the people, whoever they are, will receive 'pay' without or barely any work.

Then the third step ensues. Verse 43 informs us that there were twelve baskets full of broken pieces of bread and fishes. After describing the leftovers, the narrative immediately tells us that Jesus and his disciples dismissed the crowd (v. 45). An OFW hermeneutic helps us understand that the information about the leftover bread and fish is not tangential/appendix information. Rather, the third step of OFW hermeneutics finds this information, the leftover of twelve baskets full of food, as the crucial conclusive element of the narrative. These twelve baskets are remittances or food intentionally set aside for their folk back home. Their engagement with Jesus gave them the chance to bring home not just the remittance of teaching and compassion but also the broken pieces of bread and fishes for their families. Family is important for the OFWs as it was for the migrants during ancient times. Mobilization/migration decisions are done as a family and not just by the individual. The family and/or the community probably weighed many factors before migratory decisions are made. Since decisions were made as a family/community, the migratory workers are deeply enmeshed with their home community/nation. In expounding the importance of connecting back with home/*patris*, Laurens E. Tacoma and Rolf A. Tybout (2016, p. 347) worked through 142 Greek (funerary) epigrams found in Asia Minor, Syria, Palestine and Arabia. Through these epigrams, they have uncovered 'the immense efforts undertaken to return the ashes of the deceased home … [demonstrating] a person's birthplace was regarded as the place where one belonged' (Tacoma and Tybout, 2016, p. 356). Returning home is both for the living and the dead.

Again in 8.1–9, a 'great crowd' (*pollou ochlou*; v. 1) has gathered and approached Jesus to receive compassion and lessons from Jesus (first and second steps). The same situation happened as well: the crowd got hungry and have nothing to eat. So Jesus and his disciples gathered seven loaves of bread and a few small fish. After blessing them, Jesus and his disciples distributed them to the crowd (second step). They were filled and have seven baskets full of leftovers (vv. 2–8). Then Jesus sent them home (v. 9) with the leftovers/remittance of food to bring back to their families (third step).

The leftovers/remittances remind me of *sallim*, a Korean word that means 'living'. Jin-Ho Kim (2013, p. 223) points out that Ahn Byung-Mu expresses *sallim* as 'getting over killing'. In other words, *sallim* describes minjung theology's anti-necropolitics or against the exploitative systems that turns individuals and communities into objects of abuse, extraction and killable. Minjung as *sallim* is about becoming *shik-gu* (family; which literally means 'food-mouth'). For Koreans and Filipinx, eating is a communal event that helps us realize our connectedness with each other and with the world. It is a chance for us to check in on each other, hear each other's stories, and console one another over a hot bowl of rice. Jesus treated the crowd like *shik-gu*. That is why in Mark 3.31–35, Jesus calls the *ochlos* his family members. As their shepherd, Jesus 'feeds' his sheep/family members: 'I have compassion for the crowd, because they have been with me now for three days and have nothing to eat. If I send them away hungry to their homes, they will faint on the way – and some of them have come from a great distance' (8.3). For Jesus to feed the *ochlos*/OFW is to provide *sallim*. It also acknowledges their drive to survive and find *sallim* even when it means they have to travel a great distance. For the *ochlos* to be hungry for 'three days' echoes the difficult working conditions of the OFWs. Some of them might have literally been in constant state of hunger or at least malnutrition as they work for their remittances. And yet they persist for themselves and for their families.

This persistence, the desire to help their families back home, perhaps is the reason why Jesus equates the 'sign' (8.11–13) with the leftovers of the two feeding narratives. The Pharisees demanded a sign from heaven in order to test Jesus. Jesus sighed and responded that he will not provide them with another sign. Then he left with his disciples on a boat. Still fresh on his mind, Jesus blurted: 'Watch out – beware of the yeast/leaven of the Pharisees and of Herod' (v. 15). The disciples were confused with Jesus' utterance. They thought that Jesus was angry with them for not bringing the leftovers ('any bread'; v. 14) with them. Instead, Jesus asked them about how much leftovers were created during the two feeding narratives (vv. 17–21). Here, OFW hermeneutics connect vv. 11–13 with vv. 14–21. By doing so, the narrative flow highlights the importance of the leftovers. These leftovers are not tangential information. Rather, the leftovers are the sign of the identity of Jesus as the messiah and the kin(g)-dom of heaven. That is why Mark continues the narrative in vv. 22–26 with the healing of a blind man in Bethsaida. The sign is when the people bring a blind man, a leftover of the community, to Jesus to be healed. After Jesus heals the blind man, Jesus sends him home. The blind man, his healing, and his return/healing culminates with the confession of Peter that Jesus is the messiah (vv. 27–30). The messiah is with the leftovers.

Reading the rest of Mark with an OFW hermeneutic

If OFW hermeneutics invites an understanding of the messianic with the leftovers, then I also see in other passages of Mark resonances of OFW/migratory messianic relationality. Here, as I said before, I am not claiming that the OFW hermeneutics is the scientific formula that deciphers the entire Gospel of Mark. Rather, I hope to provide avenues for the OFWs to find themselves in the passages. Thus, my readings below find the minjung/OFW of Mark not just wherever the word *ochlos* is mentioned. Instead, I find the minjung–*ochlos* dynamic wherever I see/read the movements of the people/individual who seek Jesus for help/hope. Furthermore, certain passages even narrate explicitly how the recipients of help/hope are invited to go back to their communities.

In a few cases, the individual represents the *ochlos*. Such relationality though does not imply that individuals did not have a voice apart from the *ochlos*. Rather, I follow Mitzi J. Smith's assertion that 'without the voice and testimony of individuals who emerge from the crowds we could not know the minjung' (2013, p. 112). Smith calls this communal and reciprocal relationality between the *ochlos* and the individuals in the narrative as 'soteriological hermeneutical circle' (2013, pp. 113–14). Although Smith focuses on the Gospel of Luke, her analysis reverberates in Mark as well. I agree that when a person is healed, the community is healed. When a person is 'saved', the community is delivered as well.

The Gospel of Mark begins with a migratory-like movement: the people of the 'whole Judean region and all the people of Jerusalem' (v. 5) travelled all the way to the river of Jordan to meet John the Baptist (first step). They did so because they want to confess their sins and be baptized by him (second step). The pericope (1.1–8) does not provide the third step of the OFW hermeneutics in which the people of 'the whole Judean region and all the people of Jerusalem' (v. 5) are depicted to return home with remittance. Nevertheless, one can deduce/assume from this narrative that they/some were baptized, were able to repent, and go back home with a sense of forgiveness for themselves and their families. The Markan narrative implicitly mentions that Jesus did meet people in the Judean countryside and Jerusalem later on (chapters 10 and following).

The three-step pattern occurs again with Jesus' encounter with a leper (1.40–45). A leper went to Jesus so that he could be healed (first step). Moved with pity, Jesus touched the leper and healed him (second step). Then Jesus dismissed the leper by commanding him to go to the priest so that he can be declared to be clean and ready to be integrated back to the family (third step). Perhaps one could even imagine that his healing and return is a form of remittance for his family and his wider (Jewish) community.

'The Healing of a Paralytic' narrative (2.1–12) is also conducive for an OFW hermeneutics. Many travelled and gathered together in Jesus' home at Capernaum (first step). Jesus preached the word to them. A group of four men brought their paralytic friend so that Jesus could heal him. Unable to get near because of the crowd, the four men opened the roof of the house up and let their paralytic friend down. When Jesus saw their faith, Jesus gave them what they hoped for (second step). Now, the narrative does not end here. After forgiving the sins of the paralytic, Jesus told the healed person to pick up his mat, walk, and go home (v. 11; third step). His healing and return (with his friends) are the healing remittance that he and his community needed.

A large number of people from Jerusalem, Idumea, beyond the Jordan, Tyre and Sidon (3.8), crowds (3.7–12, 20–22, 31–35; 4.1–2, 36; 6.53–56; 9.14–29; 10.1–12, 13–16), and individuals (7.24–30, 31–37; 10.46–52) travel relatively long distances to be healed/helped by and learn from Jesus. The Gerasene Demoniac narrative (5.1–20) begins with the demon-possessed person travelling to/pushed out/secluded into the tombs. Unlike those who travel intentionally to meet Jesus, he had a fortuitous encounter with Jesus. In the cemetery, Jesus healed the demon-possessed person although his method is environmentally damaging (killing pigs in the Sea of Galilee). Nevertheless, Jesus commanded the exorcised person: 'Go home to your own people, and tell them how much the Lord has done for you and what mercy he has shown you' (v. 19). Here, his healing and the message of/about Jesus are the gifts (*pasalubong*) he will bring to his family and community.

While healing/resuscitating Jairus' daughter, Jesus' encounter with the woman afflicted with haemorrhage is another narrative that resonates with the OFW hermeneutics. First, she decided that she needs to travel and ask Jesus to heal her (5.27–28). In the midst of the crowd and being one of the persons in the crowd, she pushed her way through and touched

Jesus. Then she was immediately healed. After realizing that it is she who touched him, Jesus told her to 'go in peace, and be healed of your disease' (v. 34). Here we see the completion of the three-step narrative flow. This time, though, we do not know if she will return to her community. Perhaps she lives by herself. In any case, her story redefines kinship and healing as going (back) to personal wholeness.

A pause: host nations are NOT 'saviours'

My OFW hermeneutics also invites a 'pause', or a critical take on the conditions of the OFWs and of the dangers of saviourism. I acknowledge that the Markan Jesus likes to 'dismiss' the crowd constantly. That is why I argue that Jesus is on the one hand part of the minjung and on the other he is not because he occupies the space of the 'host'.[8] For example, Jesus calls upon the crowd when he needs their mob support. In 7.14, when Jesus was being questioned by the Pharisees and scribes, Jesus reached out to the crowd and asked them to support him, be his buffer. We see this again in 11.18 and 12.12. After the crowd helped Jesus, one could read Jesus 'sending the individual or the group home/away' (see also 7.17; 11.19) as dismissive. Tat-siong Benny Liew's argument (1999) reminds us that one has to acknowledge the colonial mimicry of the Markan Jesus and his kin(g)-dom in which he subdues the Roman Empire's authority with his own version of authority, demanding everyone to follow him or else. The OFWs also know the dangers and exploitative conditions brought about by the host nations and the multinational companies. They need the remittances from the host nations and the multinational companies. And yet they are not oblivious to the pitfalls of these 'fake saviours' who are using and abusing international labour laws in order to save labour costs.

The same goes for Mark 14.43 and 15.11, where the crowd is manipulated by the authorities to do their bidding. Verse 14.43 reads, 'Immediately, while he was still speaking, Judas, one of the twelve, arrived, and with him there was a crowd [*ochlos*] with swords, clubs, from the chief priests, the scribes, and elders.' Then again in 15.11, 'But the chief priests stirred up the crowd [*ochlos*] to have him release Barabbas for them instead.' Ahn Byung-Mu explains these two discombobulating passages by arguing that there were two crowds, the Galilean versus Jerusalem. I disagree with Ahn Byung-Mu on the binarization of the crowd. Rather, I follow Greg Carey's insistence that the minjung 'do not constitute a homogenous category' (2013, p. 123). In his reading of the 'inhabitants of the earth' in Revelation as minjung, Carey insists that an uncritical sympathetic take on the minjung neglects to illustrate the complexity of being and becoming minjung. Many of those who struggle are complicit (or even support) the oppressive systems because they are forced and/or deceived to do so. Many of the minjung/inhabitants of the earth are both oppressed and (neo-)oppressors. That is why Carey invites us to 'discern the forces that divide ordinary people against one another and lead them to participate in systems that ultimately degrade their own welfare' (2013, p. 132). Moreover, David Arthur Sánchez adds a postcolonially ambivalent layer in understanding the identities of the *ochlos*. According to Sánchez, Ahn's bifurcation between the Galilean and Judean *ochloi* is about 'performance in relationship to proximity of colonial power' (2013, p. 136). The difference is on the degree of the *ochlos*' mimicry of the colonial powers as a form of survival.

Verses 14.43 and 15.11 are narratives of mimicry, albeit they are failed responses to the pressures of the exploitative. The *ochlos* is not an innocent group of persons. There were even tax collectors (2.13–16), those who are considered enemies of the people, in the *ochlos* (movement). Perhaps that is exactly why the disciples collected the leftover bread and fish into twelve and seven baskets. The disciples collected the leftovers because they probably witnessed how some members of the *ochlos* hoarded food for themselves. In order to prevent this heinous act, the disciples could have gathered as much leftovers as they can so that they can redistribute them to everyone equitably. As Elizabeth Struthers Malbon argues (1986), just like the twelve disciples of Jesus, the crowd are portrayed ambivalently by Mark.

The OFWs work so hard to make ends meet for their families. And yet they are not exempt from problematic issues. Since they have been away for far too long from their family, many (cis-)men commit adultery. Broken family is a widely known problem in many OFW circles. This problem is a result of not just individual proclivities but also of the colonial, capitalist systems that break families apart. Inasmuch as I want to uplift the OFWs in every possible way, I also have to be critical as well by revealing the colonial underbelly of this movement and phenomenon. According to Mark 6.44, only the men (*andres*) were the direct recipients of the food. Luke 9.14 and John 6.10 also have it as *andres*. Matthew found this detail disturbing enough to add 'besides women and children' (Matt. 13.21). The preferential treatment for *andres* seems to be the colonial underbelly of this narrative, or perhaps of the Markan author.

Echoing this saddening narrative, the OFWs do not always have heart-warming narratives. Like how the oppressed are crucified on the cross, Joanna Demafelis was murdered by her employer in 2018 (Talabong, 2018, n.p.). We say her name and the names of other OFWs who were crucified in the name of finding help/hope for their families and communities.

I also follow Keun-Joo Christine Pae's call to invoke the presence of the oppressed women in the *ochlos* (movement) (2013, p. 169). By uplifting the precarious lives of the 'western princesses' (*yang-gong-ju*) who are forced to work in the US military sex industry zones (*kijichon*) for livelihood, Pae admonishes that the sex workers and the silenced women in the Mark/*ochlos* should be loved and 'healed from violence and alienation' (2013, p. 183). Eleazar Fernandez also cautions us to not mimic the 'failure of the first generation of liberation theologians to see the heterogeneity of the poor (*Minjung*)' (2018, p. 213). Not adhering to this admonition might lead to the participation of the very oppressive systems we are trying to overcome. Thus, just like we remember Joanna Demafelis, Pae invites us to seek further the hauntings[9] of the hidden/suppressed voices/presences of oppressed women. We also hope to listen to the queer folx, as Min-Ah Cho asserts (2013), in the *ochlos*/minjung/OFWs and in Mark.[10]

Notes

1 The 'x' in Filipinx symbolizes my choice to be in solidarity with the queer Filipinx communities.

2 One of the most compassionate and engaging ministers who serves the OFWs is Reverend Mariesol Villalon (see Mangiduyos, 2020).

3 As of 2021, there are approximately 909,600 foreign workers in South Korea. See Statistics Korea, 2022.

4 The feeding narrative is also found in Matthew 14.31–21; 15.32–39; Luke 9.10–17; John 6.1–15.

5 I highly encourage further engagement with Suh Nam-Dong, Kim Yong-Bock, Hyun Yong-Hak and other minjung thinkers and activists who led and participated in the liberation of the oppressed.

6 All of the English translations come from the NRSVUE.

7 See also Numbers 27.17; 1 Kings 22.17; Ezekiel 34.5.

8 Ahn Byung-Mu mentioned briefly the possibility of reading Jesus and the *ochlos*/minjung through the host–guest relationship (Ahn Byung-Mu, 2013, p. 87).

9 I invoke Grace Cho's analysis (2008, pp. 3–5) of 'ghost and hauntings' in Korean diasporic consciousness.

10 Many thanks to Loyola University Chicago's Department of Theology (the Biblical Studies faculty members and their amazing PhD students) for engaging with an earlier version of this paper during their colloquium. I am grateful to Dr Olivia Stewart-Lester for the invitation.

References

Adams, Colin, 2016, 'Migration in Roman Egypt: Problems and Possibilities', in Luuk de Ligt and Laurens E. Tacoma (eds), *Migration and Mobility in the Early Roman Empire*, Leiden: Brill, pp. 264–84.

Ahn, Byung-Mu, 2013, 'Minjung Theology from the Perspective of the Gospel of Mark', in Yung Suk Kim and Jin-Ho Kim (eds), *Reading Minjung Theology in the Twenty-First Century, Selected Writings by Ahn Byung-Mu and Modern Critical Responses*, Eugene, OR: Wipf & Stock, pp. 65–90.

Aus, Roger David, 2010, *Feeding the Five Thousand: Studies in the Judaic Background of Mark 6:30–44 par. and John 6:1–15*, New York: University Press of America.

Aymer, Margaret, 2014, 'Rootlessness and Community in Contexts of Diaspora', in Margaret Aymer, Cynthia Briggs Kittredge and David A. Sánchez (eds), *Fortress Commentary on the Bible: The New Testament*, Minneapolis, MN: Fortress Press, pp. 47–61.

Banawiratma, J. B., 2018, 'The Powerless and the Powerful for the Common – An Indonesian Liberation Perspective', in Jin-Kwan Kwon and Volker Küster (eds), *Minjung Theology Today: Contextual and Intercultural Perspectives*, Contact Zone, Leipzig: Evangelische Verlagsanstalt, pp. 195–204.

Bernard, Seth G., 2016, 'Food Distributions and Immigration in Imperial Rome', in Luuk de Ligt and Laurens E. Tacoma (eds), *Migration and Mobility in the Early Roman Empire*, Leiden: Brill, pp. 50–71.

Bruun, Christer, 2016, 'Tracing Familial Mobility: Female and Child Migrants in the Roman West', in Luuk de Ligt and Laurens E. Tacoma (eds), *Migration and Mobility in the Early Roman Empire*, Leiden: Brill, pp. 176–204.

Carey, Greg, 2013, '"The Inhabitants of the Earth" in Revelation', in Yung Suk Kim and Jin-Ho Kim (eds), *Reading Minjung Theology in the Twenty-First Century, Selected Writings by Ahn Byung-Mu and Modern Critical Responses*, Eugene, OR: Wipf & Stock, pp. 120–33.

Cho, Grace, 2008, *Haunting the Korean Diaspora: Shame, Secrecy, and the Forgotten War*, Minneapolis, MN: University of Minnesota Press.

Cho, Min-Ah, 2013, '"If They Send Me to Hell, Jesus Will Rescue Me": Minjung Theology and the Iban Movement', in Yung Suk Kim and Jin-Ho Kim (eds), *Reading Minjung Theology in the Twenty-First Century, Selected Writings by Ahn Byung-Mu and Modern Critical Responses*, Eugene, OR: Wipf & Stock, pp. 184–99.

Choi, Jin Young, 2021, 'Dispersion of Minjung in Mark and Asian Diaspora in the Americas', in Jione Havea and Monica J. Melanchthon (eds), *Bible Blindspots: Dispersion and Othering*, Eugene, OR: Pickwick, pp. 105–19.

Choy, Catherine Ceniza, 2003, *Empire of Care: Nursing and Migration in Filipino American History*, Durham, NC: Duke University Press.
Constante, Agnes, 2021, 'Filipino American Nurses, Reflecting on Disproportionate Covid Toll, Look Ahead', *NBC News*, https://www.nbcnews.com/news/asian-america/filipino-american-nurses-reflecting-disproportionate-covid-toll-look-a-rcna1112 (accessed 29.09.2022).
Deleuze, Gilles and Felix Guattari, 1987, *A Thousand Plateaus: Capitalism and Schizophrenia*, trans. Brian Massumi, Minneapolis, MN: University of Minnesota Press.
Downs, David J., 2016, *The Offering of the Gentiles: Paul's Collection for Jerusalem in its Chronological, Cultural, and Cultic Contexts*, Grand Rapids, MI: Eerdmans.
Erdkamp, Paul, 2016, 'Seasonal Labour and Rural–Urban Migration in Roman Italy', in Luuk de Ligt and Laurens E. Tacoma (eds), *Migration and Mobility in the Early Roman Empire*, Leiden: Brill, pp. 33–49.
Fernandez, Eleazar, 2018, 'Empire, Global Hegemony, and The Theo-Political Practice of the Subaltern *Minjung*', in Jin-Kwan Kwon and Volker Küster (eds), *Minjung Theology Today: Contextual and Intercultural Perspectives*, Contact Zone, Leipzig: Evangelische Verlagsanstalt, pp. 205–19.
Foubert, Lien, 2016, 'Mobile Women in *P.Oxy.* and the Port Cities of Roman Egypt: Tracing Women's Travel Behaviours in Papyrological Sources', in Luuk de Ligt and Laurens E. Tacoma (eds), *Migration and Mobility in the Early Roman Empire*, Leiden: Brill, pp. 285–304.
Holleran, Claire, 2016, 'Labour Mobility in the Roman World: A Case Study of Mines in Iberia', in Luuk de Ligt and Laurens E. Tacoma (eds), *Migration and Mobility in the Early Roman Empire*, Leiden: Brill, pp. 95–137.
Hur Joo-Mee, 2018, 'Embarking on a Theological Journey with Literature – A Confluence of Two Stories of Migrant Brides', in Jin-Kwan Kwon and Volker Küster (eds), *Minjung Theology Today: Contextual and Intercultural Perspectives*, Contact Zone, Leipzig: Evangelische Verlagsanstalt, pp. 127–44.
Hwang, Yong-Yeon, 2013, 'The Person Attacked by the Robbers is Christ', in Yung Suk Kim and Jin-Ho Kim (eds), *Reading Minjung Theology in the Twenty-First Century: Selected Writings by Ahn Byung-Mu and Modern Critical Responses*, Eugene, OR: Wipf & Stock, pp. 215–232.
In, Hannah and Wongi Park (eds), 2019, *Stories of Minjung Theology: The Theological Journey of Ahn Byung-Mu in His Own Words*, International Voices in Biblical Studies, Atlanta, GA: SBL.
Josephus, 1963, *Jewish Antiquities* (Books 16–17), trans. Ralph Marcus, Loeb Classical Library 410, vol. 10, Cambridge, MA: Harvard University Press.
Kang Won-Don, 2018, 'Some Tasks of *Minjung* Theology in the Age of Globalization', in Jin-Kwan Kwon and Volker Küster (eds), *Minjung Theology Today: Contextual and Intercultural Perspectives*, Contact Zone, Leipzig: Evangelische Verlagsanstalt, pp. 65–82.
Kim, Jin-Ho, 2013, 'The Hermeneutics of Ahn Byung-Mu: Focusing on the Concepts of "Discovery of Internality" and "Otherness of Minjung"', in Yung Suk Kim and Jin-Ho Kim (eds), *Reading Minjung Theology in the Twenty-First*

Century: Selected Writings by Ahn Byung-Mu and Modern Critical Responses, Eugene, OR: Wipf & Stock, pp. 13–26.

Kim, Nami, 2021, 'When the Minjung Events Erupt: Protests from Korea to Hong Kong', in Kwok Pui-lan and Francis Ching-Wah Yip (eds), *The Hong Kong Protests and Political Theology*, Lanham, MD: Rowman & Littlefield, pp. 171–82.

Kim, Yung Suk, 2013, 'Introduction', in Yung Suk Kim and Jin-Ho Kim (eds), *Reading Minjung Theology in the Twenty-First Century: Selected Writings by Ahn Byung-Mu and Modern Critical Responses*, Eugene, OR: Wipf & Stock, pp. 1–12.

Küster, Volker, 2010, *Protestant Theology of Passion: Minjung Theology Revisited*, Leiden: Brill.

Kwon, Jiseong J., 2022, 'Minjung in Global Context', in Won. W. Lee (ed), *The Oxford Handbook of the Bible in Korea*, New York: Oxford University Press, pp. 265–87.

Liew, Tat-siong Benny, 1999, 'Tyranny, Boundary, and Might: Colonial Mimicry in Mark's Gospel', *Journal for the Study of the New Testament* 21 (73), pp. 7–31.

Ligt, Luuk de and Laurens E. Tacoma, 2016, 'Approaching Migration in the Early Roman Empire', in Luuk de Ligt and Laurens E. Tacoma (eds), *Migration and Mobility in the Early Roman Empire*, Leiden: Brill, pp. 1–22.

Malbon, Elizabeth Struthers, 1986, 'Disciples/Crowds/Whoever: Markan Characters and Readers', *Novum Testamentum* 28 (2), pp. 122–3.

Mangiduyos, Gladys, 2020, 'Filipino Pastor Aims to bring Stranded Workers Home', *UM News*, The Philippines, https://www.umnews.org/en/news/filipino-pastor-aims-to-bring-stranded-workers-home (accessed 29.09.2022).

Mapa, Dennis S., 2022, '2020 Overseas Filipino Workers (Final Results)', *Philippine Statistics Authority*, The Philippines, https://psa.gov.ph/content/2020-overseas-filipino-workers-final-results (accessed 29.09.2022).

Miller, Jack, 2022, 'Religion in the Philippines', *Asia Society: Center for Global Education*, New York, Asian Society, https://asiasociety.org/education/religion-philippines (accessed 30.09.2022).

Pae, Keun-Joo Christine, 2013, 'Minjung Theology and Global Peacemaking: From Galilee to the US Military Camptown (*Kijichon*) in South Korea', in Yung Suk Kim and Jin-Ho Kim (eds), *Reading Minjung Theology in the Twenty-First Century: Selected Writings by Ahn Byung-Mu and Modern Critical Responses*, Eugene, OR: Wipf & Stock, pp. 164–83.

Philo, 1962, *On the Embassy to Gaius (The First Part of the Treatise on Virtues)*, trans. F. H. Colson, Loeb Classical Library 379, vol. 10, Cambridge, MA: Harvard University Press.

Ryan, Jordan J. Cruz, forthcoming, 'Explorations in Filipino American Biblical Hermeneutics: Passion and Resistance in the Struggle', in Wongi Park (ed.), *Multiracial Biblical Studies*, Atlanta, GA: SBL.

Sallust, 2013, *The War with Catiline: The War with Jugurtha*, trans. J. C. Rolfe, rev. John. T. Ramsey, Loeb Classical Library 116, vol. 1, Cambridge, MA: Harvard University Press.

Sánchez, David Arthur, 2013, 'Ambivalence, Mimicry, and the *Ochlos* in the Gospel of Mark: Assessing the Minjung Theology of Ahn Byung-Mu', in Yung Suk Kim and Jin-Ho Kim (eds), *Reading Minjung Theology in the Twenty-First*

Century: Selected Writings by Ahn Byung-Mu and Modern Critical Responses, Eugene, OR: Wipf & Stock, pp. 134–47.

Smith, Mitzi J., 2013, 'Minjung, the Black Masses, and the Global Imperative', in Yung Suk Kim and Jin-Ho Kim (eds), *Reading Minjung Theology in the Twenty-First Century: Selected Writings by Ahn Byung-Mu and Modern Critical Responses*, Eugene, OR: Wipf & Stock, pp. 101–19.

Statistics Korea, 2022, 'Summary of Economically Active Population (Immigrant)', in *Korean Statistical Information Service*, South Korea, Statistic Korea, https://kosis.kr/eng/ (accessed 15.10.2022).

Suarez, Harrod, 2015, 'Maternal Diasporas and Posthuman Subjectivity in Hagedorn's "Dream Jungle" and Roley's "American Son"', *MELUS* 40 (2), p. 74.

Tacoma, Laurens E. and Rolf A. Tybout, 2016, 'Moving Epigrams: Migration and Mobility in the Greek East', in Luuk de Ligt and Laurens E. Tacoma (eds), *Migration and Mobility in the Early Roman Empire*, Leiden: Brill, pp. 345–89.

Talabong, Rambo, 2018, '"A National Shame": The Death and Homecoming of Joanna Demafelis', *Rappler*, 4 March, The Philippines, https://www.rappler.com/newsbreak/in-depth/197347-death-homecoming-joanna-demafelis-ofw-kuwait/ (accessed 12.10.2022).

Temin, Peter, 2017, *The Roman Market Economy: What Modern Economics Can Tell Us about Ancient Rome*, Princeton, NJ: Princeton University Press.

Woolf, Greg, 2016, 'Movers and Stayers', in Luuk de Ligt and Laurens E. Tacoma (eds), *Migration and Mobility in the Early Roman Empire*, Leiden: Brill, pp. 438–61.

Zerbini, Andrea, 2016, 'Human Mobility in the Roman Near East: Patterns and Motives', in Luuk de Ligt and Laurens E. Tacoma (eds), *Migration and Mobility in the Early Roman Empire*, Leiden: Brill, pp. 305–44.

9

Post-Trauma Narrative: A Path to Liberation in the Bible and Beyond

DIANA PAULDING

Narrative formation after a traumatic event is powerful. It enables individuals to adapt to the changes in perspective that trauma inevitably brings and can restore lost agency. When we acknowledge that individuals are able to speak meaningfully about their trauma and avoid imposing collective narratives that attempt to explain their trauma upon them, individual trauma narratives have the power to challenge both those collective narratives that attempt to silence them and the social systems that led to their trauma. In this, trauma narratives can be a path to liberation.

Within the biblical field, scholars who read the Bible through the hermeneutical lens of trauma theory often rely on a separation between individual and cultural trauma. David Janzen, for example, argues that collective narratives of cultural trauma always silence traumatized individuals as they impose meaning upon individuals who are incapable of narrating their own trauma (Janzen, 2019). In contrast, I argue that while collective narratives of cultural trauma can silence individuals, this is not inevitable. We see in the book of Job how Job refuses to be silenced by the collective narratives presented by the friends and instead creates his own trauma narrative based on protest against God. In so doing, the book validates the individual voice and provides an alternative response to collective narratives about Israel's national traumas. By recognizing that individuals can speak meaningfully about their trauma, we allow them the opportunity to protest against the causes of their trauma and to influence the related collective narratives.

Acknowledging the validity of protest within individual trauma narratives is also important in contemporary liberation work. This chapter concludes by comparing examples from South Africa where individual voices have been used to influence social change. The Truth and Reconciliation Commission that was set up in 1995, although significant in its centralization of individual stories, was still driven by a dominant collective narrative and did not empower the individuals involved to drive social change. By contrast, the solidarity network ACT Ubumbano makes space for individuals to tell their own stories but also gives them agency to work to change the causes of their own suffering. By refusing to impose collective narratives upon individual sufferers and hearing their voices of protest, it becomes possible to address the root causes of their trauma. Rather than being like Job's friends and reinforcing collective narratives that silence individuals who suffer, we can instead hear the voice of the sufferers and be led by them in paving the way to liberation.

Defining individual and cultural trauma

To begin the task of exploring the intersection between the individual and the collective, it is necessary to clarify what is meant by the terms 'individual trauma' and 'cultural trauma'. Individual trauma occurs on a psychological level. The human brain is primed for survival, and when an individual is subjected to extreme stress, the brain reacts in a way that maximizes the individual's potential to survive the threat, priming the body to fight, flee or freeze in the face of danger. The psychologist Bessel van der Kolk describes how the limbic system dominates the brain's response, stimulating an increase in heart rate, oxygen intake and blood pressure, and thus providing the body with the tools needed to address the threat. Areas of the evolutionarily younger neocortex (or 'rational brain') are less immediately helpful in life-or-death situations and so activity in this region becomes reduced in stressful situations; for example, the processing of language or a person's concept of time becomes diminished (van der Kolk, 2014). These responses are normal survival mechanisms in the face of acute danger. When this neurological state persists once the acute danger has passed, however, the individual can struggle to function in everyday life and we speak of them being 'traumatized'. The literary theorist Cathy Caruth describes individual trauma as being a 'failure of experience' (Caruth, 1996); the inability of the brain to process the event and to use language to narrate it or make meaning results, she argues, in the event never being properly experienced. Caruth's explanation of trauma has proved influential in biblical scholarship and the concept of trauma being a failure of narrative forms the foundation of Janzen's argument. Individual trauma, he argues, is defined by the individual's inability to narrate their trauma as a series of events that occurred in the past.

Cultural trauma, on the other hand, is all about narrative creation. Jeffrey Alexander's influential work describes cultural trauma as occurring when a social group views an event or situation as a threat to their collective identity (Alexander, 2004). Events in themselves are not *inherently* traumatic, Alexander argues, but become seen as traumatic as collective narratives that describe the event as a threat are developed and accepted by the group. These narratives seek to explain why the situation occurred and to use these explanations to preserve or reframe the group's threatened identity. It is a phenomenon that occurs on a sociological level, and the narratives that are formed create a shared sense of suffering and a reinforced collective identity. Since cultural trauma is about narrative creation but individual trauma is perceived to be about a failure of narrative, Janzen argues that individual and collective trauma are 'not two species of the same genus but two incompatible things' (Janzen, 2019, p. 6). It should be noted that, although Janzen uses the term 'collective trauma', this phrase can have a range of meanings and the form of trauma that he describes can be referred to more specifically as 'cultural trauma', a category of collective trauma that focuses upon group identity rather than broken personal relationships or threats to social structures like the economy.

Individual and cultural trauma are therefore often seen as two fundamentally different phenomena; one is a neurological state that prohibits the processing and narration of the traumatic event, while the other is a sociological drive to create meaning and promote group cohesion. Such a sharp separation, however, fails to recognize the place of meaning-making within the process of individual trauma, and thus denies individuals the opportunity to engage with collective narratives about their trauma. There is always a danger that collective narratives about trauma are imposed upon the individuals who directly experienced them, but this is a risk rather than an inevitability. Rather than individuals being incapable of forming narrative, the individual voice can in fact challenge and reshape collective narratives that silence the victims.

Within biblical scholarship, trauma theory provides a useful hermeneutical lens for engaging with the Hebrew Bible. The creation and redaction of the Hebrew Bible was shaped by national disasters including the fall of the northern kingdom of Israel to the Assyrian Empire and the fall of Judah to the Babylonians, and so collective trauma is an appropriate and helpful lens through which to study the Bible. Specifically, as cultural trauma is about narrative, the writings contained within the Hebrew Bible provide invaluable resources for understanding the way Israelite identity and theology grappled with the traumas it faced as surrounding empires fought for control of the region.

When considering the intersection between individual and cultural trauma in the Bible, Job provides an example of how the individual voice and descriptions of personal suffering are used as a challenge to collective narratives of cultural trauma, and this intersection of the individual and the cultural in Job has relevance for how we approach contemporary struggles for liberation.

Narrative formation in individual trauma

First, it is necessary to unpack our understanding of individual trauma and to consider the place of narrative within it. The view that individuals are neurologically incapable of constructing a trauma narrative falsely equates all trauma with Post-traumatic Stress Disorder (PTSD) and denies the process of meaning-making upon which many individuals embark in the aftermath of trauma. The initial stage of trauma shares the symptoms of PTSD (such as hypervigilance and dissociation), but the criteria for PTSD diagnosis stipulates that the individual must have been experiencing symptoms for a month or more (American Psychiatric Association, 2013, p. 272). This is because, in PTSD, the brain becomes neurologically 'stuck' in the moment of trauma (Howard and Crandall, 2007, p. 14), and pharmaceutical, physical or talking therapies may be required to help the individual integrate their memories and start to form a narrative. Normally, however, these symptoms pass within a month and a process of narrative formation begins without intervention.

Ronnie Janoff-Bulman, for example, discusses the way that individuals use narrative to address the 'shattered assumptions' with which one is forced to deal in the aftermath of trauma (Janoff-Bulman, 1992). The assumption that we live in a generally safe and just world is vital for everyday life and co-existence with others. Trauma, however, shatters these assumptions. In the aftermath of physical, emotional, sexual or psychological violence, a person's frameworks of safety and justice are challenged. It is difficult to manage day to day if we do not assume we are generally safe, but trauma forces people to confront the reality that we are not. Janoff-Bulman identifies the construction of narrative as a fundamental part of addressing this realization and finding ways to cope and rebuild our world views in the aftermath of trauma. A narrative of self-blame is common; although a fault of the victim is usually not, objectively, the cause of their suffering, by seeing oneself as in some way responsible the individual can continue to view the world as just and has the agency to believe they can avoid the recurrence of such traumatic situations in the future. It is easier to see oneself as at fault, Susan Brison writes, than to believe that the world is completely random and unjust and that the trauma could happen again at any moment (Brison, 2002, p. 13). In this case, the individual's trauma narrative creates an explanation that can restore justice and agency.

Narrative creation is not always, however, the development of an explanation for the trauma. Narrative formation involves ordering the events and integrating these facts with emotion, so that 'the memory of the traumatic event is a coherent narrative, linked with feeling' (Herman, 1992, p. 213). When an individual is able to say, 'This is what happened, and it happened to me', they take control of the narrative, and there can be a sense of empowerment in knowing what happened and having the language to describe it (Herman, 1992, pp. 157–8).

Narrative can be formed in different ways in the trauma process, and it is a vital stage in the move from the person one was before to the person that trauma forces one to become. To separate individual trauma from cultural trauma on the basis of narrative or lack thereof is to focus only on the initial dissociation of individual trauma and to deny the process whereby the individual seeks to regain agency and control. It is a definition of individual trauma that in itself silences those who suffer.

Trauma narratives in the Bible

We now turn to considering the impact of this understanding of trauma on the way that we read the Bible. A major point in Janzen's argument is that the Bible's collective narratives of cultural trauma, such as the explanations of exile in the Deuteronomistic History, silence the voices of individuals by imposing narrative upon them. Although in Job the individual voice is not silenced but rather central to the book's social challenge, Janzen's identification of narratives of cultural trauma in the Hebrew Bible is an important point. Questions of theodicy run throughout the Hebrew Bible and demonstrate a wider social debate about suffering that was probably provoked by the experience of exile (Rom-Shiloni, 2021). The discussion of theodical issues that is seen across genres in the Hebrew

Bible can be understood, sociologically, as different writers engaging with collective narratives of cultural trauma. While the problem of suffering is cross-cultural and continues to be an issue for individuals today, for a group whose identity was tied up with worship of YHWH, national crises in which the local deity appeared to have been defeated would have provoked a major threat to the group's identity. The justification of the deity can therefore be seen not just as a theological problem but as a sociological one. In order to maintain the group's collective identity (particularly in light of the loss of political autonomy and the land in the exilic period), it was necessary to justify continued worship of YHWH as an undefeated god. Religious collective identity relied on the justification of YHWH.

Theodicy is a 'trilemma' in which the challenge is to reconcile the existence of suffering with an understanding of God as both omnipotent and benevolent (Green, 1987). Dalit Rom-Shiloni identifies different ways in which this trilemma is addressed throughout the Hebrew Bible; Jeremiah 21.1–7, for example, focuses on the reality of suffering and God's omnipotence, but fails to mention God's benevolence (Rom-Shiloni, 2021, pp. 14–19). Another prominent solution to the trilemma is seen across the Deuteronomistic History and parts of the prophets. This solution makes use of a narrative of collective self-blame where the sinfulness of Israel is provided as a reason for the exile. For example, 2 Chronicles 36.15–16 reads:

> The LORD, the God of their ancestors, sent persistently to them by his messengers, because he had compassion on his people and on his dwelling place; but they kept mocking the messengers of God, despising his words, and scoffing at his prophets, until the wrath of the LORD against his people became so great that there was no remedy.

The Chronicler makes an explicit link between the sin of the people themselves and the fall of Jerusalem. In so doing, the disaster is presented as a just punishment enacted by a powerful and compassionate god, while the reality of the disaster is still acknowledged. All three elements of the trilemma are held to be true at the same time, as the reality of suffering is accepted while still maintaining the omnipotence, benevolence and justice of God. In so doing, the power and worthiness of YHWH is defended and continued worship of YHWH is justified. The issue is, of course, that such a narrative functions on an 'us and them' premise that blames the victims. This is not an individual trauma narrative that seeks to rebuild agency, but the imposition of guilt on to victims in order to explain the nation's suffering. We do not hear the voice of the suffering individuals; any protestations of innocence are suppressed, since this would undermine the explanation that seeks to unite the group. Janzen is correct that such narratives silence the individual sufferer. It is this problem, however, that Job addresses.

The book of Job does not contain any direct historical references and it is therefore difficult to date the text conclusively. Nonetheless, the majority of modern scholarship dates Job between the sixth century and the fourth century BCE on the basis of linguistic features and concepts such as the *satan*, which indicate that at least the prose framework dates from the Persian period (Hurvitz, 1974). Also, the theodical questions that characterize the main body of the text reflect the broader questioning that appears in other books that are explicitly exilic or post-exilic (Rom-Shiloni, 2021). In a study of the relationship between Job and Deutero-Isaiah, JiSeong Kwon points out that, despite shared ideas in the two texts, it is difficult to establish the direction of dependence. Nonetheless, Kwon states that the similarities between Job and Deutero-Isaiah indicate a 'wide-ranging network of interconnections during the broad period which the two books present' without committing to a direct literary relationship between the two texts (Kwon, 2017, p. 34). This is significant because Job's response to collective narratives of cultural trauma does not necessarily mean that Job is responding directly to the texts that we have access to today. Rather, the range of biblical texts that engage with similar issues suggests that there was a wider social debate about theodicy, probably in the aftermath of exile, with which different scribes were engaging. It is to this debate that Job provides its unique challenge.

Although Job responds to theodical narratives and has traditionally been referred to as theodicy, the book refuses to provide answers to the problem of theodicy in the way that the Deuteronomistic History or the prophets do. Job engages with and rejects explanations of suffering that are based on Deuteronomic ideas of reward and punishment, but it does not provide a counter-narrative. The character Job never receives a satisfactory reason for why he is suffering, and YHWH's failure to address Job's plight and the jarring epilogue can leave the reader feeling frustrated. Rather than attempting to create a different explanation, Job refuses to deny any element of the trilemma *or* to blame the victim. Meaning is created not through explanation but through protest. As with the individual who is able to narrate their trauma through an integration of fact and emotion, Job acknowledges what has happened to him while still voicing his anger that it has been allowed to happen. He calls God to account, acknowledging YHWH's power and demanding that justice is upheld while rejecting attempts to diminish or explain away his own experience. In this, he maintains a stubborn faith in YHWH. The problem is not solved by rejecting YHWH and dissolving the religious group (although this is, sociologically, a possible response to a threat to the group). Instead, space is created for the anger and lament of the individual in a way that challenges popular collective narratives without rejecting God. It is therefore best to follow Zachary Braiterman and to see Job as 'antitheodicy', or a refusal to justify God in the face of evil and suffering (Braiterman, 1998).

Following Gustavo Gutiérrez's liberation-based work on Job and the theme of appropriate speech (Gutiérrez, 1985), it has become common to see YHWH's statement in Job 42.7 that the friends 'have not spoken of me what is right, as my servant Job has' as praise for Job's willingness to protest. Job's answer to the problem of suffering is not an explanation that benefits the group at the expense of the suffering individual, but an outcry that demands a better world for everyone. This, God's response suggests, is an appropriate response.

In Job, the individual voice is utilized to speak to the wider debate about theodicy. Rather than having narratives imposed upon him, the character of Job forms his own trauma narrative, speaking for himself throughout, responding to and rejecting the friends' attempts at meaning-making, and holding YHWH, the cause of his suffering, to account. Job's trauma narrative is one not of explanation but of protest.

Individual voices and collective narratives in South Africa

Job's narrative of protest can inform how we respond to trauma today. Within contemporary struggles for liberation, the South African context provides a useful case study for examining the place of individual voices in collective narratives and struggles for social change.

In theory, the South African Truth and Reconciliation Commission (TRC) centralized individual voices as a way of challenging the old collective narratives of white supremacy that underpinned apartheid. The TRC called both 'victims' and 'perpetrators' to testify about their experiences of apartheid, offering reparations to victims and amnesty to perpetrators in exchange for their stories. The public hearing of these individual stories helped to break down concepts of the 'Other', and the publicity of the hearings and the publication of the final report distributed new collective narratives for a post-apartheid society.

The TRC was not without its issues, however, and although it played an important role in the response to apartheid and the country's transition to a new government, it did not necessarily lead to healing for the individuals involved. As such, collective narratives of cultural trauma continued to override individual voices. First, it should be noted that while the creation of a trauma narrative is an important stage of processing individual trauma, a public hearing is not the ideal space for this to happen. Any truth commission will run independently of individuals' own processes of healing and so, for some participants, the TRC perpetuated rather than healed their trauma. The United Nations report on truth commissions emphasizes the need for psychological support for people who testify, recognizing that the act of giving testimony to a truth commission is not necessarily therapeutic in itself (Office of the United Nations High Commissioner for Human Rights, 2006, p. 23). Although some participants of the TRC did find that giving their testimony was cathartic, Sean Field acknowledges that others felt exploited for political gain (Field, 2006, p. 33). Individual stories were at the centre of the TRC and there are anecdotes about the respect that was shown to those who testified (Phelps, 2004, p. 109), but the individual was not the primary concern. Instead, the individual stories were used to help create a new collective narrative. The final report of a truth commission is always shaped by the narrative that the writer wishes to tell and this informs the new collective narrative that is formed. Charles Maier points out that 'trying to "synthesise" a narrative from diverse sources and voices is a dangerous exercise: reduction of many voices to one coherent story line means valuing some testimonies more than others, or privileging the significance of some stories more than others' (Maier, 2000, p. 274). Since truth commissions usually take place during a period of political or societal transition, the new collective narrative has often already been formulated by the government or sponsors of the truth commission. Individual stories can help to solidify this narrative, but reports cannot truly represent each individual's narrative. Their stories become part of a larger one, exploited for a broader motive. In this, the individual has limited agency and limited control over their own narrative and the way that it is used, and thus collective narratives continue to be imposed on the individual.

Furthermore, although the new collective narratives in South Africa deconstructed the former narratives of white supremacy, continuing social and economic disparities meant that inequality remained entrenched in South African society after the conclusion of the TRC. Only victims who testified to the TRC were awarded compensation (Aiken, 2008, p. 27) and so individuals who were not in a position to testify, either because they were not at a stage in the trauma process where they felt able to narrate their experience or because of practical accessibility issues, did not benefit. Even those who received compensation often had to wait before they were paid, while perpetrators received immediate amnesty (Stanley, 2001, p. 529). The TRC was politically powerful and a new collective narrative was formed that highlighted the atrocities of apartheid, but the lack of change in social structures meant that many of the social causes of trauma remained and economic disparity and lack of opportunities for Black communities continues to be a problem today. Unless the social causes of trauma are addressed, individuals risk being retraumatized on an ongoing basis. The group may find renewed identity and unity through a new collective narrative, but if structural inequality remains there will be limited healing for individuals.

Truth commissions are often necessary but they are a way of altering a collective narrative and should not be seen as therapeutic for individuals or, in themselves, a way of creating practical change. Further work is always required and the benefits of truth commissions for individuals can be limited if they do not occur alongside a practical addressing of economic and social disparity. Within the South African context, however, the solidarity network ACT Ubumbano provides a better example of the way that individuals can be empowered to protest against the causes of trauma and drive social change.

ACT Ubumbano links communities and organizations that work for social change and justice on a range of issues in Southern Africa. The network enables groups to stand alongside one another in solidarity and to support each other's work. A central part of the way that ACT Ubumbano works is through the empowerment of individuals to tell their own stories and to be agents of their own change. Through the network's 'Solidarity Hubs', individuals are given the chance to share their stories and reflect on their struggle, meaning that organizations can learn from their 'collective wisdom, rather than through expert instruction from institutional authorities' (Sigamoney, 2022, p. 48). Rather than NGOs or partners from the global North dictating the change that should take place and how funding should be distributed, ACT Ubumbano provides a space for communities to decide the best way to change the causes of their own trauma. Resources such as the Ubumbano Voice App,

WhatsApp groups and social media provide additional ways for individuals to present their own narratives, in their own time and their own language, and find agency to enact their own change (Sigamoney, 2022, pp. 46–59). ACT Ubumbano does not edit or moderate the narratives that are told; they are the individual's stories, and the right to tell them remains with them. Nonetheless, these stories influence the direction of the organizations and communities involved and thus help to shape the collective narratives of these social groups. The social justice nature of the participants' work means that, alongside these developing narratives and the empowerment of individuals, there is also a drive to create social change and thus to change the causes of trauma.

Within Abahlali baseMjondolo, the shack-dwellers' movement in KwaZulu-Natal, there is a saying that 'We are professors of our own suffering.'[1] To tell someone how they should be suffering, why they are suffering or how they should change it is to deny the lived experience of that suffering. Just as Job rejects the friends' attempts to explain his suffering, so the imposition of collective narratives about trauma can silence the victim even when attempts have been made to give them voice. To allow an individual to truly narrate their own trauma and protest against its causes, others need to step back and avoid imposing their own narratives. Job dialogues with the friends but his protests are directed to YHWH and he eventually provokes YHWH to address him directly. YHWH does not explain Job's suffering and there are varied interpretations of Job's final response in Job 42.1–6, but Job is not told he is wrong to protest. Instead, Job's righteous protest addresses the cause of his trauma, YHWH, and in the epilogue the circumstances are changed; YHWH abides by the laws of restitution that are laid out in Exodus 22.1–9 to compensate Job for his losses and Job's fortunes are restored in Job 42.10. Job's suffering is not diminished; his former children remain dead even as new children are born, and there is no mention of Job's skin disease being healed (Guillaume, 2008, p. 493). Nonetheless, Job's social circumstances are turned around and 'YHWH blessed the latter days of Job more than his beginning' (Job 42.12). Job 42 is unsatisfactory when one seeks an explanation for Job's suffering, but the character's protests influence the cause of his trauma and lead to a drastic change in YHWH's treatment of him.

To impose narratives that attempt to make sense of disaster upon the individuals who suffer silences the victims and traps them in a cycle of abuse and trauma. Even when these collective narratives are well intentioned, they can still silence those who suffer and isolate rather than embrace them. By allowing individuals to own their narratives, agency can be restored to them, oppression can be challenged and they can be liberated from the causes of their trauma, whether it is the divine oppression that is depicted in Job or the social oppression that fractures communities and countries. By recognizing that individuals can speak meaningfully about their trauma and that protest is a valid response to trauma, we can avoid silencing those who suffer and instead allow their voices to challenge the causes of their trauma.

Conclusion

Narrative is powerful. On a collective level, shared narratives can create meaning at a time of threat to the social group and reinforce a sense of collective identity. On an individual level, post-trauma narrative is a way of recovering stolen agency and setting new foundations for life going forward.

In the book of Job, the individual voice is one of protest. Against a literary backdrop of collective narratives that sought to justify God at the expense of human integrity, Job provides an irrefutable challenge. There is no justification for his suffering, the character insists. Meaning is instead created through Job's protest, and the presentation of the individual voice creates an alternative for ancient Israel that cuts through the explanations that found unity at the expense of integrity. Job provides a way in which the people can still engage with their god without silencing those who suffer. The solution to the flaws of the supposedly unifying collective narratives is not atheism and rejection of the religious group but rather protest, a refusal to silence individuals, and a stubborn belief that a better situation is possible.

Protest and the individual voice have a powerful place today in dismantling oppressive collective narratives. When the individual is allowed to formulate and share their trauma narrative on their own terms and collective narratives are not imposed on to them, they can challenge the very systems that gave rise to their trauma. Social groups can find unity without excluding individuals who suffer if people walk alongside these individuals in solidarity. If we allow it, their protests can shape the collective narratives that bond communities and nations and, as a unified group, a route can be paved to liberation from the very systems that cause and perpetuate trauma.

Note

1 I was first introduced to this saying in a meeting of South African and British church leaders in Pietermaritzburg on 11 October 2022 but have been unable to trace the original source.

References

Aiken, Nevin T., 2008, 'Post-Conflict Peacebuilding and the Politics of Identity: Insights for Restoration and Reconciliation', *Transitional Justice Peace Research* 40 (2), pp. 9–38.
Alexander, Jeffrey C., 2004, 'Toward a Theory of Cultural Trauma', in Jeffrey C. Alexander, Ron Eyerman, Bernhard Giesen, Neil J. Smelser and Pietor Sztompka (eds), *Cultural Trauma and Collective Identity*, Berkeley/Los Angeles/London: University of California Press, pp. 1–30.
American Psychiatric Association, 2013, *Diagnostic and Statistical Manual of Mental Disorders*, Arlington, VA: American Psychiatric Association.
Braiterman, Zachary, 1998, *(God) After Auschwitz: Tradition and Change in Post-Holocaust Jewish Thought*, Princeton, NJ: Princeton University Press.
Brison, Susan J., 2002, *Aftermath: Violence and the Remaking of a Self*, Princeton/Oxford: Princeton University Press.
Caruth, Cathy, 1996, *Unclaimed Experience: Trauma, Narrative, and History*, Baltimore/London: Johns Hopkins University Press.
Field, Sean, 2006, 'Beyond "Healing": Trauma, Oral History and Regeneration', *Oral History* 34 (1), pp. 31–42.
Green, Ronald M., 1987, 'Theodicy', in Mircea Eliade (ed.), *The Encyclopedia of Religion*, New York: Macmillan, pp. 430–41.
Guillaume, Philippe, 2008, 'Dismantling the Deconstruction of Job', *Journal of Biblical Literature* 127 (3), pp. 491–9.
Gutiérrez, Gustavo, 1985, *On Job: God-talk and the Suffering of the Innocent*, New York: Orbis Books.
Herman, Judith L., 1992, *Trauma and Recovery: From Domestic Abuse to Political Terror*, London: Pandora.
Howard, Sethanne and Mark W. Crandall, 2007, 'Post Traumatic Stress Disorder: What Happens in the Brain?', *Journal of the Washington Academy of Sciences* 93 (3), pp. 1–17.
Hurvitz, Avi, 1974, 'The Date of the Prose-Tale of Job Linguistically Reconsidered', *Harvard Theological Review* 67 (1), pp. 17–34.
Janoff-Bulman, Ronnie, 1992, *Shattered Assumptions: Towards a New Psychology of Trauma*, New York: Free Press.
Janzen, David, 2019, *Trauma and the Failure of History: Kings, Lamentations, and the Destruction of Jerusalem*, Atlanta, GA: SBL.
Kwon, JiSeong J., 2017, 'Shared Ideas in Job and Deutero-Isaiah', *Zeitschrift für die Alttestamentliche Wissenschaft*, 129 (1), pp. 32–46.
Maier, Charles S., 2000, 'Doing History, Doing Justice: The Narrative of the

Historian and of the Truth Commission', in Robert I. Rotberg and Dennis Thompson (eds), *Truth v. Justice: The Morality of Truth Commissions*, Princeton/Oxford: Princeton University Press, pp. 261–78.

Office of the United Nations High Commissioner for Human Rights, 2006, *Rule-of-Law Tools for Post-Conflict States: Truth Commissions*, New York/Geneva: United Nations.

Phelps, Teresa Godwin, 2004, *Shattered Voices: Language, Violence, and the Work of Truth Commissions*, Philadelphia, PA: University of Pennsylvania Press.

Rom-Shiloni, Dalit, 2021, *Voices from the Ruins: Theodicy and the Fall of Jerusalem in the Hebrew Bible*, Grand Rapids, MI: William B. Eerdmans.

Sigamoney, Veronica, 2022, *Origins, Identity and Practice: Documenting and Learning from our Evolving Solidarity-Based Practice*, ACT Ubumbano.

Stanley, Elizabeth, 2001, 'Evaluating the Truth and Reconciliation Commission', *Journal of Modern African Studies*, 39 (3), pp. 525–46.

van der Kolk, Bessel, 2014, *The Body Keeps the Score: Mind, Brain and Body in the Transformation of Trauma*, London: Random House.

10

Post-Liberation, Stress and African Youth

THANDI SOKO-DE JONG

No grave shall hold my body down
This land is still my, my home
(Themba Sekowe/Rikhado Makhado/Thabo Martin Ngubane,
'This Land is Still my Home', 2020)

Liberation Theologies and Liberation Hermeneutics (LT&H) have existed for less than a century but have already made a major impact on social justice issues around the world. Generally, Liberation Theologies include many theological strands such as Womanist, Feminist, Latin American, Queer, Black and Disability Liberation Theologies. Liberation Hermeneutics offers methods of reading the Bible that are participatory, lead to praxis, and approach the Bible as 'a site of struggle' – of multiple, often contending ideo-theological voices. This, in turn, 'offers forms of interpretive resilience to poor and marginalised communities who are often stigmatised and victimised by dominant monovocal appropriations of the Bible' (West, 2018). Thus, LT&H aim to resist particular social, political and economic hegemony relevant to their marginalized community through faith-based approaches centred on: (a) being life-affirming, (b) encouraging holistic human flourishing and (c) being grounded in a justice-based approach. These theologies often draw on passages like Luke 4.18 to emphasize that human beings are created in God's image (*imago Dei*) and are, therefore, worth an existence in which they experience liberation from systems that seek to oppress them.

This chapter offers an interrogatory approach to LT&H, arguing that Liberation Theologies often pay less attention to the challenges faced by community members at the personal level after becoming emancipated. That is to say, Liberation Theologies appear to prevent marginalized individuals from getting the theological support they need after their liberation.

This, I suggest, leaves a theological void for helping those individuals, especially youth, who continue to seek spiritual meaning in their post-liberation struggles. To better illustrate this worry, I turn to the popular Liberation Theology method of *see, judge, act* (the pastoral spiral). The pastoral spiral can help us examine a particular struggle observable in postcolonial and post-apartheid Southern African countries today. In particular, it can help us make some critical observations on what seems to be the lack of LT&H's accompaniment to people as they struggle with what I describe as 'post-liberation stress'. Generally speaking, post-liberation stress takes up the mental health challenges that recently emancipated political communities face.

Post-liberation stress

For purposes of this discussion, we focus on Southern Africa. I intend 'Southern Africa' in its broader sense, including all countries within the economic region known as the Southern African Development Community (SADC).[1] I have chosen Southern Africa because it is a region with which I am most familiar. It is where I am originally from, and it is where I received my spiritual formation and later my theological grounding in Liberation Theology (Malawi, Eswatini and South Africa, respectively). To the best of my knowledge, Liberation Theologies played a more prominent and visible role in the political struggle against oppressive rule in South Africa than anywhere else in Southern Africa. The work of liberation theologians such as Allan Boesak, Manas Buthelezi and other figures are well known and recognized (*Encyclopædia Britannica*, 2022; Mashabela, 2004). Similarly, across the Southern African region (and beyond), Liberation Theology has played an important role in providing a prophetic voice to impact socio-political changes directly. One such example is the 1992 Malawian *Lenten Pastoral Letter* by a Roman Catholic bishop 'that shook Malawi's political landscape, helping to usher in multi-party democracy' (Samasumo, 2022).

As stated above, Liberation Theology is an umbrella term that includes many prophetic voices that advocate for marginalized groups. This chapter focuses on interrogating the expressions of Liberation Theology that aim for people's political emancipation/liberation at the national level. I argue that this powerful, prophetic expression of the LT&H tradition tends to overlook the necessity of theologically accompanying communities as they adapt to life post-liberation. Adapting to post-liberation realities requires coping mechanisms. As new opportunities arise for members of these societies, importance also needs to be placed on how members deal with the trauma of the past and the stressful realities of life post-liberation. While it is useful to apply such a critique to all contexts and sub-contexts of LT&H, our focus in this chapter, however, centres on the post-political liberation experience and its impact on mental health, especially among young people.

Young people and post-liberation stress

The African Youth Charter of the African Union defines youth as a category of individuals between 15 and 35 (United Nations, 2013). However, the terms 'youth' and 'young people' are applied very broadly in our discussion. Languages like Chichewa (spoken in Malawi and parts of Zambia and Mozambique) allow for some flexibility regarding who can be considered a young person. *Mtsikana* and *mnyamata* mean 'girl' and 'boy' (or a youth, in general), respectively. Simply adding *wa chi* (a prefix that associates one to another) to these terms describes a person of any age with youthful characteristics *wa chitsikana* (youthful woman) or *wa chinyamata* (youthful man). For our discussion, *the youth/young people* refer to anyone born close to or after the last few colonized nations in Southern Africa gained their freedom. That is, those born in the 1980s and onwards – the cohort that was too young (or yet born) to participate in the freedom struggles that saw the independence of Namibia, Zimbabwe and South Africa, nations whose political struggles impacted the whole sub-region and beyond in myriad ways.

People born during this period have been raised to understand how the generations before them contributed to the hard-won freedom all countries in this region enjoy today. However, people born in this period also live with the reality of knowing that their freedom is incomplete. The 1980s–2000s brought with them new and unprecedented challenges, such as the failures of Structural Adjustment Programmes (SAPs) (Logan, 2015). The SAPs negatively impacted employment opportunities, service delivery and so on, and significantly the HIV/AIDS epidemic that not only devastated communities but brought with it harmful practices like social stigma, virgin cleansing myths and so on. Many young people were orphaned during this period.

Thus, young people in the region were 'born free' while simultaneously grappling with the legacies of colonization and old, contextual forms of marginalization and exclusion (patriarchy/kyriarchy, homophobia etc.). They also grapple with emerging issues brought on by political, ecological, social and economic challenges. We are yet to measure accurately the negative impacts of newer and ongoing challenges such as climate change and the Covid-19 pandemic on young people. The impact of these realities on the mental health of young people cannot be underestimated, particularly when we look at the issue of trauma. Let us, therefore, turn to the 'see' part of the pastoral spiral.

'See': male youth, trauma and post-liberation stress

Recent research in the field of epigenetics suggests that the experiences of trauma caused by hardship or violence (e.g. war, famine, genocide etc.) can leave their mark (that is, change/modification in the expression of – not mutation) on the genetic code that male offspring in subsequent generations inherit through the Y chromosome (Henriques, 2019). These studies are new, and only a few have been done so far, but researchers are confident that the experience of trauma can be passed down to offspring through DNA and impacts how males in subsequent generations respond to (similar) trauma-triggers in their environment (see Dias and Ressler, 2014). Post-traumatic stress is another form of trauma passed down generationally. Joy DeGruy describes this psychosocial element of multigenerational trauma, adding that it is impacted when coupled with continued oppression and the absence of opportunity to access the benefits available in society (DeGruy, 2005, p. 125). This suggests that not all experienced trauma derives from events we have personally witnessed or gone through. Rather, some trauma is passed on to us genetically.

I wish to bracket this as the first issue to consider as we seek to understand how young people experience post-liberation stress. They may be living with the traumas of colonial and, in the case of South Africa, colonial and apartheid experiences endured by and passed down from their forebears. These traumas can remain with, and even be passed down to, future generations if there continues to be a lack of/limited professional intervention (including pastoral support based in LT&H).

Memoria miserabilis

Confirming Joy DeGruy's notion of multigenerational trauma, the South African theologian of Black Liberation Theology (BLT), the late Vuyani Vellem, argued that the memory of racism is too deep to forget. It is a memory made of historical acts that have occurred for several centuries. These acts and the ideologies behind them underpin the 'underside of modernity', making memory a noncognitive concept or *memorialization* 'but rather memory as the past that flashes right now', such as through trauma (Vellem, 2018, p. 37).

Therefore, we can understand the trauma carried into the post-liberation phase of Southern Africa as what Vellem describes as *memoria miserabilis*. This is the notion that the *ghost* of empire comes back to haunt us all and will continue to do so if it and its impact remain untouched (Vellem, 2018, p. 37). In popular culture we see, for example, in 'Monsters you Made' (by Burna Boy) how *memoria miserabilis* can be expressed in music.

Trauma and males: a brief overview

The term 'trauma' comes from the Greek word for 'physical wound or puncture' (Pollack, 2017). Psychological trauma implies a 'wound or tear into a person's psyche where unwanted emotions, thoughts, and physiological experiences are forced through' (Soko, 2022). Trauma can develop immediately, days, months or years after an event (which can be a one-time event, multiple events or long-lasting, repetitive events). Trauma can affect anyone; not all people are materially poor, all people *can* be oppressed in one way or another (Luke 4.18).

Within society, various ideas, gender roles, expectations and norms impact how individuals respond to trauma. In the case of males, social narratives and expectations of masculinities can, for example, force boys and men to 'man up'; that is, to show physical and emotional strength and dominance. This implies that a 'man's man' is emasculated when they admit/acknowledge susceptibility to physical or emotional trauma and pain (Warner, 2018; Wilcock, 2018). As such, when faced with a traumatic experience, there is societal pressure to conform to the prescribed/conventional/traditional norms of masculinity, such as the push to 'be resilient', 'not cry', 'forget about it' and/or keep trauma to oneself or numb it to avoid feeling shame about appearing weak and vulnerable to others (such as in the case of normative male alexithymia) (Warner, 2018).

Such beliefs assume that males process traumatic events – such as loss of loved ones/innocence/properties and so on; that is, (generational) violence and abuse of various kinds – differently from women. They do not need to seek and receive appropriate help to heal. One of the outcomes of this gender bias is that the mental health challenges men may face in response to trauma, such as physical and mental health problems, or coping mechanisms such as substance abuse, addictions, can be overlooked or left untreated (Warner, 2018). Trauma can also negatively impact how affected males carry out public and private gender roles prescribed by their society that may encompass community, religious and family/personal relationship roles. Often these roles demand that a man appear strong, capable and provide or sustain economic stability (be a 'provider') with little or no interest in their struggles and no effort to encourage other traits that they may have that are useful in the human-flourishing of any gender, such as 'confidence, passion, honesty, loyalty, and kindness' (Wilcock, 2018). From an LT&H perspective that emphasizes life-affirming masculinities, these traits are acknowledged in our understanding of Jesus as one who did not conform to the prevailing normative masculinities of his day (see West, 2010). For instance, he did not deny his vulnerability but was able to emotionally respond in several instances, such as in passages where he wept (John 11.35; Heb. 5.7).

According to the psychologist Debra Warner, there are fewer trauma-response resources for boys and men than for women (Warner, 2018). Additionally, the media tend to minimize or silence stories of male trauma in line with social expectations for men to appear strong and emotionally unaffected. From a theological perspective, these portrayals minimize themes that are important to LT&H, such as healing, justice and life-affirming praxis. Having laid out an overview of trauma and some of the ways it impacts male youth, let us now turn to discuss trauma and post-liberation stress.

Trauma and colonial history

Tsitsi Dangarembga's 1988 post-independence Zimbabwe novel, *Nervous Conditions*, explores trauma in a colonial setting. In the book, we encounter the teenager, Nyasha, as she goes through the daily, overt struggles that come with colonization. The author points to the extreme mental pressure that takes its toll on Nyasha, who eventually 'loses her mind' when she fails to reconcile herself with a colonized existence:

Why do they do it, Tambu, to me and to you and to him? Do you see what they've done? They've taken us away. Lucia, Takesure. All of us. They've deprived you of you, him of him, ourselves of each other. We're groveling. Lucia for a job. Jeremiah for money. Daddy grovels to them. We grovel to him. I won't grovel. Oh no, I won't. (Dangarembga, 1988, pp. 204–5)

When Nyasha's mental health declines, her parents encounter ignorant assumptions about black mental health. One psychiatrist tells them that Nyasha could not be ill, 'that Africans did not suffer in the way we had described. She was making a scene. We should take her home and be firm with her' (Dangarembga, 1988, p. 206). Her parents eventually consult a more compassionate psychiatrist.

There is much to unpack from Nyasha's story, from her recognition of identity crises in her family to the realization that she is neither at home in her own culture nor the British and Rhodesian cultures imposed on her and her community (Sizemore, 1997, p. 72). We can sum this up by describing her situation as one in which a young person recognizes that there needs to be more to their lives than ignoring the impact of their parents' traumatic experiences and thereby risking the chance of repeating harmful patterns of behaviour and passing those on to future generations. There needs to be healing from, and addressing of, the traumas that occurred before political liberation if we are to deal with and overcome the challenges that we encounter post-liberation properly.

Let us now turn to the 'judge' part of the pastoral spiral to better understand some of the current challenges impacting young people.

'Judge': discerning the post-liberation stress among young people

Popular culture provides us with insights into mental health discourses and young people in Southern Africa. In popular music, the news of South African hip hop artist Jabulani Tsambo's (better known as Hip Hop Pantsula, HHP) death by suicide (2018) was received with shock. HHP succumbed to depression at the age of 38. From some perspectives, as an icon, he was not the 'typical' person likely to die by suicide (see Lepodise, 2018).

This chapter suggests that his suicide, and that of other well-known young people in the region, is emblematic of a mental health crisis evidenced by a rising incidence of suicide, suicide attempts and ideation that appears skewed towards those who self-identify as (young) males. Without denying the factor of clinical depression in some of these cases, however, as this chapter argues, there are other psycho-social factors that we need to 'discern' in this 'judge' step.

In 'judging' the situation, I am drawn to how celebrities utilize their platform to speak out and draw attention to suicide and mental health issues (Jimfoxx07, 2022). Lucius Banda (a Malawian reggae, afro-pop artist), for example, released a Facebook video in which he shared concerns about rising suicide rates and urged his fans to seek help and not resort to suicide (Banda, 2022). The video garnered thousands of views and multiple reactions, shares and comments within days of posting. Similarly, at the international level, artists like Kendrick Lamar (album: *Mr. Morale & The Big Steppers*) are bringing themes around males and emotional pain into focus (2022). The artist Stromae (also known as Paul van Haver, Rwandese-Belgian) 'opens up' about this reality in *L'enfer* (Hell), in the hope that other young people will feel less alone and access help (see Bradshaw, 2017). He sings (in part) the following:

> I've considered suicide a few times.
> And I'm not proud of it
> Sometimes you feel it'd be the only way to silence them
> All these thoughts putting me through hell.[2]

Returning to the Southern African context, historically, early research into suicide in the region was limited to the forms of suicide we today describe as assisted suicide/euthanasia cases. This occurred particularly among the very elderly struggling with poor health. Early accounts exclude information about suicide among young people. Also, the types of knowledge produced in early accounts of suicide were heavily biased towards an imperialist perspective (see Samuelson, 1929). Therefore, it is difficult to rely on such accounts – which often emphasize the writers' perceptions of 'cruelty' and 'strangeness' – as they leave out the fuller contextual issues, such as evidence of the effects of colonization and apartheid on the mental health pressures of the elderly in that period.

Against this background, to 'judge' some of the influences on post-liberation stress, we will focus on discourses today that range from popular music to publications. As an exhaustive list is out of this chapter's scope, we will limit our focus to gender norms (kyriarchy and its influence on how girls and boys are socialized from an early age), spirituality, racism, and social status. Beginning with gender norms, the lyrics from the song in the prologue, 'This Land is Still my Home', contains an important clue in the following lines:

> I tried to bend my knees
> But my knees were already bent
> I haven't stood like a man for such a long time now.

While Riky Rick (Rikhado Makhado, 1987–2022) – who himself died by suicide – does not elaborate on what 'standing like a man' meant for him, Janta (Sukulani Mwachumu, a Malawian singer and producer) and AKA (Kiernan Jarryd Forbes, a South African rapper and producer) offer some clues. In his song 'Chisoni' (Sorrow), which he wrote after contemplating suicide and deciding against it, Janta gives insights into the experience of heartbreak from a male perspective (2020). Heartbreak brought on by losing a relationship because of a change in financial circumstances can cause harm to the mental health of men who are accustomed to the gendered expectation of being a provider for their spouse or families. Janta asks in the song, 'Was this how it was for past generations?' It was not necessarily the same for past generations. Functional social institutions tended to offer some stability for families that ensured that, for example, sudden loss of family income was not the norm. However, Southern African social institutions' historical disruptions (the legacies of slavery, colonization, apartheid etc.) have negatively impacted family income, especially among the poor. For instance, the 'land grabs'[3] of the past have a continued negative effect on livelihoods, gender roles and social conflict today.

Racism as social disruption and mental health

Underpinning this history of disruption is racism. Generations of Africans have fought and continue to fight the notion that attaches a negative value to black skin, a notion that 'considers black frightening, dangerous, repulsive, and a prime candidate for destruction' (Williams, 1993, p. 28). Thus, young people are growing up around these ideas that associate 'illegality and disaster' and 'intellectual and moral inferiority' with Black people as perpetuated through various media (Williams, 1993, p. 28). Therefore, it is not a surprise that young people living in the post-liberation period face the stress of having to both resist and try to overcome the negative expectations imposed on them. What young people experience today may be different from the experiences of slavery and political colonization. However, the potency of racism on mental health remains a serious obstacle to young people's mental health.

According to Vuyani Vellem, the Black Theology of Liberation (BTL) perspective has never started with racism as a natural human phenomenon, but with the historical justification of racism, structural domination, violent oppression and the denial of Black people's humanity (Vellem, 2018, p. 34). Thus, BTL 'judges' racism as an ethos built on prejudice that creates legal, philosophical, theological, economic and cultural structures undergirded by a concealed spirit of the superiority of the white race. BTL 'judges' white supremacy as not worthy of having finality in epistemological and cultural disputes among civilizations as its claims and scientific validations have long been debunked (Vellem, 2018, pp. 34, 42). Vellem admits that BTL has not been altogether effective in its prophetic call but it is 'sterilised' and 'castrated' by the reality of a falsely created impression of triumph against racism that has been falsely created (Vellem, 2018, pp. 31–4).

The impact of historical legacies on mental health

Leaving aside the systemic factors that inhibit the healing of traumas and post-liberation stress, let us now turn briefly to the impact of factors at the individual level. Hope Mezuwa, a social researcher in Malawi, describes how we, as individuals, may be participating in perpetuating the problems left by the historical legacies discussed above. In the wake of the suicide death of an online personality from neighbouring Zambia, Mezuwa writes about the Malawian context (but probably applicable elsewhere in Southern Africa):

> While suicidal deaths are not entirely a new phenomenon, present statistics are unprecedented. Medical professionals, often and rightly, attribute them to prevalent high levels of unemployment, persistent deep poverty, and poor health that in turn catapult poor souls into depression and stress. Doubtless, stress levels out here are unparalleled. But rising numbers of suicides are only one of the multiple signs pointing to the fact that there is something the current dominant generation isn't doing right. (Mezuwa, 2022)

Based on his research, the current dominant generation (the youth),[4] unlike previous generations, emphasizes individualism for the independence and wealth creation opportunities such a lifestyle facilitates. Thus, as he explains below, other themes that were more common in the past, such as empathy and 'love, kindness, and compassion', are now restricted to an individual's nuclear family or circle of friends. He therefore urges us to consider that:

> Our departed friends did not take their lives because a [e.g. love] relationship ended, they did so because they did not see the rest of us as of any help at all. Not that they are entitled, but we must create a society that assumes the responsibility of preserving a sense of belongingness and community for its members. Psychologists, counselors and other professional formal mental health support mechanisms are necessary but they will mostly be a successful avenue if they build on existing natural and traditional support systems built within families and personal relationships. We will have to invest in relationships and be intentional and deliberate about love, empathy, compassion and kindness. (Mezuwa, 2022)

Popular artists and post-liberation stress

The above-highlighted themes of love, kindness and compassion align with LT&H's emphasis on Jesus' compassion for the poor and oppressed in Luke 4.18.[5] Our belief that justice is love (and kindness) in action needs to lead us into praxis that acknowledges that LT&H has taken a back seat on the issues outlined in this chapter so far (see Freire, 1993). Young people are noticing the need for life-affirming[6] theological traditions. That is a challenge LT&H needs to take up. AKA, reacting to the death of Riky Rick, sums up, in my view, the spiritual need of the youth as follows:

> I hope that very soon, we can address the issue of how damaged and broken the men in this country are. We have no one to talk to, we just pat each other on the back and say, 'get on with it, be strong my boi,' but in reality, we are traumatised. Generational trauma passed down to us. … Can we (myself included) start going to church again. … Something has to change. (AKA, 2022)

Notably, other themes that AKA raised in the rest of the quote conform to those raised by Riky Rick and Janta. Thus, conforming to the expectations of patriarchal gender norms, AKA seems to accept uncritically the undue pressure on men to be providers (even when they are not capable in light of post-liberation stress). He drives this point home by writing:

> Ladies, we are not perfect by any means [but] we are crying out for your approval, your love and affection. Please, can we reset and go back to family values? ... Please, can we start some sort of dialogue about men in this country because it's our duty to protect you, to provide and care for you. (AKA, 2022)

Post-liberation stress from an LT&H perspective

These lyrics reveal a problematic interpretation of the role and duty of males as sole providers – rather than co-contributors to family income and welfare (see Moyo, 2017). From an outside perspective, this view can be criticized for being maladaptive to current trends in scholarship about gender and sexuality. Scholars address a range of issues on the topic, such as the social constructions of gender (and sexuality) and gender fluidity; or the opening up of dominant African imaginations of gender to be more inclusive of other ways of being other than the strict male/female frameworks alluded to so far in this discussion (see van Klinken and Chitando, 2015; Khumalo, 2014). Notions of masculinity (and sexuality) remain contextual (and for some, very personal) and tied to ethical choices, personality traits, desires, belief systems, intersectionalities and so on. For the present chapter, we keep in mind that there are multiple expressions of masculinity in Southern Africa. Thus, we do not take a prescriptive approach, but rather our focus is a descriptive one that aims to take into account the particularities of masculinities in the Southern African context as impacted by the ruptures and disruptions in the social and personal fabric of life in what Vuyani Vellem calls the *longue durée* of colonization and, in the case of South Africa, Apartheid (Vellem, 2018, p. 31–48). One of the major impacts of the disruption and ruptures is that the life-affirming attributes of African cultures have been undermined together with those that were proved to be problematic (baby thrown out with the bathwater). Gustavo Gutiérrez offers strong opposition to the denigration of culture by stating that:

> In addition to this physical and economic death from poverty, there is a cultural side, a cultural death. Anthropologists say that 'culture is life.' When we despise a culture, a religion, a race, a gender, and ethnic group, we are killing persons – culturally speaking – belonging to that sector of humanity. (Gutiérrez, 2007, p. 11)

Thus, the impact of the disruption and rupture centres around systemic aspects that harmed what was positive. This is/was through what Vellem calls *epistemicide, spiritualicide* (Vellem, 2018, p. 34). This reality is what makes post-liberation stress important to tackle as the disruption and rupture have an impact on culture in as much as culture plays an important role[7] in the 'affirmation of Black, African actuality, the dignity of being a historical people with its traditions, heroes, art and religion' (Vellem, 2018, p. 42). Against this background, a prophetic LT&H stance acknowledges that the processing of trauma – past and present – needs to include a cultural lens that conforms to what Bénézet Bujo describes as African ethics 'articulated in the framework of community, which involves remembering one's ancestors' (Bujo, 2003, pp. 56–7).

Vellem's discussion above leaves room for the understanding that culture and cultural norms – or what is left of them, are held on to by some because, often, they are the only constant – of a people's history with its roots plunged into the material conditions of a people (Cabral, 1974, p. 84).[8] Thus, culture plays an important role in giving meaning to identity, meaning from which individuals and communities can draw agency.

From this perspective, we can infer that the point which the artists cited so far aim to make is that trauma and stress are major concerns among young people, particularly those who identify as males – with all the trappings of what masculinity entails in Southern Africa. This is, therefore, a call for action to LT&H (and all with the capacity to intervene in life-affirming ways) to recognize that we lack a unified theological approach that is hope-filled, holistic, life-affirming and responsive in ways that offer hope, meaning and a spirituality that validates young people struggling to cope with the challenges of life post-liberation struggles.

'Act': a call for action

Having considered the 'see' and the 'judge' aspects of the pastoral spiral in light of post-liberation stress, this concluding aspect – 'act' – serves as the call for LT&H to respond to the impact of trauma and stress as outlined in this chapter. I wish to make two suggestions as a contribution to the many options that we collectively already have in mind.

The first suggestion is to theologize in ways that recognize that although the reality outlined above is relatively new (compared to past generations' experiences), we have at our disposal a rich history of literature from such fields as psychology, theology, fiction that covers themes relating to the current topic. Resources from psychology include the recent *Pan-Africanism and Psychology in Decolonial Times* by Shose Kessi, Floretta Boonzaier and Babette Stephanie Gekeler (2021). Non-fiction literature includes Frantz Fanon's *The Wretched of the Earth* (1961) and Kwasi Wiredu's *A Companion to African Philosophy* (2004); while important works of fiction on topics related to the present one include Chinua Achebe's *Things Fall Apart* (1958), Cheikh Hamidou Kane's *L'Aventure Ambiguë* (1961), Ngũgĩ wa Thiong'o's *The River Between* (1965), Mariama Bâ's *Scarlet Song* (1981), Zakes Mda's *The Heart of Redness* (2000), and *Nervous Conditions* and its sequel *The Book of Not* (2006) by Tsitsi Dangarembga.

Similarly, we have a rich store of theological works from the African continent and its diaspora addressing topics that touch on the issues raised. Such works give us the 'shoulders to stand on' in this task. Examples include Musa Dube's 'Postcolonialism & Liberation' (2004), Mercy Amba Oduyoye's 'Reflections from a Third World (*sic*) Woman's Perspective: Women's Experience and Liberation Theologies' (1983), Ezra Chitando and Sophie Chirongoma's *Redemptive Masculinities: Men, HIV and Religion* (2012); and from the diaspora, Dolores S. William's 'Sin, Nature, and Black Women's Bodies' (1993).

My second suggestion is that we would need to take care to translate the outcomes of our reflection – based on the 'standing on the shoulders of giants' – into our liturgies in local churches. This would be relevant, especially in a climate where young people such as AKA call for members of society to start 'going to church again'. Without well-reflected liturgies, we risk the chance of congregants and visitors encountering some of the existing, problematic messages that teach that victims of suicide are sinful, killers, and worthy of God's punishment (eternal damnation). LT&H needs to counter such a message and generally fill the void by providing supportive, educative and hope-filled liturgies that recognize all who are struggling with mental health as God's image-bearers and acknowledge the impact of post-liberation stress on their lives.

This chapter therefore suggests that time and space during church services must intentionally be given to collectively discuss, share, testify, educate, pray and intercede with one another on mental health issues. Liturgies could include, for example, an emphasis on interrogating/discussing how generational trauma and/or stress can be passed on intergenerationally. Reference can be made to biblical texts/stories that demonstrate examples of this. The liturgy could also include reflections on how biblical solutions to trauma can be used in conjunction with other methods such as psychological/medical interventions. This approach may also call for designing a safe, healing section within the liturgy (or a separate healing liturgy) that includes affirming one's identity in Christ and symbolic actions such as:

- cleansing (depending on cultural relevance) and restoration prayers for the mind;
- writing down issues and burning them in a 'letting-go' ritual mid-service before the cross of Christ at the altar (psychological and spiritual processes/themes are likely to overlap here);
- prayers for renewing one's dedication and commitment to a life strengthened by God;
- opportunities for story-telling; that is, providing a space for people who are willing to share their struggles or stories that encourage, affirm and support others to do so.

Such liturgies can play an important role in facilitating discussion of mental health issues and current challenges in general, as well as those arising directly (and indirectly) from post-liberation stress. They can also be impactful for facilitating an inclusive and collective approach to dealing with post-liberation stress and trauma that complements the separate, private interventions which are also important and needed. A positive outcome would be that such liturgies would help in efforts to destigmatize the topic of mental health; overcome shame; address loneliness/suffering in silence; allow for collective empathy and compassion; and support those who are struggling to cope and have little hope or have lost hope.

Conclusion

In conclusion, it is high time LT&H took up a prophetic role on these issues directly. Such a role seems to be already exemplified by the young people as in the example of YoungstaCPT (also known as Riyadh Roberts), who provides a non-judgemental, empathetic, compassionate and prayer-filled response to suicide in his song 'Dear Rikhado, love Riyadh', which is summarized in the final lines of the song, 'I know it's a temporary existence/I'm sorry *broer* [brother]/Lord have mercy on you' (Youngsta-CPT, 2022). It would be impactful, relevant and meaningful to see such theologies and liturgies developed in LT&H as soon as possible, even as we continue to fight for liberation in other spheres and contexts.

Epilogue

An example of song lyrics that offer a useful reminder of 'life-affirming responses' (e.g. confidence, kindness, perseverance, etc.).

> '*Maury*' (Translated)
> [...]
> My heartache was worse,
> I wanted to hang myself.
> But that is now all gone my brother,
> Nothing lasts forever my sister.
> It hurts but the pain goes away, my brother,
> And the wound heals.
> [...]
> You are still blessed.
> Just be brave, life is like that.
> One day you will be well...
> (Namadingo, 2021).

Acknowledgements

I am grateful to Julie Soko, Indileni Hilukiluah, Mohamad Al-Hakim, Tawonga Gondwe-Nkosi, Folkert de Jong, Dumisa Mbano and Matchona Phiri for all their helpful insights, comments and criticisms on earlier drafts. Thanks also to the participants at the Council for World Mission's

Discernment and Radical Engagement (eDARE) conference 2022 for their constructive feedback.

Notes

1 SADC member states are Angola, Botswana, Comoros, Democratic Republic of Congo, Eswatini, Lesotho, Madagascar, Malawi, Mauritius, Mozambique, Namibia, Seychelles, South Africa, United Republic of Tanzania, Zambia and Zimbabwe.

2 Original text: *J'ai parfois eu des pensées suicidaires. Et j'en suis peu fier. On croit parfois que c'est la seule manière de les faire taire. Ces pensées qui me font vivre un enfer.* Translation available online: https://tekst-sanderlei.com/2022/01/AD12/L%E2%80%99enfer-Song-Translation-and-Lyrics-Stromae-en-GB.html.

3 According to Borras et al. (2011), 'Land grabbing is the contentious issue of large-scale land acquisitions: the buying or leasing of large pieces of land by domestic and transnational companies, governments, and individuals.'

4 According to The Organisation for Economic Co-operation and Development, 'Malawi's population is largely youthful with 80% of its population aged below 35 years and with a median age of 17' (OECD, 2022).

5 'The Spirit of the Lord is on me, because he has anointed me to proclaim good news to the poor. He has sent me to proclaim freedom for the prisoners and recovery of sight for the blind, to set the oppressed free, to proclaim the year of the Lord's favour' (NIVUK).

6 Life-affirming refers to interventions that have an emotionally or spiritually uplifting effect. For Liberation Theology interpretations, see Pillay, 2020.

7 According to Jesse N. K. Mugambi, 'Culture is the total manifestation of a people's self-understanding and self-expression, through politics, economics, ethics, aesthetics, kin-ship and religion' (Mugambi, 2003, p. 119).

8 The denigration of cultural cores, according to Vellem, leads to a social situation in which, in the words of Chinua Achebe, 'Things Fall Apart' (Vellem, 2018, p. 39).

References

AKA (Kiernan Jarryd Forbes), 2022, 'Let's keep it 100' (24 February), Instagram, https://www.instagram.com/p/CaWGuDet9MR/?utm_source=ig_embed&ig_rid=415044dd-3179-4cfc-82d5-86172d0e3d60 (accessed 24.02.2022).

Banda, Lucius C., 2022, 'A problem shared must be halfway solved. Do not abuse your brothers' trust in you', Facebook, https://www.facebook.com/SojaBandaLucius/videos/2161505920663688 (accessed 30.04.2022).

Borras, Saturnino M., Jr et al., 2011, 'Towards a better understanding of global land grabbing: an editorial introduction', *Journal of Peasant Studies* 38 (2), pp. 209–16.

Bradshaw, Lisa, 2017, 'Stromae nearly committed suicide after taking malaria drug', *The Bulletin* (13 November), https://www.thebulletin.be/stromae-nearly-committed-suicide-after-taking-malaria-drug (accessed 5.05.2022).
Bujo, Bénézet, 2003, *Foundations of an African Ethic: Beyond the Universal Claims of Western Morality*, Nairobi: Paulines.
Cabral, Amilcar, 1974, 'Spirituality and Struggle: African and Black Theologies', in Charles Villa-Vincecio and Carl Niehaus (eds), *One Nation: A Festschrift for Beyers Naude*, Cape Town: Human & Rousseau.
Chitando, Ezra and Sophie Chirongoma (eds), 2012, *Redemptive Masculinities: Men, HIV and Religion*, Geneva: WCC.
Dangarembga, Tsitsi, 1988, *Nervous Conditions*, London: Women's Press Trust.
DeGruy, Joy, 2005, *Post Traumatic Slave Syndrome: America's Legacy of Enduring Injury and Healing*, Milwaukee, OR: Uptone.
Dias, Brian G. and Kerry J. Ressler, 2014, 'Parental olfactory experience influences behavior and neural structure in subsequent generations', *Nature Neuroscience* 17, pp. 89–96, https://doi.org/10.1038/nn.3594 (accessed 23.07.2022).
Dube, Musa W., 2004, 'Postcolonialism & Liberation', in Miguel A. De La Torre (ed.), *Handbook of U.S. Theologies of Liberation*, St Louis, MO: Chalice.
Encyclopaedia Britannica, 2022, 'Allan Boesak: South African clergyman', https://www.britannica.com/biography/Allan-Boesak (accessed 23.06.2022).
Freire, Paulo, 1993, *Pedagogy of the Oppressed*, New York: Continuum.
Gutiérrez, Gustavo, 2007, 'Liberation Theology for the Twenty-First Century', in Pilar H. Closkey and John Hogan (eds), *Romero's Legacy: The Call to Peace and Justice*, Lanham, MD: Rowman & Littlefield.
Henriques, Martha, 2019, 'Can the legacy of trauma be passed down the generations?', BBC, 26 March, https://www.bbc.com/future/article/20190326-what-is-epigenetics (accessed 5.05.2022).
Janta (Sukulani Mwachumu), 2020, 'Chisoni', YouTube, 28 September, https://www.youtube.com/watch?v=VPHfuJPE3Uc (accessed 20.05.2022).
Jimfoxx07, 2022, 'Lasizwe finally opens up after Riky Rick suicide watch the video', *Opera News*, March, https://opera.news/za/en/entertainment/ddfceeca b4866045bb89897a25ef39cd (accessed 5.06.2022).
Kessi, Shose, Floretta Boonzaier and Babette S. Gekeler, 2021, *Pan-Africanism and Psychology in Decolonial Times*, London: Palgrave Macmillan.
Khumalo, Minenhle N., 2014, 'The Non-Origins of Queer Blackness: Queering African(a) Temporalities', Fourteenth Transdisciplinary Theological Colloquium, Madison, New Jersey.
Lamar, Kendrick, 2022, *Mr. Morale & The Big Steppers* [CD], Santa Monica, CA: Interscope Records.
Lepodise, Orateng, 2018, 'HHP was a legend who did so much for the youth of Mahikeng', *Opera News*, 26 October, https://www.dailymaverick.co.za/opinionista/2018-10-26-hhp-was-a-legend-who-did-so-much-for-the-youth-of-mahikeng/ (accessed 5.05.2022).
Logan, Fraser, 2015, 'Did structural adjustment programmes assist African development?', *E-International Relations*, 13 January, https://www.e-ir.info/

2015/01/13/did-structural-adjustment-programmes-assist-african-development/ (accessed 6.05.2022).

Mashabela, James Kenokeno, 2004, 'Buthelezi, Manas', *Dictionary of African Christian Biography*, https://dacb.org/stories/southafrica/buthelezi-manas/ (accessed 22.06.2022).

Mezuwa, Hope, 2022, 'On suicidal thoughts and deaths', *The Nation Newspaper*, 23 February.

Moyo, Fulata, 2017, 'Interrogating religion in search of gender justice: in conversation with Fulata Moyo', https://www.thefreelibrary.com/Interrogating+religion+in+search+of+gender+justice%3a+in+conversation...-a0500197249 (accessed 12.05.2022).

Mugambi, Jesse N. K., 2003, *Christian Theology and Social Reconstruction*, Nairobi: Acton.

Namadingo, Patience, 2021, 'Maury', YouTube, https://www.youtube.com/watch?v=5Ze8AmyqTMY (accessed 23.05.2022).

Oduyoye, Amba, 1983, 'Reflections from a Third World Woman's Perspective: Women's Experience and Liberation Theologies', in Virginia Fabella and Sergio Torres (eds), *Irruption of the Third World: Challenge to Theology*, Maryknoll, NY: Orbis Books, pp. 246–55.

Organisation for Economic Co-operation and Development (OECD), 2022, 'Malawi's population is largely youthful with 80% of its population aged below 35 years and with a median age of 17', https://www.oecd.org/dev/inclusivesocietiesanddevelopment/malawi-youth.htm#:~:text=Malawi's%20population%20is%20largely%20youthful,a%20median%20age%20of%2017 (accessed 5.05.2022).

Pillay, Jerry, 2020, 'Wither black theology of liberation? Perspectives from the late Professor Vuyani Vellem', *HTS Teologiese Studies/Theological Studies* 76 (3), https://doi.org/10.4102/hts.v76i3.6232 (accessed 23.07.2022).

Pollack, Tami, 2017, *Treating Children with Autistic Spectrum Disorder: A Psychoanalytic and Developmental Approach*, Oxford: Routledge.

Samasumo, Paul, 2022, 'Malawi: Lenten Pastoral Letter seeks to awaken the consciences of politicians and citizens', *Vatican News*, 8 March, https://www.vaticannews.va/en/africa/news/2022-03/malawi-catholic-bishops-pastoral-letter-meant-to-awaken-politi.html (accessed 2.05.2022).

Samuelson, R. C. A., 1929, *ZULU#18 Godusa: The Old Woman and the Ant-Bear's Hole*, https://ethicsofsuicide.lib.utah.edu/tradition/indigenous-cultures/african-traditional-subsaharan-cultures/zulu18/ (accessed 19.05.2022).

Sanderlei, 2022, *L'enfer*, https://tekst-sanderlei.com/2022/01/AD12/L%E2%80%99enfer-Song-Translation-and-Lyrics-Stromae-en-GB.html (accessed 26.05.2022).

Sizemore, Christine, W., 1997, 'Negotiating between ideologies: the search for identity in Tsitsi Dangarembga's "Nervous Conditions" and Margaret Atwood's "Cat's Eye"', *Women's Studies Quarterly* 25 (3/4), pp. 68–82, http://www.jstor.org/stable/40003373 (accessed 26.07.2022).

Soko, Julie, 2022, 'Trauma among Males', Interview (18 May).

Stromae (van Haver, Paul), 2022, 'L'enfer', YouTube, https://www.youtube.com/watch?v=DO8NSL5Wyeg (accessed 15.01.2022).

United Nations, 2013, *United Nations Youth: Definition of Youth*, https://www.

un.org/esa/socdev/documents/youth/fact-sheets/youth-definition.pdf (accessed 22.06.2022).

van Klinken, Adriaan and Ezra Chitando, 2015, 'Masculinities, Religion and HIV in Africa', in Emma Tomalin (ed.), *The Routledge Handbook of Religions and Global Development*, London and New York: Routledge, pp. 127–37.

Vellem, Vuyani, 2018, 'Cracking the Skull of Racism in South Africa Post-1994', in Roderick R. Hewitt and Chammah J. Kaunda (eds), *Who is an African?*, London: Lexington, pp. 31–47.

Warner, Debra, 2018, 'Breaking the silence of male trauma survivors', TedX Palo Alto College, https://www.youtube.com/watch?v=I3SyzQJJhvA (accessed 22.06.2022).

West, Gerald O., 2010, 'The Contribution of Tamar's Story to the Construction of Alternative African Masculinities', in S. Tamar Kamionkowski and Wonil Kim (eds), *Bodies, Embodiment, and Theology of the Hebrew Bible*, New York, London: T&T Clark, pp. 184–200.

——, 2018, 'The Bible as a Site of Struggle', 2018 De Carle Lecture Series (videos), https://biblicalstudiesonline.wordpress.com/2018/08/10/gerald-west-the-bible-as-a-site-of-struggle/ (accessed 22.03.2022).

Wilcock, Landon, 2018, 'Reimagining masculinity; my journey as a male sexual assault survivor', TEDx Queens University, https://www.youtube.com/watch?v=BWWPZlaq35U&t=638s (accessed 19.06.2022).

Williams, Delores S., 1993, 'Sin, Nature, and Black Women's Bodies', in Carol J. Adams (ed.), *Ecofeminism and the Sacred*, New York: Continuum, pp. 24–9.

YoungstaCPT (Riyadh Roberts), 2022, 'Dear rikhado, love riyadh', YouTube, https://www.youtube.com/watch?v=Ms_xwwOizII (accessed 3.05.2022).

(rel)*ease*

11

Our Practices Preach: The Church-Industrial Complex and The United Church of Christ

SHERYL JOHNSON

'United in Spirit and inspired by God's grace, we welcome all, love all, and seek justice for all.' This is the mission statement of the United Church of Christ (UCC), a progressive mainline Protestant denomination in the United States, formed in 1957. Progressive politics are a defining feature of the denomination. A 2014 Pew Research survey found that, of the mainline Christian denominations, UCC members were the most Democratic-leaning by way of political party affiliation (Lipka, 2016). The United Church of Christ also celebrates several historic 'firsts' related to social justice, including being the first Christian denomination to have ordained a woman and the first historic denomination to have ordained an openly gay person. It is clear that justice is central to the self-understanding and identity of the United Church of Christ. The denomination's website homepage (www.ucc.org) features many vibrant images and statements that focus on issues of equality, inclusion and justice. Amid images that feature racially diverse people, rainbow LGBT pride imagery, and appeals to take action on current social issues, it states: 'Doing justice, seeking peace and building community are central to the identity of the United Church of Christ. Our actions to create and foster economic, environmental and racial justice are rooted in the teachings of scripture and the policies of our General Synod.'

Certainly, having online images and messages that highlight justice concerns and releasing denominational statements that speak to these issues can create the perception that social justice is an all-encompassing and central concern in the UCC; however, it is also important to consider whether – and how – these values inform the day-to-day life of the church in a practical sense. Do these commitments to justice inform the administrative practices at the level of individual congregations? Do values related to justice inform every aspect of the church's life, including financial decisions and practices? If not, what are some of the barriers and explanations for this? How might the concept of Industrial Complex aid our understanding? For those who might desire that justice values be lived into more fully in their church, how might this be realized?

This chapter will focus on the intersection of justice commitments and congregational financial practices in the UCC. Specifically, it will consider the perspectives of ministers serving UCC congregations in California based on interviews conducted in 2022. Although one geographic region may not be representative of the church as a whole, California is considered a progressive-leaning state politically and therefore justice concerns are likely to be especially pertinent in this region. Additionally, ministers have a unique perspective on congregational life, but their views may not be representative of others in the churches that they serve. Focusing research on a bounded subset of a broader community – in this case, ministerial leaders – can provide some consistency and help to reveal some common themes, even if their beliefs may not be shared universally.

My interview research shows that denominational commitments to justice, even when deeply significant to ministers, can be very difficult to integrate into congregational financial practices for a variety of reasons. These include an uncritical adoption of more mainstream financial values; justice work being viewed as something for programmatic engagement rather than an all-encompassing value and approach; and the difficult positionality of ministers concerning financial deliberations. These elements point to the Church Industrial Complex at play. The theoretical framework of the 'Industrial Complex' explores how institutions can become focused on their own self-aggrandizement – pursuing power, growth and profits – in ways that may well contradict and undermine their expressed purpose and stated mission. The logics of capitalism overtake systems and institutions and introduce practices such as profit-seeking and hierarchical leadership (Best, 2011, p. xx). Significant theorizing has engaged phenomena such as the Military, Healthcare, Academic and Non-Profit Industrial Complexes, and there are particularly salient connections between the situations of churches and academic and non-profit organizations due to the shared mission to, in part, enlighten, educate and serve.

In regard to the Church Industrial Complex, we can see that even churches with well-established critiques of economic inequality, profit motives and prevailing socio-economic structures can be shaped by moneyed interests and assumptions such as the notion that financial resources are inherently a sign of success, and financial struggles are a sign of inferiority or failure. However, there is a deep desire among at least some UCC ministers to resist this Complex and live into their justice commitments more fully in church financial practices, as an expression of their faith. While many Christian theologians and ethicists have articulated the importance of economic justice, my research reveals some nuances of the challenges that are faced by ministers and local church communities who strive to do this work, resisting the sway of the Church Industrial Complex.

Methodology and population studied

To better understand the relationship between commitments to justice in mainline/progressive church contexts and congregational financial practices, I conducted ten interviews with UCC clergy presently serving congregations in California. These interviews were conducted by online video meetings. My interview subjects serve a variety of congregations in locations ranging from rural to suburban to urban and that vary in size from about 30 active participants in worship on a Sunday to about 200. Six interviewees identify as female and four identify as male; however, I will refer to them all in this chapter with the pronoun 'they' in order to preserve greater anonymity. Some serve as solo ministers while others serve multi-staff churches.

My interviews consisted of a semi-structured interview schedule that varied based on the subject and the context of the conversation, but the basic shape of the interviews and the focus of my questions were similar throughout. I began by asking my interviewees to share some basic demographic information about themselves and their churches as well as their background in ministry/church involvement. I then asked them to articulate their understanding of Christian values related to social justice. Next, I asked them to share their perception of their congregation's orientation towards justice and any particular commitments, involvements or practices that demonstrate that orientation. I then asked them to share about their church's financial decisions and practices, including whether or not they felt these were informed by their commitments to justice. If they responded affirmatively, I requested more details and examples. If they responded negatively, I inquired about why they believed that was so, what barriers or limitations existed from their perspectives, and whether they had attempted to address these. In some cases, interviewees felt that their churches' financial practices did embody some, but not all, of their commitments to justice, which I then explored through additional questions. Other questions and conversation topics arose from the material shared by my interviewees, but this description provides a basic overview of the interview schedule.

On the whole, my interviewees seemed very eager and willing to speak with me. Many expressed gratitude for the opportunity to have this conversation and to speak about these subjects. One even stated that the interview helped them to identify a longstanding but unnamed sense of personal discomfort arising from their perception of a deep disconnect between their church's stated public identity as a justice-committed church and the financial practices that were not just failing to live up to those commitments but, in their view, actually undermining these stated commitments.

To be clear, my interviewees are not fully representative of the clergy of the UCC as a whole and are not even representative within California. My sample was relatively small and was also limited by those who were willing and able to speak with me. Additionally, many of my subjects were recommended to me by an Associate Conference Minister, by interviewees themselves, or were known to me previously because of my connections to the UCC in California. It is also possible that, although our interviews were confidential and anonymous and I primarily asked open-ended questions, interviewees may have shared what they thought I wanted to hear, or thought were the 'right' answers to some of my questions. Additionally, as I stated in the introduction, congregation members might have different perspectives from their ministers on some of these matters. Despite these limitations, my interviews do illustrate some important issues and phenomena concerning church financial practices. Even as individual cases with partial perspectives, they still serve to illuminate critical facets of the challenges and possibilities for church finance as well as varied perspectives on these matters.

After conducting my interviews, I coded the material and organized it based on the various themes that emerged. I will highlight some of that thematic data to bring the various interviews into conversation with one another, and I will do so with an overall focus on how church finance and social justice intersect in mainline/progressive church contexts.

Data analysis and findings

Justice is central to UCC ministers' sense of vocation

In introducing themselves to me, eight of my interviewees began by sharing how their commitments to social justice led them into ministry generally and to the UCC specifically. One of my interviewees, for example, shared how it was their undergraduate activism work – pushing their university to divest its holdings from fossil fuels – that contributed to their emerging call to ministry (Interviewee 2, 14 February 2022). Another shared that learning about the participation of the church, and clergy specifically, in the civil rights movement is what brought them into the church and to ministry in the UCC (Interviewee 3, 15 February 2022). A third interviewee shared about being a member at a UCC church before attending seminary where there was significant work for justice that was engaged both in the community and through the church's financial practices and governance arrangements. They shared that this orientation was a significant draw for many new members and was significant for their call to ministry: 'At [name of church], any growth we experienced was because of the justice work, I don't think we had a single new member or visitor who did not cite that as the reason they came. And that was true for me as well, and that led me to go to seminary myself' (Interviewee 5, 3 March 2022). While social justice may not be a universal factor in all UCC ministers' experiences of vocation, justice is closely aligned with the identity of the UCC. Because the UCC is also a relatively small denomination, it is likely that many who have chosen to serve it in ministry are doing so because of its unique identity and place within the broader scope of Christian denominations.

Social justice is key to UCC congregational self-identity, but may be inflated

Most of my interviewees (nine out of ten) also shared that social justice is key to their congregations' self-understanding and reputation within the community: 'We're the church with the pride flag, the Black Lives Matter sign, the "immigrants welcome here" slogan. All of these things are what bring new people to us and what differentiates us from the other churches in the area. Our people are very proud of these things and very public about them' (Interviewee 7, 2 April 2022). A common theme across these interviews was that ministerial leaders see any engagement with justice work as a net positive and as more significant than many other churches in their communities, which leads to an admitted sense of complacency with even relatively minor initiatives. One interviewee shared how their church's hosting of various recovery/12-step groups is seen as major work for justice even though these groups do pay to rent the space because there is the sense that other churches would not want to rent to these groups (Interviewee 2, 14 February 2022). Another shared that their church allows people to park overnight in their vehicles to sleep, noting that this service is referred to continually as a sign the congregation is very justice-orientated. However, in the minister's opinion, this programme does not involve any significant time/costs as it is managed by an external organization that screens those who park in the lot and supports their practical needs. The minister describes that, despite the little risk or demands for the church, the programme is described by church members as though it is a huge sacrifice (Interviewee 4, 1 March 2022). Another interviewee concluded, 'A lot of churches I've served talk about justice ... but very little if anything from their budget goes to work that is not rooted in the charity model' (Interviewee 9, 28 April 2022).

Most of my interviewees shared specific examples of justice work that they feel their churches are proud of and reference often, yet for the most part, they felt that much more justice-orientated work could be done. A common theme was that while these programmes were often cited as critically important to the church's identity, the programmes were relatively insignificant within the broader life of the congregation concerning the amount of time, budget and congregational involvement offered. This could be related to the Church Industrial Complex, as a profit orientation de-emphasizes initiatives that do not directly produce its metrics of success, such as power, profit and influence. However, because there are churches (and many other organizations in society, such as businesses etc.) that do even less work for justice, small efforts can play an oversized role with respect to perception and self-identity and understanding. A further connection can be seen in work related to the Non-Profit Industrial Complex where it is noted that language and images related to liberation and revolutionary movements are appropriated by non-profits whose practices tend to be more institutionally orientated and reformist in nature (Rodriguez, 2007, p. 34). This imagery can serve to mask the reality of the situation and suggest that the organizations are more radical than they are in actuality.

UCC churches don't live up to their commitments to justice in financial practices

While some of my interviewees did share some positive examples of commitments to justice informing financial practices in relatively small ways, nine of my interviewees strongly asserted that, on the whole, they believe that their congregations fall short in significant ways concerning having their commitments to justice inform and undergird their financial practices. The one exception to this commonality shared that they understood their church to be unique in this regard. When I asked for examples or illustrations of this 'falling short', their answers varied.

Three clergy interviewees focused on staff compensation. 'No church I have served has paid me [as the minister] enough to live in the church's local community' (Interviewee 1, 10 January 2022), said one. Another shared about their church's recent decision to shift from having a salaried custodian on staff to using a cleaning company: 'Our custodian role used to come with benefits, pension, stability, all that. Now the cleaning company we use pays their staff minimum wage with no benefits. One cleaner told me that her schedule changes every week, and she never gets enough hours to pay her bills' (Interviewee 6, 5 March 2022). This interviewee lamented that the congregation has been very receptive to their preaching on topics relating to worker justice and labour rights, but when it comes to their employment practices, the congregation and board have a primary commitment to keeping costs as low as possible. This is directly related to business mindsets and the Church Industrial Complex, where expense minimization is a primary goal, even when it might conflict with other values.

Five interviewees focused on issues related to budgeting and priorities. 'Outreach is the first thing to go from the budget when money gets tight. We think of these other organizations as secondary. We preach telling people to keep giving even when they feel the pinch in their own budgets, but what do we do as a church? The opposite' (Interviewee 10, 30 April 2022). Another noted that the congregation's budget is split into two separate funds, one focused on 'internal' church funding (building, staffing, programmes etc.) and the other on 'external' initiatives (outreach programmes, denominational contributions, justice work etc.), and members are explicitly encouraged to give most of their contributions to the first fund and just about 10% of their total contribution to the other. The minister admitted that many congregation members do not give any to the second fund, which is treated as completely optional and much less important than the first: 'It's as if they think we cannot be a church without the things in the first fund and so people should feel obligated to give, but the other fund is totally about personal choice and isn't core to who we are' (Interviewee 4, 1 March 2022).

Four interviewees spoke about investments in relation to church funds. 'There is no such thing as ethically 'clean' investing – if you are investing and you think it is totally clean you haven't dug far enough', shared one (Interviewee 1, 10 January 2022). They elaborated that they do not believe that congregations should be sitting on a great deal of investment funds because there are so many urgent needs that people have right now. Another minister stated, 'The role of money is not to make more money, especially not at the cost of the planet' (Interviewee 4, 1 March 2022). Two others disclosed the reticence they have experienced when they've tried shifting the congregation's funds into more ethically orientated investment portfolios. One of them stated, 'They are afraid of anything that might cause us to earn less or that might make it seem like we are critical of the business and banking industries' (Interviewee 9, 28 April 2022). This person shared that their congregation is willing to discuss social justice in more abstract ways, but when discussions more directly implicate the actions and values of specific individuals or the local church (and might risk the Industrial Complex-related priority of financial growth/security), there is a great deal of anxiety and resistance.

Speaking broadly, my interviewees identified many areas where their own church's commitments to social justice were not reflected in congregational practices. These areas included: staff compensation, budgeting/priorities, investments, messages about donations/giving to the church (and embedded assumptions about members' financial situations), costs related to church activities (such as expensive youth mission trips that individual families are expected to pay for), rental groups (that is, trying to earn as much as possible without taking into account the needs and realities of different organizations), and several others. However, it was not only the fact that these issues exist that was significant for various ministers; many expressed the overall sense that topics related to social justice did not arise in church finance conversations even when justice is central to the church's overall identity and is featured prominently in its preaching, education and community engagement. Henry A. Giroux, in describing the Academic Industrial Complex, argues that professors are increasingly pushed on to a treadmill of creating revenue for the university, while at the same time, they find their own salaries and job security reduced, in part due to increased use of part-time roles and term-limited contracts (Giroux, 2007, pp. 120–1). Similarities can be seen in churches where pastors and other leaders face increased pressure to create revenue, even when that does not align with their values, while at the same time they may be struggling to pay their own bills or have their hours reduced.

Conventional economic values inform UCC congregational financial practice

When I asked those who identified a disconnect between their church commitments to justice and their financial practices why they believed this issue existed, I received a variety of hypotheses and articulations of the dynamics at play. Primarily, they observed that their churches' financial practices are rooted in 'conventional' economic values such as financial stability, growth, risk avoidance, consumerism and individualism. Five interviewees stated that institutional survival seemed to be the primary value. One minister offered, 'They really want to save as much as they can to ensure the church is present for future generations, but I'm usually trying to push them to spend money on mission because there won't be a church in 30 years if we aren't doing something like living the church's mission' (Interviewee 3, 15 February 2022). This statement identifies some of the tensions embedded within the desire for church survival: risk-aversion may ultimately undermine survival. Still, this urge to maintain the institution at all costs was especially prevalent in the interviews: 'People confuse keeping the faith to pass along to future generations with maintaining the institution, and more specifically, the building' (Interviewee, 10 January 2022). The desire to save money for the future and preserve the church as an institution is not simply one factor among many others; it exposes the deeper question of what comprises the church: does it require features such as paid staff and a building, or is it more about less tangible aspects such as faith, community and mission?

One interviewee identified three primary barriers to imbuing church finance with justice commitments: 'congregational individualism, siloed thinking between justice and administration, and entrenched patterns' (Interviewee 7, 2 April 2022). When I asked them to explain more about this siloed thinking, they reflected: 'It's like they categorize everything related to justice under "outreach" rather than seeing it as something that needs to inform every part of our church's life. I think it is connected to white or Western culture … this idea that topics can be so separate.'

Regarding entrenched patterns, they shared that so much of their church's financial practices are just a recapitulation of what was done the year before and involve the same people in leadership: 'There is the sense that things have gone fine in the past and so they will continue to be fine if we just stay on the same path with the same "captains at the helm".'

Similar budgetary patterns and a sense of 'defaulting to what has been done before' (Interviewee 1, 10 January 2022) were named by two others as well. This same interviewee, along with three others, spoke about the issue of 'congregational individualism', which I loosely define as being primarily concerned with one's congregation and not with others or the wider church/denomination. Some felt that this approach is embedded within the overall structure and polity of the UCC. One stated:

> Look at [name of municipality]. There are six UCC churches. All of them are struggling for money and competing with one another. We talk a lot about sharing and collaboration, but yet here they are all fighting for survival and using up a lot of money that could be going to mission doing so. I think someone from the denomination needs to come in and say there will just be one UCC. But we're Congregationalists so that will never happen. (Interviewee 1, 10 January 2022)

Relatedly, three interviewees mentioned a reticence to support the UCC denominationally and attributed that sentiment as arising from problematic values. One minister stated, 'People always want to ask, "What are we getting from the denomination?" and if we should really support it if we give more than we seem to get' (Interviewee 2, 14 February 2022). They found that this sentiment was rooted in an approach that was contrary to a spirit of sharing, collaboration and fund redistribution. Another shared that their congregation appreciated being a part of the UCC because they found it comparatively less denominationally orientated and therefore required less by way of denominational financial contributions from congregations. The minister shared their frustration with this sentiment because they believe 'in both the importance of government to serve society and denominations to support congregations, especially the most marginalized ones' (Interviewee 8, 3 April 2022).

Although ministers may not perfectly understand all of the factors that undergird their congregation's financial approaches and additional or differing factors may be involved, these responses are helpful to begin to understand why justice does not feature more prominently in local church financial conversations. In many cases, the primary influences seem to stem from a particular understanding of ecclesiology/what the church is: the individual congregation persisting into the future with a building and paid staff informed primarily by the practices and leaders of the past. Although some interviewees acknowledged that this perspective is not necessarily incompatible with a social justice-informed church, they do have complex personal feelings about some of these aspects (i.e. arising from relying on their church budgets for their salaries). On the whole, it seems that many of these values relate to a particular expression and understanding of church, of which my interviewees were vocally critical.

The issue of competition is also addressed by Andrea Smith in her scholarship about the Non-Profit Industrial Complex. She describes how non-profits, in their orientation towards money, are pressured to compete with one another for funding and adhere to the wishes of major donors (Smith, 2011, pp. 142–3). Similarly, but in describing the Academic Industrial Complex, Henry A. Giroux asserts that this phenomenon transforms everyone into an 'entrepreneur, customer, or client' (Giroux, 2007, p. 104). Relatedly, in churches we can see the push to view members and rental groups as fickle customers who need to be satisfied in accordance with the level of their giving and contribution to the overall budget. This means that the desires of the privileged are likely to be prioritized, contrary to a justice-rooted ethic. Giroux critiques that in academia, the line between student and consumer is becoming blurred, such that 'customer satisfaction is a surrogate for learning' (Giroux, 2007, p. 106). We might ask if the same is true for congregation members with respect to discipleship and church membership.

Change is possible: church finances could – and should – be more aligned with justice

It is important to note that each of my interviewees openly expressed that church finances could and should be considered through a lens of commitments to justice. None of the nine who expressed a strong sense of disconnect between practices and commitments believed that this current state of affairs was inevitable or unavoidable. One, for example, shared that their current priority for their ministry is to 'bring forth the question of how must our commitments to becoming an anti-racist church inform our finances' (Interviewee 3, 15 February 2022). Another shared something quite similar; their church council just completed a study on Ibram X. Kendi's *How to be an Antiracist*, and the minister is now preparing to lead a workshop where each line of the church's budget will be considered through the lens of anti-racism. They plan to ask the council to consider 'how would a decrease or increase in each line item promote greater equity or help us live our mission to put our faith into action more fully' (Interviewee 4, 1 March 2022). This is a fascinating exercise and could be a significant bridge between a more educationally orientated endeavour (book study) and the actual financial practices of the church, thus potentially bridging the 'silos' that others identified between 'justice' and 'administration'.

Some interviewees shared specific examples where this alignment of justice and finance already exist in their churches. One shared about some unexpected income that the congregation received and then was invested in ethical funds and used to support community programmes. They shared that this case was treated differently from the regular finances of the congregation, but it freed them to begin to think about money in a new way (Interviewee 2, 14 February 2022). Another interviewee recalled the entrance fee sliding scale that was used for a church fundraising dinner, which helped make the event more accessible and furthered conversations about income inequality within the church community and society at large (Interviewee 9, 29 April 2022). Additionally, one minister offered the example of 'giv[ing] the plate offering away each week to community justice organizations and just hav[ing] pledges sustain the operating budget' (Interviewee 6, 3 April 2022). This approach also suggests a willingness to forgo potential income in service of work for justice in the community. Finally, another interviewee described how their church was beginning to pay people to do certain types of work that had previously been done by volunteers. They shared: 'It's one thing for the white retiree with a generous pension to volunteer but it's totally different for the young Black artist who is trying to piece together enough paid work to survive – and who has to deal with the impacts of the legacy of slavery and ongoing racism' (Interviewee 3, 15 February 2022).

In general, my interviewees were excited to share these examples of justice work and programming at the local level and were proud of those moments when they experienced the values of the church being put into practice. While many lamented that these examples were relatively minor and did not represent their congregation's overall approach to money, they did feel that these incarnations of justice were significant and had helped expand their congregation's minds as to what was not only possible but also ethically necessary. One minister also expressed the hope that these examples would not be used as an excuse to limit the more challenging work of integrating justice into finance (that is, that these small instances were enough and could be raised as evidence that the congregation had taken justice into consideration; Interviewee 10, 30 April 2022). But on the whole my interviewees found these examples hopeful and signs that their congregation could do more in the future.

Still, many of the interviewees felt unsure of how to move forward in a large-scale way, other than simply raising smaller-scale possibilities in specific cases when the opportunities arose. Some expressed frustration that their community engagement and teaching and preaching about theology and social justice did not seem to have much of an impact on aspects related to administration and finance. One person felt that their preaching was their primary opportunity to share their views as their guidance was not welcomed in meetings or conversations specific to finance: 'There is the general sense that I am there for spiritual guidance but that financial wisdom is the arena of the real professionals – accountants, business leaders, older well-off guys, you know, the types that serve on the trustees and finance committees' (Interviewee 7, 2 April 2022). This comment also indicates the sense that the particular social location (concerning age, gender and so forth) of certain ministers may also contribute to their perspectives on finance being less welcomed. It also suggests a sense of separation between the 'spiritual' and 'secular' realms that might contribute to the overall divide between justice-orientated work and church finances. In any case, while my interviewees were largely proud of the smaller-scale examples their congregations had been willing to enact, the ministers were mostly unsure of the next steps or how to move from token actions to deeper paradigmatic shifts.

Critiquing the system that pays your bills: ministers' complex positionalities

One additional, common theme is the desire of many of the ministers to increase the profile of social justice in their church's financial processes. When I asked my interviewees whether their position as church employees impacted their ability to bring up considerations of justice in the context of discussions and deliberations over church finances, eight out of the ten said that it did, at least to some extent:

> It's so tricky to talk about this because, at the end of the day, they pay my bills. I need this job to survive. I don't have a previous career and I haven't been able to save very much, so I feel vulnerable on a very

visceral level. And then there is also the reality of just knowing that a lot of what I am advocating for costs money, meaning, in some people's minds, leaving less for my salary. (Interviewee 1, 10 January 2022)

Many of the interviewees reflected extensively on how difficult it is to criticize one's employer, which is magnified when the minister is experiencing forms of greater vulnerability. For example, one shared: 'As a queer person, I know that there aren't a lot of other churches that would hire me. And I have at least 30 years until retirement. It might be easier for a straight minister who is about to retire to have these conversations, maybe less risky. But for me, I have to tread very carefully' (Interviewee 3, 15 February 2022). When I asked how they deal with their positionality in these conversations, many of them shared that it has been very helpful to work collaboratively with congregation members to offer critiques, to be upfront about the potential awkwardness that might arise from their ministerial position, to be sure to offer praise for what the church is already doing, and also to offer general statements or suggestions about what needs to be done so that congregational members can feel they are in charge of making any shifts. One interviewee, for example, shared that they often introduce biblical teachings as a way to bring up justice concerns but not directly criticize what the congregation is doing.

For most of my interviewees, this issue of their positionality with respect to the congregation was a central concern as they reflected on their work to try to encourage the church to integrate justice concerns into their finance and budgeting decisions. Many shared that they wanted to do more to support these efforts but felt constrained by their vulnerability in not wanting to jeopardize their employment and not wanting to be seen as self-serving or overly self-negating. Some felt that bringing up justice concerns around finance meant advocating for greater salary and benefits for themselves and other church staff, which could be seen as self-serving on the part of the minister. Others felt that bringing up justice concerns could mean that the congregation might want to reduce their salary by, for example, allocating more funds for outreach or social justice initiatives. Giroux, in describing the university context, also notes that professors are increasingly pressured to not speak about controversial matters because of the ways that it might impact the university's bottom line (Giroux, 2007, p. 160). Several of my interviewees felt somewhat unsettled about their salaries in relation to the church budget and justice concerns and felt that these feelings impacted their abilities to have open conversations about justice issues in their churches.

Conclusion

My interviewees' descriptions and analysis of their congregations largely align with the work done by scholars who study the practices of mainline and progressive churches; however, these interviews reveal the particular challenges and perspectives of ministers serving congregations, which offers nuance and perspectives regarding the realities of the Church Industrial Complex. It is useful to know that the phenomena experienced by these ministers on a local level are connected to broader trends, and my interviewees were able to specifically articulate the particularities of the challenges of living into alternative economic values in congregational settings. Christian theologians and ethicists make a strong case for the necessity of this work, but my interviewees provided useful data on why this gulf persists between stated commitments to justice and the approaches to finance in congregational administration and how elements of the Church Industrial Complex impede work for justice both within a congregation and more broadly.

Although the sample size of this research was relatively small and the findings may not be universalizable to all contexts and all UCC ministers, the issues raised were nevertheless critically important. These interviews revealed that a commitment and desire to do justice is not sufficient, in and of itself, to ensure that it will inform all aspects of the life of a church, particularly in the area of finance. Even UCC ministers in California, many of whom have chosen ministry in the UCC precisely because of their commitments to justice, experience numerous constraints in their efforts to infuse justice concerns into all aspects of the congregation's lives, including financial decisions. These specific constraints include complacency with small instances of work for justice, a sense of separation between the congregation's work for justice and the everyday business of the church, deeply embedded norms and values that inform how financial work is engaged, and the minister's complex positionality in their congregational systems. We can connect these constraints to the profit-centrality of Industrial Complexes and see how these phenomena operate similarly in other sectors of society. Still, importantly, each of the interviewees articulated some optimism about the possibilities of achieving greater justice in their congregational settings but simply noted the need to be careful and strategic in these conversations.

Future work might consider the perspectives of members of UCC congregations with respect to issues of justice and finance and particularly the views of those most involved with the financial life (i.e. trustees, treasurers, finance committee members) and social justice life (i.e. outreach/justice/mission committee members etc.) in these communities. It could also consider perspectives from other regions of the UCC as well as of people from other denominations and even other faith and non-faith traditions. Additionally, it would be useful to explore case studies of churches (as well as non-profits, academic institutions etc.) that have taken bold action to resist Industrial Complexes and align their commitments to justice with their financial practices to see what might be learned and applied to other contexts.

On the whole, it is clear that stating a commitment to do justice is not sufficient to ensure that it will happen. It is often the case, as the familiar saying goes, that 'Actions speak louder than words'. Perhaps, in this case, our financial practices may *preach* louder than our words, be those 'words' found in our sermons, pronouncements, theologies or elsewhere. It is critically important to consider not only what we say we believe but how all of our practices, taken together, either align with and bolster or undermine that message. Making change can be much easier said than done, but understanding the dynamics, values and barriers at play is an important first step. Ministers have a unique perspective on these challenges from a grassroots level and their analysis and reflections provide critical insight into both what is currently taking place, why that is so, and what could be in the future.

References

Best, Steven, 2011, 'Introduction: Pathologies of Power and the Rise of the Global Industrial Complex', in Steven Best et al. (eds), *The Global Industrial Complex: Systems of Domination*, Lanham, MD: Lexington, pp. ix–xxv.

Giroux, Henry A., 2007, *The University in Chains: Confronting the Military-Industrial-Academic Complex*, Boulder, CO: Paradigm.

Lipka, Michael, 2016, 'U.S. religious groups and their political leanings', *Pew Research Center*, 23 February, https://www.pewresearch.org/fact-tank/2016/02/23/u-s-religious-groups-and-their-political-leanings/ (accessed 8.12.2021).

Rodriguez, Dylan, 2007, 'The Political Logic of the Non-Profit Industrial Complex', in INCITE! (ed.), *The Revolution will Not be Funded: Beyond the Non-Profit Industrial Complex*, Durham, NC: Duke University Press, pp. 21–40.

Smith, Andrea, 2011, 'The Revolution will Not be Funded', in Steven Best et al. (eds), *The Global Industrial Complex: Systems of Domination*, Lanham, MD: Lexington, pp. 165–79.

12

Liberation at the Cusp of Apocalypse: A Small Move from Making More to Making Beauty

S. LILY MENDOZA

In a world full of grief and trauma, unmetabolized and metastasizing into cancer-like growth that is wreaking havoc on the Earth's ecosystems and auguring the end of life as we know it, what is left for us to do? 'We make beauty anyway' is the fierce and stubborn reply of original peoples who still carry a measure of intactness in their lives amid our modern culture's unrelenting assault. This moment not being their first holocaust – many in fact have not ever *not* been in one since modernity's assault on their homelands, fighting the corporate giants that would, for example, dam their waters, clear-cut their forests, pave over their farmlands, bulldoze their sacred places for real estate development – their call is not just to fight but to keep the seeds of real culture alive through the hard lesson of learning to suffer with grace, beauty and dignity.

This chapter will explore such a witness, beginning with my own journey as a born-again Christian convert auspiciously getting interdicted by a mid-30s encounter with Indigenous magnificence in an ethnomusicology classroom at the University of the Philippines – one that spoke profoundly to my body before my head could comprehend and constituted a sensual 'conversion' away from civilization's hollow trappings into an ever-deepening embrace of land-taught wisdom and grace by original peoples both in the USA where I now reside (and teach) and the homeland to which I return with regularity. In the mix, I will trace the way liberation has become an adventure out of the grip of our species' delirium of supremacy (gone hyper in colonialism's development conceits and mainstream Christianity's convictions of universalism) and into a 'small ordinariness' shot through with the grand potency of a seed.

But first, the big question: 'Liberation from what?'

Liberation from what?

As I was preparing to write this chapter, I came across a provocative book by the Canadian journalist and author Andrew Nikiforuk, *The Energy of Slaves: Oil and the New Servitude* (2012). It wasn't the first time I encountered the term 'energy slaves'. Ivan Illich, writing in 1974, had used the same term in his slim but insightful volume, *Energy and Equity*, grappling, even as early as then, with the inevitable problem of inequity that arises once energy use and production reaches a certain threshold.

Nikiforuk, following closely on Illich's track, makes the claim that underneath contemporary modern humans' relationship with energy is a master–slave dynamic, no different from that of the monarchies in the Middle Ages whose opulent lifestyles were enabled by the muscle power of hundreds of thousands of labouring human (and animal) slaves. Contrary to the notion that we have now finally done away with slavery, given that we now have all these mechanized machines to do the labouring for us, Nikiforuk argues that our settled, convenient, richly resourced lifestyles that we have come to take for granted in our modern world (and which the poor are constantly urged to aspire to), are in fact just as dependent on the energy of slaves, if not more so – only now in the form of coal, oil and natural gas, not to mention the human muscle power that is still ubiquitous in sweatshops, plantations, mining and some of the most dangerous extractive operations of industrial production around the globe. There are no winners in this game, Nikiforuk asserts, certainly not for the slave whose degradation is stark, but neither for the master, whose ultimate loss of freedom and gross dependency on the slave makes him 'lazy, unhealthy, dumb, and unskilled in the basics of survival' (in Riches, 2016, p. 152).

I open with this reference given that one of the challenges in grappling with the theme of liberation is first gaining a clear sense of the nature of our enslavement. The question, 'Liberation from what?' demands that we first recognize – as starkly as possible – our condition of captivity, to make visible the bars of the holding cell that incarcerates us. This is hard to do when the very condition of captivity has now become, in our modern world, coterminous with human life itself. Without recognizing the aberrant nature of our condition as a modern civilization – having erased from memory the hundreds of thousands, if not millions, of years when we lived very differently as a species on the planet – when confronted with the apocalypse of collapse and extinction, our well-trained instincts are likely to make us cling to our chains even more tightly, rather than breaking free.

In this chapter, then, will be a two-pronged probing: the first, into the cultural logic of an energy slave system that in my own life has shown up as a colonizing regime, one that I now see is responsible for introducing a dynamic of restlessness and instability into what has heretofore been a largely relatively stable equilibrium in the world prior to agricultural settlement and civilization-building, and on the other, the constant press of natural peoples (that is, those living a very different ethic of relation to the Wild) to return to balance, to keep the cycle of life going – their practice of beauty-making a discipline they keep as a form of repayment of the debt owed to the natural world for nurturing and keeping them and life alive. But the weaving of the narrative argument will necessarily meander through my story of colonial subjection – growing up – to the epistemic terror of the civilizational mandate as introduced to our people by Christian Protestantism and its modern secularized version of Western progress, advancement and growth and my subsequent tutelage to the world of our Indigenous kin in my Philippine homeland where I was drawn auspiciously to a radically different way of seeing and being in the world. The lessons from this latter encounter will form the alternative ground for re-imagining a future no longer captive to the seductions of 'more' (bigger, better) but rather compelled by a force much stronger and more powerful: that of beauty and love. As my partner, James Perkinson, likes to say, 'You cannot exit one cultural formation without tutelage to another.'

Captivity in the key of Christian subjectification

I still remember the moment of my Christian born-again conversion. It was in the home of my Sunday school teacher and youthful idol, Ate Leni ('Ate' is Tagalog for 'big sister'), then a brilliant upper-class student at the University of the Philippines and one of the leaders in the State Varsity Christian Fellowship, an Oxford-originated Christian student organization where I was newly introduced as an incoming college freshman. Ate Leni was every bit my role model – bright, articulate, passionate. Both her family and mine were from the same province (Pampanga) in the Philippines, with both our fathers serving as pillars of our local United Methodist Church.

I had grown up in Sunday school, my father being one of the early converts to Protestant Methodism. My mother, a convert from Catholicism, served as the church's organist upon marrying my father. All six of us siblings sang in the church choir, took our turns leading the Methodist Youth Fellowship, and faithfully sat – and eventually taught – in Sunday school. Living in a majority Catholic neighbourhood, church was our life and community. 'Culture' for us was innocuous at best; church life was all. 'Filipino' signified even less; if ever, what it signified were the ways that we (as a people) needed to cease being: 'superstitious', 'idolatrous', 'backward', in short, 'uncivilized'. But although we were immersed in Bible study and church teachings, there was a lot that felt mostly rote and routine even while being scrupulously demanding psychically. I remember pledging 'to be good' after each church communion, to love God above all else, only to be plagued with acute awareness of failure every single time.

Ate Leni, being the consummate spiritual mentor that she was, was not remiss in noticing both my anxiety and earnestness, and that afternoon, in a scheduled one-on-one time, sat me down on the sofa next to her in their home's living room, opened the Bible and, line-by-line, read Isaiah 53 to me:

> [4] Surely he took up our pain
> and bore our suffering,
> yet we considered him punished by God,
> stricken by him, and afflicted.
> [5] But he was pierced for our transgressions,
> he was crushed for our iniquities;
> the punishment that brought us peace was on him,
> and by his wounds we are healed.
> [6] We all, like sheep, have gone astray,
> each of us has turned to our own way;
> and the LORD has laid on him
> the iniquity of us all. (NIVUK)

I'm not sure now if it was just me who concluded, or if it was something that she herself articulated, but listening to those words, I remember being hit with the thought that Jesus, the prophesied messiah, was not just dying for the world in general, but *for me* in particular; that it was *my* sinfulness that had – literally – pinned him on that cross. It didn't matter if I were the only person alive in the world, Ate Leni remarked, Jesus would still have had to die for me and my sins – that's how much I was loved by God. At that, a dam broke, and overcome by a mix of sorrow, indebtedness and gratitude, I sobbed uncontrollably. It was then that Ate Leni put her arms around me and led me to pray the sinner's prayer and accept Jesus as my lord and saviour.

It was a paradigm-shifting experience, my conversion, from thereon reorientating my entire life's purpose and energy towards the one goal of 'missionizing' the world – to 'save' the world as I had been 'saved', to learn that the debt I owed (for failing to measure up to God's demands) had already been paid for by Christ meant I no longer had to be constantly tormented by my moral failure. God loved me unconditionally – that should be enough, indeed, a liberating thought. And, cognitively, I was all in.

For decades thereafter, I faithfully followed in the footsteps of Ate Leni (and a host of other brilliant spiritual mentors), becoming an ardent apologist for the Christian faith, building my own quite successful ministry among the intelligentsia while working as a scholar, researcher, writer and, eventually, a faculty member, at the University of the Philippines.

But somehow, unbeknown to many, whatever cognitive liberation my born-again conversion afforded me refused to translate to an affective, experiential release. Deep within, the torment remained, with the nagging accusation (of not being enough) continuing to wreak havoc on my psyche. The constant refrain was that of being 'weighed and found wanting', in the Tagalog language, *tinimbang ka nguni't kulang*. It was a mysterious affliction the roots of which I had no way of figuring out, but one that I nonetheless sought to make my peace with by counting it as my own version of St Paul's 'thorn in the side', with God hopefully perfecting his power in my weakness – or so I rationalized.

When the invitation came for me to join the Inter-Varsity Christian Fellowship national staff at the conclusion of my undergraduate studies, my overscrupulous conscience would keep me from saying yes, secretly fearful of 'being found out'. For how can one purporting to be a Christian leader continue to be so tormented in their innermost being? Sadly, not even Isaiah's promise of God's heart being tender and forgiving in the passage that says, 'A bruised reed He will not break and a dimly burning wick He will not extinguish' (Isaiah 42.3, NASB 1995), had power to break the stranglehold of self-accusation and judgement that clung like a barnacle to my psyche, stifling my soul's freedom.

Freedom and release from a most unexpected place: irruption of the fugitive 'anomaly'

The rationalist individualism in North American Protestantism had no way of accounting for such malaise (as I suffered) beyond its relegation to the personal; that is, if ever, *I* – no one else – was responsible, and if I were to be freed from such an affliction, it had to be from my own effort and exercise of responsibility. And so I continued to power through, choosing a secular job as a researcher/writer for – of all things – a 'Cultural Liberation Program' under the auspices of an outfit within the country's premier state university (from where I also graduated) commandeered by then Philippine President Ferdinand Marcos to serve as his administration's policy research centre. To equip myself for the work, I enrolled in an MA programme in Philippine Studies – this all while continuing my clandestine missionary work among doctoral students and those training as diplomats and ambassadors. My immersion in the centre's cultural work lent a nationalist inflection to my Christian faith, but evangelicalism's totalizing and universalist orientation would leave no quarter – all cultural knowledge had to be sifted through and brought 'under the reign of Christ', thus making 'the' biblical lens serve as the unbending arbiter for what could and could not be affirmed based on its perceived in/commensurability with the Truth (with a capital T) of God in Christ.

That is, until a fateful encounter with another world unexpectedly ripped open my iron-clad certainties, shaking the very foundations of my belief and faith and calling into question all I had ever taken for granted as life's meaning and purpose. I called it 'The case of the fugitive "anomaly" escaping subjection despite the mind's near-total epistemic capitulation' (Mendoza, forthcoming). As I wrote of that moment of awakening in another essay:

> The occasion was a graduate course in the humanities titled 'The Image of the Filipino in the Arts', taught by an ethnomusicology professor, where I encountered for the first time the amazing artistic creations of our indigenous communities that were least penetrated by modern development and Christian missionisation – their intricate weaving designs, the wild vibrant colours of their textiles, their basketry, dances, songs, chants, mythic stories and so on – and what they signified in terms of a different way of being in the world. I was stunned! Nothing prepared me for the power of that encounter with wild, untamed beauty: complex geometric designs that mathematicians noted could not have been

wilfully conceived by the rational mind, mellifluous melodies able to call up grief out of all its hidden places, polyphonic sounds and rhythms coming from native instruments that not only sounded but looked utterly beautiful, dances as diverse as their ecologies of origination, intricate architectural structures that used not a single nail to bind parts together and so on, and all of these creations of beauty ritually sourced, many given in dreams, with materials taken from the wild only with the accompanying respect, honouring and asking for permission, and, always, in service of beauty.

I still remember walking back to my dorm room bawling my heart out, not knowing what it was that hit me from all the innocent descriptions of those works of art. It was as if my body knew something that my mind could not (yet) fathom. (Mendoza, 2018, pp. 89–90)

The impact of that encounter with Indigenous beauty took time to percolate into my conscious understanding. It was at once exhilarating and epiphanic, but also disconcerting. As a Christian, one after all was not supposed to fall in love with the 'pagan' or 'primitive' – that abjected figure of the historical past whose destiny, 'as we know', is to vanish, to be superseded by superior, more evolved ('civilized') humans (cf. Mendoza, 2013). Such was the unspoken assumption in my religious socialization. These land-dwelling Indigenous kin who still retained their ecologically moulded cultures and ways of being epitomized a human subjectivity that we modernizing Filipinos were told – in the stories we heard in the churches, in the schools and in the public discourse – to regard as retrograde, inferior and 'less-than'. Furthermore, within the logic of the country's modernizing economy, these retrograde beings did not count, since they were predisposed neither to buying nor selling and, as such, were non-contributors to the market economy and therefore superfluous, unless assimilated and converted. And yet there I was, falling hopelessly in love despite myself. Sophisticated cynics would call it 'romantic', a kind of 'primitivist nostalgia'; but for me it was more a case of 'deep calling to deep' (Psalm 42.7) – an undeniable, if confounding, truth-recognition mediated not via rational cognition but somatically, through a kind of powerful, affective, and embodied knowing. Irrupting ironically in the heat of my Christian missionary fervour and devotion, the rip it caused in my otherwise perfectly coherent Christian world view would, over time, give way to a thoroughgoing rupture, like having a veil torn asunder to reveal a whole other world hitherto forbidden from consideration as a possible way of human *being*.

I sometimes wonder how I would have responded differently to such hailing had my incorrigible psyche not harboured that intractable 'thorn in the flesh' (that is, the bane of being under constant scrutiny and surveillance) – that fugitive part of me that refused to be at ease with the totalizing Christian disciplining. Would I have had courage to venture into that other world talked about exclusively – within the terms of the dominant discourse – only as our country's 'past', to be transcended and left behind, now that we have joined the rest of the civilized world's march to progress? So stark were the prohibitions – from that world is 'primitive', 'superstitious', 'no way to live as a human being' and, simply, 'such a miserable form of existence', to 'it's 'idolatrous', 'demonic', an 'abomination to God'. Stay away – the only permissible mode of relation one could have with that world is to make it a target for missionization. In fact, growing up, that was all I remember of that world when I would tag along with our family's White American missionary friends while on their proselytizing sorties in the remote parts of our province: scenarios of dark-skinned, kinky-haired, pitiful-looking native peoples being preached at and then compelled to pray the sinner's prayer inside concrete church structures that stuck out conspicuously in their rural abodes.

That fateful encounter in the humanities classroom did change me for ever. So powerful was its impact that I was compelled by its witness of radical otherness and beauty – somatically mediated – to devote all my subsequent time and energy to learning more about the provenance of that beauty, one that had – literally – 'startled' me into healing and release, overwhelming me with a new kind of longing and desire. I quickly learned that to love that other world was a dangerous thing, for one, because it called into question Christianity's exclusive claim of being the sole articulator of the 'Truth'. Graduate study would supply the conceptual tools for me as I learned concepts such as frameworks of intelligibility, ideology, hegemony, doxa, canon-formation, power-knowledge, regime of truth, colonial gaze, subjectification, post/modernity, post/colonialism, post/structuralism, but it was actual encounter, relationship, and tutelage with Indigenous elders and teachers that became the ultimate source of deep insight and inspiration for me.

Indigenous beauty as a counter-mirror: recognizing terror in Christianity's salvific narrative

The cultural theorist Fred Moten once remarked in an interview (19 October 2018):

> Anybody who thinks they can come even close to understanding how terrible the terror has been without understanding how beautiful the beauty has been against the grain of that terror, is wrong.

Indeed, it was the witness of Indigenous beauty that flung open the door for me to a totally different way of apprehending the world than I had been taught growing up. It is also what helped me begin to understand that the mysterious affliction that I suffered for years actually had roots somewhere – not in an imagined psychological neurosis that had no basis save for my 'lack of faith' in God's unconditional love, but in what turned out to be the very real after-effects of centuries of epistemic colonization visited upon an entire people – at the heart of which is the salvific narrative of EuroWestern Christianity. Although it is true that assimilation, when successfully accomplished, can manifest in what may appear as a seamless narrative or, in Bourdieu's formulation, a kind of doxa that makes the imposition not seem like one but simply something of the order of nature, it is also true that under conditions of oppression and power domination, there is always the possibility of the 'fugitive anomaly' erupting from underneath the quiescent surface, awaiting its moment of escape from ideological subjection when the moment is ripe. That moment came for me in that humanities classroom.

But why terror?

The tradition itself, in its provenance as a movement of escaped slaves, exiting Egypt and re-learning ways to live on the land as pastoral nomads, before amalgamating with peasants revolting from Canaanite city-states and becoming 'Israel' is a redeeming narrative. Movements led by John the Baptist and Jesus of Nazareth both built on that history, seeking to return peasants in their day to a more reciprocal relationship to land. Under Paul's influence (among others) it became an outlaw religion inside the Roman Empire, until Emperor Constantine adopted it as the official religion of Rome and began using it as a tool of domination and conquest. That domination dynamic was enshrined in what came to be known as the Doctrine of Christian Discovery, stipulating that European Christian nations had the right to claim lands and subjugate native populations not already under the rule of other European Christian nations.

The quintessential outcome of that kind of imperial project became a reign of terror for native/Indigenous peoples around the globe, decimating their numbers by as much as 95% (in the case of the Americas) and wreaking havoc on their land-based cultures and sacred traditions. In the Philippines, half a million to a million Filipinos were massacred (out of a population of about six million at that time) during the US invasion of the country at the turn of the twentieth century, justifying colonial takeover as a noble and righteous cause, its purpose, the civilizing and Christianizing of a 'senile and savage' people otherwise unable to govern themselves (see MacKinley's speech to the Methodist delegation in Schirmer and Shalom, 1987, p. 22).

That domination doctrine remains in effect up to the present; it has never been abrogated. In the USA it forms the basis of property laws. In the Philippines it took the name *Jus Regalia*, Regalian Doctrine, dating back to the Spanish regime that decreed ownership of Philippine territories by virtue of 'discovery' and conquest. Today it remains enshrined in the Philippine constitution with the state taking over as 'the source of any asserted right to ownership of land', often to the disadvantage of Indigenous communities that are likely to get the short end of the stick when fighting for their ancestral territories, notwithstanding the institution in 1997 of the Indigenous People's Rights Act intended to protect their rights.

Further devastating is the central tenet known as *terra nullius*, the concept of 'empty lands'. No matter the prior presence of peoples in the places that Europeans claimed to have discovered, if such peoples were not Christian, or if they were not settled and not actively exploiting the land for wealth creation and the production of surplus, they were deemed less than human and the lands they occupied effectively 'empty', the inhabitants treated merely as part of the flora and fauna. The reasoning is that subsistence living is no better than animal-like existence and failure to aggressively pursue wealth and create surplus meant failure to maximize the use of the land for the glory of God. Peoples living as hunter-gatherers, pastoral nomads or subsistence farmers were therefore cast as poor stewards of God's creation, deserving to be dispossessed of their lands, enslaved and, in many cases, outright eliminated.

The invention of the monotheistic notion of a transcendent God – a singular, all-powerful sovereign being separate from the world he is believed to have created – likewise proved devastating in that it cast the nature-based spirituality of Indigenous peoples as idolatrous; that is, as 'worshiping creation rather than Creator'. Where the mountains, rivers, trees, forests, plants and animals were themselves regarded as expressions of the divine (deities), the notion of a transcendent God inaugurated the widespread desacralization of the natural world, making possible the objectification and exploitation of nature as non-living and inanimate (mere 'resource' for humans' disposition). Interestingly, one former Christian mentor of mine once categorically declared, not without a tinge of pride, that Christianity is to be credited for the rise of modern science given its understanding of God as transcendent rather than residing in trees, rivers, mountains, rocks or animal beings, and it is this – the distancing of Creator from creation – that allowed for the full exploration and exploitation of the natural world for human good, without fear of reprisal from the spirit beings formerly believed to inhabit all of creation. The result is the replacing of relations of honouring, mutuality, and respect with the natural world with those of conquest, domination, objectification and use and, in addition, the demonization and pathologizing of modes of communicative transactions with the non-human (or more-than-human) world and the world of spirits (via trance, possession, shamanic and other 'techniques of ecstasy' [cf. Eliade, Trask and Doniger, 2004]) that among native peoples were not only an important resource for survival and thriving but ritual observances that helped them remember the 'Original Instructions' for living in a good way on the land.

Herein lies the epistemic terror of Christianity's civilizational narrative as introduced to our people by Christian Protestantism. Not only did it denigrate and pathologize native spirituality – turning earth-honouring peoples into 'sinners' destined for hell unless given access to salvation through submission to Christ, but, together with its modern secularized version of Western progress, advancement and growth, it also imposed its ethic of anthropocentric rationalism, hard work and ceaseless striving upon our people in an endeavour to recreate us as industrious workers for a modern economy. The effect is to reproduce a once thriving people (us Filipinos) as 'lazy', 'indolent', 'lacking in motive power and easily content' – the unnamed frame of reference being what the historian William McNeill (in Mann, 1986/2012) characterizes as the restless instability constituting the 'true uniqueness of Western civilization'.

To our detriment, our national elite were a quick study, setting out – post-independence – to create a modern, progressive nation state, convinced of the utter necessity of weaning ourselves away from our curse of easy contentment, what Nick Joaquin (1988), one of our renowned Filipino writers in English, described as the bane of our 'heritage of smallness', a subsistence-prone sensibility that has kept us from striving for more. Suggesting that it is high time we got over the insults of our colonized past, the same writer urges us to marvel instead at the incredible opportunity afforded us: 'the compelling of our native physique, psyche, and personality to undergo revolutionary (and evolutionary) change that otherwise would have been imprisoned in a timeless, unchanging state of fixity' (cf. Mendoza, 2013, p. 14). As I wrote further:

> Europe in this discourse is represented as the Hegelian dynamic that propels a languorous, self-content, and 'unmotivated' people to fulfill their spirit and their destiny. In concrete terms, it means being driven by the colonial impetus to diligence and progress as realized in the mastery of nature, the development of technology, and the ceaseless production and accumulation of material wealth ... [T]hanks to European colonization, the prehistoric Filipino managed to transform himself into a modern rational human being. Through the introduction of the tools of civilization, a ragtag group of tribal folk living in isolation from each other gained identity as a nation, attaining economic transformation from a 'subsistence culture' to 'the first world economy of modern times'. (Mendoza, 2013, p. 14)

A small move from making more to making beauty

I, on the other hand, would argue that it is this hankering for more that is in fact the curse. The accumulation of surplus that formed the foundation of civilization-building (roughly 5,000 years ago) is not innocent; by necessity, it entailed the massive use of slave labour, whether in the moving of boulders to build palaces and temples, the digging of irrigation canals for agriculture, or the ceaseless working of land for extraction of metals for tools and weaponry and, as well, for food production to feed an ever-expanding population. Every empire built, every civilization created, is dependent on the enslavement not only of other humans but of animals, plants and mineral beings that have had to be coerced, forcibly made to function in a manner other than their own willing without so much as the courtesy of asking for permission and without acknowledgement of indebtedness or gratitude. Not to say that every innovation or human invention is under indictment, *tout court*. Rather, what is damnable about any empire- and civilization-building project is precisely the shunting aside of all ethic of courtesy, reciprocity and limitation vis-à-vis the natural world, having turned the Earth and her beings into nothing but dead inanimate objects there exclusively for human use and disposition. Gone are the rituals of beauty, gratitude and honouring that in still-intact cultures are meticulously observed as a way of feeding that which feeds and keeps them alive, the magnificent Holy in Nature. The Indigenous writer Martin Prechtel exemplifies this different way of being in the world thus:

> Technological inventions take from the earth but give nothing in return. Look at automobiles. They were, in a sense, dreamed up over a period of time, with different people adding on to each other's dreams – or, if you prefer, adding on to each other's studies and trials. But all along the way, very little, if anything, was given back to the hungry, invisible divinity that gave people the ability to invent those cars. Now, in a healthy culture, that's where the shamans would come in, because with every invention comes a spiritual debt that must be paid, either ritually, or else taken out of us in warfare, grief, or depression.
>
> ... Human ingenuity is a wonderful thing, but only so long as it's used to feed the deities that give us the ability to perform such extravagant feats in the first place. (in Jensen, 2001)

This is what the ritual way of living is about: the offering of beauty – whether in the form of eloquent speech, beautiful grieving, a gift made by hand – as a gesture of gratitude to the Earth from whom all things come.

This sense of an earth-grounded sacrality is also what finally shed light on the larger meaning of my epiphanic hailing in that classroom, one made evident as well in my subsequent encounters in the flesh with the cultures of our Indigenous peoples. It was not just about the politics of representation – the liberatory feeling that comes from being presented with an alternative, more redeeming, report on one's native subjectivity, helpful as that framing may have been in my initial attempts to make sense of such a powerful experience, but the realization that what I was witnessing had to do finally with questions of ultimacy, of what life was about, and what it meant to be a human being in the world. And what I understood is that for intact original peoples, life was not about them but about this sacred mystery that some call the Holy in Nature. And the task is to maintain balance by observing the ritual courtesy of not taking anything without giving something back. Thus, their concern then, as now, is how their manner of walking, speaking, relating, cooking, weaving and ritual-making feeds the Holy in Nature, the ultimate Beauty-Maker and Life-Giver. It is for this reason that such cultures had no separate domain for 'art', 'religion' or, for that matter, 'nature'. All of life is art and all manner of being is sacred, and everything *is* nature, including us humans. Thus, beauty-making is not primarily for display of unique talent or ability as a means of securing one's worth or place in the world; rather, it stems, first and foremost, from a desire to live worthy of the generosity one has been given (in simply being born and given life) by the Holies in Nature. And because the primary relationship is with the living world as related to intimately within the particularities of a people's given ecology and geography of habitation, such is also what gives shape to the unique teachings, ritual forms, musics and other distinctive cultural practices of a tribe or native community (e.g. the bear ceremonies of the Ainu peoples, the bean and corn dances of the Tzutujil Mayans, the elaborate ritual food offerings among devotees of Voudun in Haiti, the binanog/eagle dance among the Panay Bukidnon in the Philippines).

Beauty-making, in this sense, is not the specialized function of those called to be 'artists' but the obligatory responsibility of every living being to feed life and maintain the Earth's delicate balance. It is also key to understanding the indescribable uniqueness and originality of Indigenous works of art – from the dizzying array of colours and designs of their woven textiles, the polyphonic nature of the sounds and rhythms of their musical instruments, the intricacies of their dance movements both subtle and vigorous, and the complex layers of meaning in their cosmic narrations and mythic stories, among others. It turns out that the forms and designs themselves are not human-originated, but land- and spirit-taught, many reportedly given in dreams (as in the case of the T'boli dream-weavers in Southern Philippines), trance-induced (as in the sinuyaman embroidery tradition of the Manobo in Mindanao Philippines), or in mimetic responses to the movements of beings in the ecology (as in the *bwang* and *tsonggo* dances of the Ayta in imitation of bees and monkeys or in the graceful undulating hand movements of the Yakan *pansak* dance evoked by the movements of birds, the waves of the sea and other nature elements). In the words of the ecophilosopher David Abram, 'The [artistic forms] respond directly to the land, as the land responds directly to the spoken or sung [or danced] stories' (1997, p. 177).

That life is ultimately not about us but about being part of this grand orchestra of beings all engaged in keeping life alive through living beautifully and magnificently according to their nature is what I suggest here as the key to our liberation from our captivity to our modern culture's insatiable greed and narcissism. Martin Prechtel warns that attempting to strike a better bargain than this makes a culture murderous. It is for this reason that land-rooted cultures typically orientate their energies towards other than surplus production and material accumulation – not only to avoid incurring heavy indebtedness to the Earth but because they elaborate meaning elsewhere. Prechtel speaks of one native Mayan village in Guatemala:

> The Tzutujil were not trying to build a nonsuffering world. The world they were part of was not run by humans, and it had only live things residing in it. There were no dead things. Instead of eradicating all the misery of the world, the Tzutujil were trying to suffer together creatively in a beautiful way to keep their world of delicately balanced live things more vital by feeding it the grief of their human failures and stupidity. These failures were made beautiful by the ornate and graceful way the people dedicated their suffering to the earth and to that which made life live, in a proven ritual attitude of great antiquity. (Prechtel, 1999/2004, p. 198)

Andrew Nikiforuk, whose work was mentioned in the introduction, locates the crisis of our time not in diminishing energy resources or even in the threat of climate change (for which it may be argued that the solution is simply finding low-carbon emitting 'green' energy alternatives that could keep the party going) but rather in the damnable master–slave dynamic at the heart of our relationship with the natural world, one that has effectively turned the Earth and her beings into our minions, with the blowback now coming back to bite us. Confronted with the direness of our predicament, the question I pose in this chapter is no longer how to save us but how to recognize the terror in our heavily indebted lifestyle of ease and comfort that most have disastrously declared 'non-negotiable'. How to find ways to metabolize such terror into tear-soaked offerings of grief and sorrow that can birth new desires and new understandings is the challenge, the re-learning once more of the ancient art of beauty-making that alone feeds the Holy in Nature. It is the compelling call I hear from the teachings of all antique peoples around the globe. Beleaguered on every side, they resolutely say, 'Even to the end, even if we don't make it, we keep making beauty anyway.'

References

Abram, David, 1997, *The Spell of the Sensuous*, New York: Vintage.
Eliade, M., W. R. Trask and W. Doniger, 2004, *Archaic Techniques of Ecstasy*, Princeton, NJ: Princeton University Press.
Illich, Ivan, 1974, *Energy and Equity*, London: Calder & Boyars.
Jensen, Derrick, 2001, 'Saving the indigenous soul: An interview with Martin Prechtel', *The Sun magazine*, http://thesunmagazine.org/issues/304/ (accessed 08.04.2024).
Joaquin, Nick, 1988, *Culture and History: Occasional Notes on the Process of Philippine Becoming*, Pasig City, Philippines: Anvil.
Mann, M., 1986/2012, *The Sources of Social Power: Volume 1, A History of Power from the Beginning to AD 1760*, New York: Cambridge University Press.
Mendoza, S. L., 2013, 'Savage Representations in the Discourse of Modernity: Liberal Ideology and the Impossibility of Nativist Longing', *Decolonization, Indigenization, Education, and Society* 2 (1), pp. 1–19.
———, 2018, 'Babaylan Healing and Indigenous "Religion" at the Postcolonial Crossroads: Learning from Our Deep History as the Planet Grows Apocalyptic', in S. Debeer (ed.), *Just Faith: Glocal Responses to Planetary Urbanization*, Series on Religion and Society, Durbanville, Cape Town: AOSIS, pp. 72–102.
———, forthcoming, 'Theorizing at the End of the World: Transforming Critical Intercultural Communication', in T. K. Nakayama and R. T. Haluanani (eds), *The Handbook of Critical Intercultural Communication*, rev. edn, Oxford: Blackwell.
Moten, F. and S. Hartman, 2018, 'To refuse that which has been refused to you: An Interview by Chimurenga', *Chimurenga*, 19 October, https://chimurengachronic.co.za/to-refuse-that-which-has-been-refused-to-you-2/ (accessed 19.03.2024).
Nikiforuk, Andrew, 2012, *The Energy of Slaves: Oil and the New Servitude*, Vancouver: Greystone.
Prechtel, Martin, 1999/2004, *Long Life, Honey in the Heart: A Story of Initiation and Eloquence from the Shores of a Mayan Lake*, New York: Tarcher.
Riches, Dennis, 2016, 'Review of the book *The Energy of Slaves: Oil and the New Servitude* by Andrew Nikiforuk', *Social Science Research* 11 (2), pp. 149–60.
Shirmer, Daniel B. and Stephen Rosskamm Shalom (eds), 1987, *The Philippines Reader: A History of Colonialism, Neocolonialism, Dictatorship, and Resistance*, Cambridge, MA: South End.

13

Being Moved: Pina Bausch's Incarnational Dance and Divine Desire's Queer Choreography[1]

ÁNGEL F. MÉNDEZ-MONTOYA

Before immersing myself in undergraduate and graduate academic studies, I was a professional contemporary dancer for ten years. During my studies for a BA in dance, and then for an MA in theology and MA in philosophy, I was able to manage my time and energy to continue dancing and choreographing. However, once I started my PhD studies in philosophical theology, it became difficult to keep up with dance training. I choreographed a few pieces for professional dancers but had to stop dancing in order to fully dedicate time and energy to my doctoral studies. Now that I am a full-time professor and researcher, I am starting to get back to my dance roots. This is mainly because I am currently looking for possible dialogues between dance and theology, taking as a primary aim growing in knowledge and wisdom from such a fascinating dialogue. As a theologian, I consider it imperative to integrate the experience of dancing bodies and of learning from dance on its and their own terms.

Since 2017, I have restarted dance training and choreographed a solo dance that I perform in theological conferences and academic gatherings. At the same time, researching as a theologian from a dancing body horizon, and from the language and the world of dance, helps me to rehearse diverse ways of being first moved by an epistemology (somatic cognition) of dance.[2] In this chapter, I focus on some choreographic proposals made by Pina Bausch, which, I suggest, could provide heuristic insights on the primacy of 'desire' in dance and in theology. I understand that the notion of desire is quite complex and contains multiple meanings. Herein, I invite the reader to stretch theological imagination by learning from some choreographic proposals by Pina Bausch, and her understanding of human desire, which becomes the main impulse for her dancing. Her proposals could be excellent food for thought for an articulation of divine desire in theology.

The German postmodern choreographer Pina Bausch (1940–2009) destabilized many conventions in the language of dance and the performing arts, incorporating novel intimations regarding the body's complexity and desire's queer motion – a perplexing desire that moves body, heart, mind and spirit, rather than the other way around. I propose allowing theology to be moved by Bausch's choreographic provocations in a search of theological expression that incarnates divine desire without trying to possess it or retaining it just for ourselves. How can glimpses of the emergence of theological impulse be caught, intimating an extravagant pulsation that non-identically resonates with the perpetual motion of the gift of divine desire? How to be deeply moved to incarnate a theology of such queer desire? Even more subversively, how to encounter divine desire interwoven in the flesh of those who are rejected because of the colour of their skin, their ethnicity, gender, sexuality, migratory status and other supposed 'indecencies'? The final section of this contribution visits some theological alternatives to counter the critical conditions of the extreme violence experienced in Mexico, which is systematically implemented by the ongoing iteration of heteronormative, patriarchal and abusive/ destructive desire. Against such a gloomy backdrop, can we envision 'another' choreography emerging from the pulsations of an extravagant divine desire that disrupts the flux of hegemonic violence and rejection, re-signifying human desire with transcendental and ever-inclusive love?

Pina Bausch: a brief biography

Born in Solingen, Germany in 1940, from early childhood Pina Bausch trained as a ballet dancer. In 1955, she entered the Folkwang School in Essen, under the teaching and direction of Kurt Jooss, an important figure in the European modern dance scene of that time, along with Rudolf Laban and Mary Wigman. Laban, Wigman and Jooss were a breath of fresh air for dance. They searched beyond the balletic structure and the rigid grammar of dance in order to capture the human body's expressive potential. Their emphasis on expressive gestures and the dramatic power of ordinary movement sowed the seed of German *Tanztheater* (dance theatre), the springboard to so-called Expressionist Dance (*Ausdruckstanz*) (van Schaik, 2013).

Artistically, Bausch was also influenced by the modern dance movement in the United States, particularly in New York, during her studies at the Juilliard School of Dance. During her residency in New York, she became familiar with the works of modern dance pioneers, such as Martha Graham, José Limón and Antony Tudor. These three choreographers echoed the *Ausdruckstanz* in Germany, exploring the evocative and emotional communication power that the dancing body enjoys. Furthermore, American modern dance witnessed by Bausch during her stay in New York was also the seed of a more abstract exploration of choreography, reliant on pure movement rather than emotions. George Balanchine through ballet and Merce Cunningham through modern dance both pioneered an exploration that greatly influenced the formalist trend in American modern dance. Finally, Bausch also witnessed the American visual and theatre scene, which started to experiment with improvisation and 'performances' known as 'happenings', the sheer visceral intent of performance, from which would emerge the early postmodern dance movements in the United States and internationally (Climenhaga, 2009, pp. 3–8).

In 1962, after experiencing New York, Pina Bausch returned to Germany. Jooss invited her to become the leading soloist in the Folkwang Ballet. It is worth noting that during those years modern dance in Germany had started to incorporate the legacy of experimental theatre, greatly influenced by Bertolt Brecht, Antonin Artaud, Samuel Beckett and Jerzy Grotowski, among others. For this reason, by the time Bausch was offered a position as director of the Wuppertal Ballet – renamed Tanztheater Wuppertal in 1973 – she had already been exposed to a very broad experimental interweaving of dance and theatre. As director of Tanztheater Wuppertal, her early works were pieces based on operas, such as *Iphigenia in Tauris* (1974) and *Orpheus and Eurydice* (1975). She also created a choreography based on Igor Stravinsky's *Le Sacre du Printemps* (1975), *The Rite of Spring*. In *Pina Bausch*, Royd Climenhaga points out that in these choreographic works Bausch did not follow the linear patterning of original opera or ballet, but rather:

> [she t]ook the fundamental condition operating in each story to act as an overriding metaphor from which movement and bodily attitudes grow. Her collage techniques surrounded the ideas to create a multi-faceted perspective of the story, re-creating the condition and mood of each story rather than telling it through a more conventional linear narrative. She drew on her own and her dancers' personal experiences to

create presentational movement patterns formed from emotive gestures and derived from a response to, rather than in service of, formal story structures. (Climenhaga, 2009, p. 10)

After these early works, Pina Bausch grew less interested in technique or the formal qualities of dance, and instead concentrated on the essential emotional gesture that is full of metaphoric value. In particular, she focused on expressing everyday actions that reveal a sense of ourselves as individuals relating to a complex network of social interactions. This break from a formalist language into a more neo-expressionist language within dance and theatre also coincided with:

> Emancipatory dance movements in Japan, where Butoh dancers reacted against the tradition of formal theatre in which every bodily movement, from nail to nose, had its precise meaning. The Butoh dancers sought the human being in their experiments. In this respect, a striking similarity can be seen between Bausch and Butoh: both are forces of liberation. … The relation between Ausdruckstanz, Butoh, and dance theatre is their longing to be free from tradition and to be open to new creative pathways. (van Schaik, 2013, p. 51)

Furthermore, Bausch was not that interested in how dancers move, but rather she wanted to discover *what* moves dancers, what drives them to move. Her later works developed from the individual dancer's experiences as well as from the individual themes that Bausch was so interested in exploring at a given time and for a given choreographic work. Her pieces explore humour as well as drama, displaying an intense realistic and everyday expression as much as more metaphoric or poetic imagination. They often even lack any logic, or a particular fixed meaning (Servos, 2008, pp. 11–16).

Bausch attempted to move beyond the formal language of dance technique, and instead concentrated on the complexity of human emotions, or psychological projections, searching to reflect life and reality from multiple perspectives. For this reason, her company is composed of a broad spectrum of performers, including performers from different age groups, body types, nationalities and ethnic backgrounds. At times, dancers are asked to only express themselves through non-verbal and often repetitive bodily gestures, but they can equally be asked to express themselves through using their voice to state text fragments, utter random words, or even sing on stage. Sometimes dancers repeat very fast movements over and over until they literally reach physical exhaustion. Other times, they enter into trance-like slow motion, or even just remain motionless, as if portraying a still photograph rather than a filmed sequence in movement. Moreover, the dancers also explore their feelings and sense of embodiment through coming in touch with a broad variety of themes, as well as through their interaction with a wide spectrum of spatial situations beyond the conventional theatre space, performing outdoors and in unconventional environments. Likewise, Bausch was not concerned with merely displaying an exclusively German cultural identity, for in fact she was often invited to establish a work while in residence abroad, which gave her the opportunity to explore a multiplicity of cultural world views (Climenhaga, 2009, pp. 26–30).

Bausch's death in 2009 was a great loss to the artistic community in general and to the dance community in particular. Through her unceasing creativity, she produced about 40 choreographic pieces. She was internationally renowned and became a great inspiration to dancers and choreographers, as well as to a wider public. Not only did she become a great influence in the field of dance and the performing arts, but she further inspired people working in diverse arts media. Because of Bausch's multiple perspectives on human life, embodiment, and unconventional methods for her choreographic presentations on matters related to the body, gender, sexuality, age, culture, arts and so forth, the impact of her work moves beyond the disciplines of the arts, reaching a larger public and the broad territory of the humanities. How could her proposals inspire theological thinking? I now turn to focus on Bausch's method of searching for that which moves the dancers, in order to also ask about what moves the theologians, and so contribute to an exploration on a theology of divine desire.

Being Moved: what moves the theologians?

One of the main axioms of Pina Bausch's works appears in her statement, *I am not interested in how people move, but in what moves them* (Servos, 2008, p. 25). Her choreographic themes did not arise from a concern for technical virtuosity, or the impersonal formal qualities of dance movement. She wanted to immerse herself more deeply into the performers as real agents with concrete desires, emotions, fears, hopes, dreams and questions. By concentrating on the fundamental elements of subjective expression, and searching for the motivating impulse from which movement begins in a given situation, Bausch's work explores the very roots of dance and theatre, the origins of art as a communicative expression of human existence, understanding dance as a way of incarnating the emotions, desires and profoundly lived human experiences in the flesh of the performers. After all, choreography is an epistemic discourse of the flesh. The physical action and the emotional intensity of the performers on stage spring from the dancers' experiential impulse, letting themselves be moved by the ineffable, extravagant, queer motion of desire.

And what moves the theologian? What drives theological reflection? Pina Bausch's work inspires and provokes theological thinking insofar as Christian theology searches beyond the technical and formal capacities of theological discourse, moving into the depths of God's desire underlying human desire.[3] Discipline, intense critical research and study are required components in order to achieve an effective theological discourse. But theological expression is much more than that. The core impulse of theological reflection may spring from a profound and authentic experience of being moved by divine desire.[4] And incarnational theology – of God fully embracing humanity in the incarnation – is particularly moved by the divine experience of radical vulnerability as well as the delight of just being human.

Let's remember that Pina Bausch was a child of the post-war era, wondering how to dance after Auschwitz. In the face of a meaningless world, Bausch was not afraid of materializing in and through the body the depths of a lack of meaning so that the performing body could become an epiphany of primal epistemic meaning with and through a dancing body. Theology may as well emerge from the human existential angst of experiencing the absence of God, of wondering how to theologize after Auschwitz and Hiroshima, while living in our current world wounded by hunger, violence and ecological crisis. Even there, in what seems a total absence of God, a profound and authentic theological expression can emerge.

In Mexico, for instance, we are disturbed by a violent desire that perpetuates the abjection of human bodies because of the colour of their skin, their ethnicity, gender, sexuality, migratory status, for defending social justice and protecting the rights of humanity and the planet, or for other supposed 'indecencies'.[5] Indeed, a sinister face of exploitation and carelessness appears in the great gap between a small elite of the wealthy and the great majority of Mexican people living precariously. In Mexico, hate crimes against women, members of the lesbian, gay, bisexual, transgender and intersex, plus (LGBTI+) community, indigenous people, migrants, journalists and human rights defenders are alarming (Pantoja, 2015; Muedano, 2017; Ávila, 2018). Violence in Mexico is implemented by the ongoing iteration of heteronormative, patriarchal and abusive practices.

One cannot help but be moved, shiver and quake in the face of such atrocities. These movements are profoundly visceral, but they can also move and touch the heart (affectivity, emotionality) and the head (intellection, reasoning). When theologians close their minds, ignore their gut feelings and the messages of the heart, deafen their ears and shut their eyes, their bodies become paralysed, incapable of being touched by untouchable and rejected bodies. When this happens within theological reflection, then, walls are raised, castles of normativity and supremacy are rigidly constructed, people and communities become invisible, subordinated, and/or de-territorialized. Consequently, theological impulse is interrupted, paralysed by fear and hatred.

Despite hegemonic rejection, the untouchable bodies touch God as they are touched by divine desire.[6] Being touched and embraced implies a queer movement beyond oneself, beyond the frontiers of self-identity into otherness, that which is not 'I', yet with the ineffable capacity of touching and embracing 'me' – an interpellated self. Divine desire evokes an ecstatic dance of God moving beyond God into otherness, dancing with the other's desire that palpitates through and with God's loving embrace.[7] By touching the untouchable, God is also touched by the other, so that divine transcendence is touched by immanence, while immanence is touched by infinite divine desire.[8] Theological vocation emerges from this carnal and bodily cadence, a dance of a hybrid human–divine desire. God's desire is not indifference, for it is profoundly moved by those who are rejected and live precariously. God's desire for humanity and creation – particularly those who live in the diaspora of society, and an injured planet – moves the guts, hearts and minds of theologians, gifting it theological reflection and practice with a queer theological dance. A queer theological dance moves us when we find the courage to embody erotic-agapeic divine desire; when even in the midst of violence and hatred we embrace the power to speak up, go into action, touch and be touched by the 'indecent' untouchable bodies. For God abides in *this* body and in *this* flesh (Isherwood, 2013). This is a queer movement, for it comes beyond the ego, and this strange movement emerging from otherness, twists, queers our being paralysed by the hegemony of violence, hatred, indifference and exploitation. The theologian is thus moved by a kinetic human and divine desire that moves one beyond oneself, embracing/ touching and being embraced/touched by the other, moving the self with an incarnational dance. In this caressing movement of both human and divine desire we can envision the dance of theology and the theology of dance.

Pina Bausch used to say, *Dance, dance, otherwise we are lost.* Even in the absence of hope in post-Auschwitz Germany, she believed that dancing was a way of coping, or resisting against human violence, rigid norms and hegemonic relationships. Counter to such negativity, Bausch encountered human desire as the kinaesthetic *positum* that moved her and the performers to dance. In exploring the complexities of human desire by asking the dancers to explore the depths of their desires, fears, anxieties and emotions, Pina Bausch allows a sense of human contingency, a sense of crisis and existential angst, yet without causing depression, for it provides courage to embrace humanity with all its contradictions, absurdity and finitude, dancing both the comedy as well as the tragedy of ordinary and extra-ordinary human life. For Pina Bausch, dance is all about inflaming the desire to dance, while letting ourselves be moved by desire ... Otherwise we are lost.

Theology, like dance, is all about desire. It is a desire to relate to one another, interpersonally, as well as our desire to relate to creation as a whole (see Jantzen, 2006). St Francis of Assisi, for instance, expressed his desire to relate to the whole of creation as a brother and a sister. His theological expression was an embodied gesture of his own liberating theological desire for God and creation (see Boff, 1982). St Francis, and many other mystical and mostly queer theologians from both today and the past, illustrate that if there is a theological expression at all, it is because it first starts with God's own desire for intimacy with us, turning us into agents, participants of a loving relationship; so plentifully that our own agency moves beyond us, sharing queer, excessive love with others. Humanity desires God because God first desired us. Theological expression is thus a response to God's initiative to communicate, making us all participants of divine desire.[9]

The Christian God is certainly a God of desire: God is both *eros* and *agape*. God is love and the lover, a loving community. Christianity envisions God as relationality, a Trinitarian community of love. God desires God, but because of God's superabundance or plenitude, there is nothing lacking in God's desire. God is not an isolated 'thing'. God is *perichoresis*, the choreography of an erotic-agapeic trans-participatory dance. Divine desire moves into otherness, unfolding creation, the flux of finitude, contingency and immanence. Therefore, the self, as all creation, is in perpetual flux, immersed in the eternal pulsation of divine desire, dancing with God's infinite love. That is why all creation is an expression of God's superabundant desire; God shares divine love and desire with all creation.[10] In this Trinitarian interweaving of harmonious love, God is both lover and love. Dancer and dance are one and the same. As W. B. Yeats mused, *How can we know the dancer from the dance?* Theology may invite the whole of creation to partake of this same desirous dance.

In Christian theology, God's desire is radicalized by *kenosis*, God's movement into otherness, becoming human, even to the point of undertaking a monstrous death, unfolding within the monstrosity of the violence and mistreatment of people and the crucified planet. But God's kenosis does not nullify divine desire, for Christ's resurrected flesh queers (transfigures and re-signifies) the hegemony of death and opens a fissure for the emergence of the gift of a resurrected life, a more 'livable life' (see Butler, 2004). Through incarnation, the invisible God becomes visible and touchable flesh. Right there, in the most humanly visible gesture of the flesh, is the invisible divine embracing of humanity's flesh. Humanity is further embraced by divinity, a gesture of desire whereby humanity is transfigured by such a queer, divine impulse (see Keller, 2006). It is true that there is no explicitly theological theme in Pina Bausch's works. Nevertheless, her radicalizing somatic desire may also evoke and provoke a theological reflection upon the pulse of a kinetic flesh, adventuring into the ceaseless question and mystery of what moves, what is the impulse of the theologian's invocation.

In our current situation of extreme violence and exploitation of people and the planet, we are lost if we don't let our flesh, gut and head – which are also constituted by mind and spirit – be moved by such a sinister choreography. But counter to this dance, there is another *momentum*, a rather queer impulse emerging from excessive love, a choreography of resistance to violence and hatred, and an incarnational dance of personal and communal transfiguration.

Just as Pina Bausch's choreographies were in a way an expression of her own biography, letting the vicissitudes of daily life move her, every theology is also some sort of biography. God's story, as it inscribed in the sacred scriptures, for instance, is also inscribed in our own daily narratives and stories. From a theological horizon, then, God's story is intertwined with human narratives, co-creating a human–divine flux, an ever-perplexing choreography (see Loughlin, 1996). This means that the art of doing theology implies the theologian's self-involvement with the world. Theology, as well as Pina Bausch's choreography, is not an impersonal performance, but a performing that voices and embodies the depths of our planetary existence. The theologian cannot be indifferent or aloof to these corporeal and kinetic insights, nor can the theological corpus remain unaffected or untouched by both the daily suffering and the joy of the world. Otherwise, we are lost.

Notes

1 This chapter is drawn from discussions in a book that I published in Spanish, *Teopoeticas del cuerpo: la danza, la teología filosófica y las intermediaciones de los cuerpos* (Ciudad de México: Universidad Iberoamericana, 2023).

2 This notion of 'an epistemology of dance' emerges from my personal experience as a dancer and choreographer, exploring dance and cognitive embodiment or somatic experience as a way of knowledge and wisdom. The main inspiration for an epistemology of dance comes from a dance and neuroscience approach, such as that developed by Minton and Faber (2016).

3 While here desire is named *eros*, as an attraction to the other, love is named *agape*, as the unconditional love kenotically given to the other. In God, desire and love, though distinct, complement one another, as God's desire arrives, simultaneously, with God's love. From a theological perspective, humans are *imago Dei* (God's image), which implies that human desire – albeit contingent and finite – is also participant in God's erotic-agapeic love. For a further theological reading on God's *eros* and *agape*, cf. Benedict XVI, 2005.

4 On the emergence of human desire for God and the resonance of divine desire in theology, see Catherine Pickstock, 2012.

5 The term 'indecency' is inspired by Marcella Althaus-Reid (2004, p. 19), who suggests a connection between material bodies (gender, sexuality, race and so forth) with matters related to economy, politics, theology and practices of resistance in the midst of *decency* – control, normativity, subordination, colonization and hegemony.

6 For a further reflection on theology as a way of re-signifying hegemonic and violent desires into divine desire, see Isherwood and Althaus-Reid (eds), 2004.

7 On God's ecstatic dance and theology's dancing with God, see Johnson, 2005.

8 For an inspiring argument about touching God and God being touched by us, see Rivera, 2007.

9 For a further analysis on God's desire and the relational dimension of divine love that opens up a space for personal and inter-personal agency, see Ward, 2003, pp. 183–218.

10 As Catherine Pickstock states, 'God is lover, *eros* and *agape*; the mutuality of the Father and the Son and the emergent unilateral gift of the Spirit. But the latter expresses the mutuality of Father and Son, and the mutuality only arises as the further emergence of the Spirit. Moreover, the mutuality is itself the birth of the Son from the Father in anticipation of and communion with the Spirit, which will arise

from the bond of Father with Son. Desire as aspiration and desire as emergence are complexly interwoven' (Pickstock, 2012, p. 112).

References

Althaus-Reid, Marcella, 2004, *Indecent Theology: Theological Perversions in Sex, Gender, and Politics*, New York: Routledge.
Ávila, Jonathan, 2018, 'Homofobia, el Odio que Prevalece', *Reporte Indigo*, https://www.reporteindigo.com/reporte/homofobia-odio-prevalece-expresiones-odio-violencia-comunidad-lgbt-colectivos-alerta/ (accessed 28.03.2018).
Benedict XVI, 2005, 'Deus Caritas Est', Vatican, http://w2.vatican.va/content/benedict-xvi/en/encyclicals/documents/hf_ben-xvi_enc_20051225_deus-caritas-est.html (accessed 7.09.2018).
Boff, Leonardo, 1982, *Francis of Assisi: A Model for Human Liberation*, New York: Orbis Books.
Butler, Judith, 2004, *Undoing Gender*, New York: Routledge.
Climenhaga, Royd, 2009, *Pina Bausch*, New York: Routledge.
Isherwood, Lisa, 2013, 'Es en la Encrucijada que la Sabiduría Toma su Posición', in Genilma Boehler, Lars Bedurke and Silvia Regina de Lima Silva (eds), *Teorías Queer y Teologías. Estar... En Otro Lugar*, Costa Rica: Editorial DEI, pp. 221–39.
—— and Marcella Althaus-Reid (eds), 2004, *The Sexual Theologian: Essays of Sex, God and Politics*, London: T&T Clark International.
Jantzen, Grace, 2006, 'New Creations: Eros, Beauty, and the Passion for Transformation', in Virginia Burrus and Catherine Keller (eds), *Toward a Theology of Eros: Transfiguring Passion at the Limits of Discipline*, New York: Fordham University Press, pp. 271–87.
Johnson, Jay Emerson, 2005, *Dancing with God: Anglican Christianity and the Practice of Hope*, New York: Morehouse.
Keller, Catherine, 2006, 'Afterword: A Theology of Eros, After Transfiguring Passion', in Virginia Burrus and Catherine Keller (eds), *Toward a Theology of Eros: Transfiguring Passion at the Limits of Discipline*, New York: Fordham University Press, pp. 366–74.
Loughlin, Gerard, 1996, *Telling God's Story: Bible, Church and Narrative Theology*, Cambridge: Cambridge University Press.
Minton, Sandra Cendry and Rima Faber, 2016, *Thinking with the Dancing Brain: Embodying Neuroscience*, London: Rowman & Littlefield.
Muedano, Marcos, 2017, 'Imparable, el Crimen contra las Mujeres; Cifras del Inegi', *Excelsior*, http://www.excelsior.com.mx/nacional/2017/10/22/1196308 (accessed 28.03.2018).
Pantoja, Sara, 2015, 'Mexico, Segundo Lugar Mundial en Crímenes por Homofobia', *Proceso*, http://www.proceso.com.mx/403935/mexico-segundo-lugar-mundial-en-crimenes-por-homofobia (accessed 28.03.2018).
Pickstock, Catherine, 2012, '*Eros* and Emergence', in Gerard Loughlin (ed.), *Queer Theology: Rethinking the Western Body*, Oxford: Blackwell, pp. 99–114.

Rivera, Mayra, 2007, *The Touch of Transcendence: A Postcolonial Theology of God*, Louisville, KY: Westminster John Knox.

Servos, Norbert, 2008, *Pina Bausch: Dance Theatre*, Munich: K. Kieser.

van Schaik, Eva, 2013, 'The Mistrust of Life – Relations in Dance: Connections Between Butoh, *Ausdruckstanz* and Dance Theatre in Contemporary Experimental Dance', in Royd Climenhaga (ed.), *The Pina Bausch Sourcebook: The Making of Tanztheater*, New York: Routledge, pp. 49–54.

Ward, Graham, 2003, *Christ and Culture*, Oxford: Blackwell.

14

Liberation of Things: Accessing to the Agency of Thing

ILJOON PARK

Entanglement: what anthropocentrism and biocentrism miss

Anthropocentrism is that which we have tried to overcome since Rachel Carson's ecological provocation in *Silent Spring* (1962), in which she especially described how pesticides can disrupt the human-animal-plant-soil-worm-microbe networks, destroying the ecology of the environment. The pesticides, which are intended to kill weeds, had a devastating effect on the ecological networks of beings including humans. In order to produce more crops, farmers used pesticides, but they did not know that it would cause environmental diseases to them and even kill them. What draws our attention here in her pioneering book, although it provoked our ecological awareness of being, is that being is 'entangled' with other beings including the non-human and the material beings.

Our anthropocentric view of the world, beings, life and so on conceals the existential fact of entanglement, viewing 'being' only in the image of an individual and independent (living) agent. In the modern Western tradition of humanism, individualism has become the doctrinal definition of human beings, accompanying the surging of human rights discourse all over. Thus, we are living in a world in which the discourses of human rights have transformed our civilization into a more human world. However, as the crises of the climate and ecology have been mounting, the beneficial discourses on human rights have turned into a violent discourse for non-human beings. For the conception of human rights focuses upon the rights of human beings, overlooking the existence and power of non-human agencies. The current crises we are now facing, such as the ecological crisis, the climate crisis, the crisis of ocean current by the melting of glaciers, and so on, have decisively witnessed the agential powers of non-human beings as well as the so-called hyperobjects like the climate and the oceanic current systems. Upon reflecting on these crises, one is now realizing that the scheme of our human civilization has derived from the dualistic schemata of living and non-living, of the animate and the inanimate, thus discriminating the non-living as passive and dead matter. This dualism is indeed a marker for our biocentrism. Our common-sensical definition of being exclusively hinges upon the concept of life, regarding inanimate matters as dead stuff.

However, as the case of pesticides has shown, material beings can exert their own agencies, now threatening exclusively human-centred civilization. Pesticide is not a living being but material stuff. However, one can read the scene of the *Silent Spring* as the effects of the agential power of the material being. Matter is not dead and passive but it has its own agential power. That is, being is more than life. As a matter of fact, the non-living matter with its own agency or capability for being is inextricably entangled with living forms of being. Indeed, 'being' consists of the entanglement of the living and the non-living.

In fact, the so-called posthuman discourse points us to the fact that the event of human 'being' is a hybrid assemblage of human organism and non-human beings. Andy Clark describes this as 'the extended mind' and defines human being as 'natural-born cyborg'. The thesis of the extended mind by Clark and Chalmers is that 'when parts of the environment are coupled to the brain in the right way, they become parts of the mind' (Chalmers, 2011, p. x). Here, the mind does not refer to the unique faculty of human rationality but rather to the assemblage of human brain and parts of the environment. That is, human agency is not the bodily puppeteer of the brain as the control tower. Human capabilities for being lie in their extension over other beings, including non-living materials and systems. In this context, Clark describes humans as 'natural-born cyborgs' (Clark, 2003, p. 6). Humans cannot work without tools and devices, and these artificial tools are none other than their bodily extension. However, this bodily extension is connected to the brain, forming a brain-body-tool network. This means that 'human being' is none other than 'actor-network' (Latour, 2007, pp. 10–11). 'Being' is already and always in doing, and this 'doing' works in a network of actors. This actor-network includes non-human beings as well as human agencies.

One of the painful lessons from the Covid pandemic and the climate disasters is that being is not a process confined to life or organic or animate being. Rather, being is entangled with the inorganics. In fact, the direct cause of the outbreak of the Covid pandemic was corona virus, which is not an organism but rather something between organism and the inanimate. This inorganic being has massively disrupted our civilization. The tiny virus has decisively interfered with human life. What matters here is that human life is already and always entangled with non-human beings. Further, non-human beings have their own agencies to interact with human agencies through actor-networks in the entanglement of beings. In this sense, Merlin Sheldrake says that any sense of the 'we' is already and always 'ecosystems that span boundaries and transgress categories', 'emerg[ing] from a complex tangle of relationships' (Sheldrake, 2021, p. 20). Indeed, we are 'entangled with' other forms of existence, including non-human forms of being. In fact, minerals, viruses, bacteria, fungi and so on significantly influence what humans think as well as what they behave. The condition of the inner visceral intestines significantly produces some effect in human's decision-making process.

In this sense, although Sheldrake did not mention it, the 'we' as ecosystem is already and always plural, being entangled with the non-human beings including inanimate beings. For example, methane out of the burps of cows and sheep that humans breed for meat has been disrupting the ozone layer of the planet, and this disruption has threatened the existence of living on the planet, including human civilization. Our life depends upon the critical balance of the atmosphere on Earth. Plants need carbon dioxide (CO_2), emitting oxygen as excretion. Organisms on earth, including humans, need oxygen for their respiration, discharging carbon dioxide. This is the balance of being and at the same time the entanglement of beings. Living and non-living are entangled through diverse forms of being. This entanglement of life and non-life shows us a reason to think of alternative ways beyond biocentrism. Being is more than life or living.

Response-ability

Being is not a static or fixed substance but rather a process or, more exactly, the circulation of energy. In this sense, being is none other than energy transformation. In this circulation of energy with its transformational power, being is already and always in a ceaseless process or movement(s) through each being's response-ability, the ability to respond to other beings. Entanglement means that beings interact with each other, meaning that they respond to each other. With this response-ability, beings 'intra-act' in the entanglement. Thus, the existential process of being is a constant movement of response-ability. It means that a being can 'prehend' other beings.

A. N. Whitehead (2007) applies the concept of prehension to all kinds of beings, including electrons. Note that this is not a kind of animism. Animism exclusively binds to the notion of living or organism. However, in Whitehead's philosophy of organism, prehension is not confined to biological organisms. Thus, Whitehead's concept of organism does not only refer to the biological concept of organism but also to any being with prehension or response-ability, including tiny electrons, quirks, rocks and so on. If one can use the word 'life' or 'living' to describe the whole cycle of being between life and the non-living matter, one should use it with the erasure, as Heidegger signifies 'being' (*Sein*) with the erasure.

Put differently, being is extension. What exists is none other than a state of being associated with other, not in the form of noun but in a form of verb; that is, either 'connects' or 'being connected'. When Andy Clark and David Chalmers proposed their concept of 'the extended mind', what is extended over with connectivity is, they thought, 'the mind' emergent from the extended connections. For they see the extendibility from the perspective of neuroplasticity. One with common-sensical knowledge cannot imagine intelligence without the brain. However, intelligence can emerge just out of connectivity without the brain and the central nervous system. For example, during the Covid pandemic, the corona virus showed their intelligent and adaptative evolutionary strategies through their variations, responding to the strategies of human disease control. In another example, fungi collectively and intelligently behave just by their connectivity. Indeed, mycelium, a root-like structure of a fungus, seems 'to possess a directional memory' (Sheldrake, 2021, p. 53) when it explores the way it is supposed to proceed. Connectivity is intelligence. What is striking in the case of fungi is that their connectivity is not confined to their species, but it is extended over other beings, especially other species of fungi and plants. By making different members of species, other species, and other beings being connected, fungi behave with their intelligent and adaptive strategies, but it is surprising that they have no brain structure. In *The Power of Movement in Plants* (1880), Charles Darwin mentioned that the root tips of plants integrate 'signals from different parts of the organism', given that the root tips 'determine the trajectory for growth'. According to Darwin, root tips act 'like the brain of one of the lower animals … receiving impressions from the sense-organs, and directing the several movements' (Sheldrake, 2021, p. 66). What Darwin means with this is that the growing tips are 'the place where information comes together to link perception and action, and determine a suitable course for growth', and this is like the work of the brain in higher organisms. Here one can see that intelligence can be exerted by connectivity, and the brain structure in higher animals makes this collective intelligence more efficient, especially on the level of individual animals. However, the point here is that intelligence is not necessarily based upon the brain structure. Given that the term 'swarm intelligence' refers to 'the problem-solving behaviour of brainless systems' (Sheldrake, 2021, p. 74), intelligence works through connectivity to and association with other beings, although it is more efficient when it has a brain system, partly because the brain can store much more information.

Connectivity itself can be a form of intelligence, and it is none other than the extendibility of being. Any being's extendibility over other beings can exert intelligence for their own well-being and prosperity, and the connectivity is none other than their response-ability to the changes of their environments. Clark and Chalmers explain this extendibility of being with their virtual case of Patient Otto. Otto knows that he suffers from Alzheimer's. That is, he knows that his memory capacity has been damaged. So in order to complement his damaged memory, he carries a notebook all the time. Whenever he has things to remember, he writes notes and puts them in a place he can easily see, like on the refrigerator. In this way, Alzheimer Otto catches up his so-called normal life. The point Clark and Chalmers suggest is that the notebook Otto carries with him complements the deficiency of his biological brain and functions as an external brain (Clark, 2011, pp. 226–7; Clark and Chalmers, 1998). What matters is that the intelligence Otto exerts with his notebook is not different from that of the so-called normal person, Inga. Because Inga does not have any memory problems in her biological brain, she does not carry external devices to complement her memory. However, Otto and Inga do almost the same things and, in this sense, human mental capabilities are not confined to the biological skull but can be extended over other tools and devices. Here the point is not just that we are natural-born cyborgs but also that intelligence can be carried out by the hybrid assemblage of the damaged brain and the notebooks. When they are connected in functional ways, they can do intelligent works. Thus, connectivity can be an extension of intelligence or mind, and it in this sense is none other than extendibility of being. Put differently, extension is a desire of being to be associated with other forms of beings, and intelligence is none other than a desire of being to respond to and associate with other beings. Being is association with the other, and

Sheldrake calls it 'long-lasting intimacy of strangers' (Sheldrake, 2021, p. 91).

Being as collective assemblage

Being is not a singleton but the collective assemblage of element, things, microbes, bacteria, fungi and so on. The existence of eukaryotic cells bears witness to this collectivity. Eukaryotic cells consist of the collective assemblage of bacteria, in which mitochondria were the ones swallowed but not digested by the other bacteria. The predator and the prey negotiated to live together. They are living together, making life together. This can be called sympoiesis, in Donna Haraway's term (2016, p. 58). 'Being' is already always this making-together – one can call it a spatial sympoiesis. They share a space of living together with each other. Fungus is another example of sympoiesis. Fungi live with plants, extracting minerals from rocks and phosphorus and nitrogen from the soil and supplying them to plants, with whose radicles they are entangled through their mycelia. In return, they receive carbon nutrients, such as carbohydrates, that the entangled plants produce through photosynthesis. It is called mycorrhizal symbiosis. Further, fungi connect plants to a network so that the whole forest can communicate through the mycorrhizal networks. In this fungal network, it is meaningless to ask who is the subject and who is the other. In fact, a hyphal network, which is developed into a mycorrhizal network of fungi, does not know the distinction of the self and the other. It lives and functions on the basis of associating with others. Given that human civilization has inextricably entangled with fungal species in fermenting food stuffs such as yeast, beer, kim-chi and so on, one may call being 'symborg' (Sheldrake, 2021, p. 103) like lichen, which is the witness to the co-living of fungi and algae.

Yet there is another form of sympoiesis – that is, temporal sympoiesis. Life and death make being together. Indeed, the living becomes the non-living when it does its own duty as the living. It turns into material elements for other forms of the living to come. In this way, sympoietic entanglement of being constitutes the transformative circulation of energy. That is, the living and the non-living are entangled together in the circulation of energy. Put differently, being is the flow and change of energy. Energy 'cuts across multiple thresholds of existence, and it is always dynamic, always changing' (Crockett, 2022, p. 2). In this sense, Crockett says, 'being is energy transformation' (Crockett, 2022, p. 2). From the perspective of energy, the dualism of life and death is very anthropocentric and/or biocentric. Suppose we think about the principle of the sanctity of life in bioethics. In the flow of energy, death or dying is as much precious and sacred as life or living. In fact, life and death constitute the cycle of being with energy and change. The flow of energy connects living to the intrinsic dynamic of matter as well as that of hyperobjects.

Living and non-living are connected by the existence of decomposers like bacteria, viruses, microbes, fungi and so on. The decomposers decompose the dead bodies into material elements so that other forms of being can utilize them for their own living. In this sense, death can become a contribution to (other) beings with the help of decomposers. Decomposition is 'the disassembling of a form of being into elements in assimilated forms into other beings when certain beings are finally fully exhausted and lost their directionality of movement' (Tatsushi, 2022, p. 20). Decomposition is a process of being that disassembles exhausted forms of being in order to (re)compose them into other forms of being. It is none other than the circulation of energy or the transformation of energy.

However, this viewpoint should be used very carefully in order not to be confused with the logics of Nazism, fascism and/or imperialism. The perspective of the circulation of being is the perspective of nature, not any human perspective. We live only once, and there lies the preciousness and uniqueness of our life. Nonetheless, nature is 'indifferent' (Corrington, 1996, p. 12) to individuals' pain and suffering as well as joyfulness and ecstasy. Nature embraces things within itself, including life and death. In fact, life and death are the ways nature embraces all beings in a way to circulate in energy transformation. It means that nature does not know waste. However, certain forms of being can matter to human survival, well-being and prosperity. Beyond human perspective, being in nature is an entanglement of the multiples on the one hand and of life and death on the other hand.

The Anthropocene as the collision of two kinds of time

The Anthropocene is the age in which the temporal sympoiesis is disclosed as the collision of two scales of time: the geological time and the human-centred time of historicity (Chakravarty, 2021, p. 49). The timescale of human history is so small in comparison with that of geology. Now the beings of the geological time show themselves up in the disguise of climate crises: climate change, ocean conveyor belts, tectonic movements and so on. These non-human geological agents are very different from the human agent in that they do not have consciousness, reason, intention and so on. They are not rational decision-making agents at all. Rather, they are agencies with their own response-abilities.

Then, the human body is entangled with beings of the geological time. For example, almost 70% of the human body consists of water. Where does the water in the body come from? The water in our body witnesses to the 5-billion-year history of the earth. Through the body, beings of geological time such as water are connected to the present being of human history. The body may be a medium connecting geological time and human history as well as connecting the brain and the external environment, and in this sense the body can be termed 'the between'. Through the body, the extensive continuum of the brain-body-device-environment network is interconnected. Now the water is severely damaged. For example, the breast-feeding milk of mothers in North America is already polluted. If one tried to sell it in stores, the FDA would not allow it because the milk is seriously contaminated and polluted (Neimanis, 2017, p. 33).

Due to the climate crises and ecological devastation, we humans seek a sustainable civilization with renewable green and carbon-free energy. However, the transition from fossil fuel to electrical energy may not be a final solution. For our concept of sustainability still clings to anthropocentric perspective of overcoming crises. According to Chakravarty, what matters in the notion of sustainability is 'the question of sustaining human civilization' (Chakravarty, 2021, p. 82). Thus, the question of sustainability asks us humans if one can manage production within the range of sustainability. It means that the word 'applies only to humans' and only to 'the interactions we have with our environment' (Chakravarty, 2021, p. 83). In other words, the notion of sustainability does not contain any care of non-human beings. Thus, expressions like 'sustainable civilization' miss what really matters in this Anthropocene: non-humans and their agential powers. In the warnings of the sixth extinction, one forgets that some non-human beings like viruses, bacteria, fungi and material beings will survive the mass extinction. This is an ironical warning that humans will not survive this mass extinction if they do not responsibly care for non-human beings. This is what sympoiesis really means for human beings on the earth.

The crises in the Anthropocene really matter to human civilization and survival. The climate disaster will bring an end equally both to the rich and the poor, and to the developed and the developing countries. It means that the concept of justice that humans imagine is not the same as how nature works. It may be said that nature is indifferent. However, our discourse on climate justice seems to cling on the dualistic understanding of the rich and the poor, of the developed and the developing countries, and of the privileged and the marginalized.

However, as Bruno Latour once quoted Margaret Thatcher, 'There is no such thing as society' (2007, p. 5), so one could say that there is no such thing as the rich, the privileged, the developed and so on in uniforms. For example, the US citizen does not uniformly refer to the privileged. According to Amartya Sen, the average life expectancy of Afro-Americans is shorter than labourers in China (Sen, 2013, p. 44). Society consists of actor-networks, which are the collective assemblages of humans and non-humans. There is no society in which only the privileged live. Society as the extension of actor-networks just refers to some non-humans-matter-humans-institutions-environment-culture. It is not a single network, but there are multiple overlayered-overlapping networks under the name of society. Actor-networks do not exist under the name of society, but the truth is opposite; that is, society is just an assemblage of multiple actor-networks. The privileged depend for their living upon the underprivileged, such as illegal immigrant workers, the socially marginalized and so on. However, it does not mean that there is no social injustice but rather that there is plenty. Nonetheless, the stubborn fact is that we as the privileged and the poor and oppressed are entangled.

What makes our situation unique in this Anthropocene is that the ecological disasters, the climate crises and their consequences are indifferent to human prosperity and well-being, regardless of the rich and the poor, of the privileged and the marginalized. It may be said that we are all doomed regardless of race, sex, gender, ethnicity, class and so on in this critical period of the Anthropocene. The term 'Anthropocene' refers to the fact that we humans have become geological agents in this age, leaving inerasable footprints upon the earth, and thus upon us, not *us*. This is what the collision of the two scales of time, the geological sense and the historical sense of time, means.

The discourse on climate justice ignores the geological sense of time that is colliding with our historical or critical sense of time, displacing the geological agent issue with historical or critical issue. In fact, it may not be a fault or mistake of people or scholars issuing the call for climate justice, because this collision of two senses of time is an unprecedented event in human history. What matters is that we cannot ignore this collision if we want to find a way to live with it. We may not overcome these crises of climate and ecology due to the lack of enough time or of our comprehensive understanding of the complex, overlayered and overdetermined workings of the hyperobjective systems. In this context, today one needs a theology beyond the dualism of success and failure.

As Whitehead said, 'All we know of nature is in the same boat, to sink or swim together' (Whitehead, 2007, p. 148). Indeed, being is none other than sympoiesis (making-with) of beings. That is, being is what beings make together. In this sense, existence consists of multiple overlayered 'intra-action(s)' in the entanglement of beings including hyperobjects. There is nothing outside of this ontic entanglement.

We need to change our perspective to see being in this Anthropocene from exclusively focusing on organic forms of life to the entanglement of being(s) with the inorganic, and also from the individuated form of organism to the entangled network of actor(s). Any being never lives alone, because 'being' is a collective event of assemblage. Being is 'entangled', but it is not a heap or a commingling of agencies but interconnected networks of agencies. According to Karen Barad, being is primarily entanglement of the living and the non-living. Out of this entanglement of being(s), individual agencies of networks emerge. What one sees as a subject or an object is none other than an 'agential cut' (Barad, 2007, p. 175) through the being of the entanglement. It is a perspective, from which an agency sees and observes things. According to Barad, the entanglement of being(s) is none other than the interactions of agencies, but she prefers the term 'intra-action' to that of interaction, for interaction presupposes the existences of subjects and/or objects. What she wants to say with intra-action is that agential interaction comes first and then the subjective or objective phenomena follow, because when being is entanglement, it means that there is nothing outside of the entanglement. So every interaction is already and always intra-action within the entanglement. A being is never alone but already and always with other forms of beings, intra-acting with each other through agential network(s) within the entanglement.

In this entanglement, being exists with its own response-ability. In other words, the interactions or intra-actions within the entanglement of being is none other than a response(s) from all entangled beings. Given that the current climate disasters may be the responses of matters to what we humans as geological agents have done in this Anthropocene, these crises may be the window for us to see and access to the agencies of things.

Theology of becoming-humanity (與人) by neighbouring-with-things

A Korean poet Lee Gyu-Bo, in the Goryo dynasty in the Middle Ages, proposed a notion of *yeo-mul* (與物), which means 'neighbouring with things'. One day, he found that one of the legs of the desk he had been using had broken. Instead of replacing it with a new one, he decided to fix it and continue to use it. While fixing the broken leg, he talked to the desk, saying, 'When I was alone and painful in writing, you saved me. Now you are in pain due to the broken leg, I save you by fixing your broken leg. In this way, we are saving each other with the commonality of pain.' With this story, he suggests a concept of *mul-ah-sang-gu* (物我相求), which means that 'I' and matter save each other (Park, 1999, p. 124).

In Lee's *yeo-mul* (與物, 'neighbouring with things'), he was treating things as if they had person-like agencies; that is, as companions to his life. So, he responded to the pain and suffering of the desk, as it responded to his loneliness and pain while he was writing. However, their response-abilities are not the same, and the human subject seemed to have some initiative in their intra-action within their entangled lives. Nevertheless, the demonstration of their intra-active response-abilities can be exerted and interacted due to their common existential capabilities of 'neighbouring with'. Humans can exert their own existential capabilities by neighbouring with things.

In Lee's attitude to things, I can see an emergent momentum to become humanity by neighbouring with things. I can term it as *yeo-in* (與人). We become humanity, when we treat our neighbouring beings as human-being. It means that humanity is not given but that it is to be cultivated with care.

Cultivating humanity is needed more than ever, especially when democracy seems to be impotent in solving or overcoming the crises we are facing, such as climate crises, global warming, melting down of glaciers, ecological devastations all over the world and so on. Our political system has been based only upon the human subjects; that is, voters who have their own citizenship, a legal right to vote. Political representatives are supposed to represent 'us' the commons, but they actually reflect their interests first in politics, cunningly mastering us. This is the political problem our current democracy system has. This is why our world has been more inhuman than ever.

Our urgent political problem in this Anthropocene is that non-human agencies like the climate system, ecosystem, current circulation system and so on seem to speak with their own agential powers. However, their voices have not been politically represented. Unless we humans find a way to represent the political voices of the non-human agencies, there would not be any exit out of the crises that we humans are facing.

Can humans politically represent the non-human agency of the earth, including numerous non-human agents on the earth? Becoming humanity can be realized through our neighbouring with things. Without listening and responding to them, we humans cannot become humanity. It means that we humans must find a way to listen and respond to the voice of non-humans, including material things. That is, we are humans only when we are on behalf of them. So we become each other, as we humans treat and respect things. We may have been wrong all along when we talk of the image of God. For YHWH calls Godself the plural: 'Let us make humans in our image' (Gen. 1.26). God is sympoietic being all along, listening and responding to other beings. This may be the meaning of the image of God. Our political representation of non-human beings now becomes our theological task for the Anthropocene.

References

Barad, Karen, 2007, *Meeting the Universe Halfway: Quantum Physics and the Entanglement of Matter and Meaning*, Durham, NC: Duke University Press.

Chakravarty, Dipesh, 2021, *The Climate of History in a Planetary Age*, Chicago, IL: University of Chicago Press.

Chalmers, David, 2011, 'Foreword', in Andy Clark, *Supersizing the Mind: Embodiment, Action, and Cognitive Extension*, Oxford: Oxford University Press

Clark, Andy, 2003, *Natural-Born Cyborgs: Minds, Technologies, and the Future of Human Intelligence*, Oxford: Oxford University Press.

——, 2011, *Supersizing the Mind: Embodiment, Action, and Cognitive Extension*, Oxford: Oxford University Press.

—— and David Chalmers, 1998, 'The Extended Mind', *Analysis* 58 (1), pp. 7–19.

Corrington, Robert S., 1996, *Nature's Self: Our Journey from Origin to Spirit*, Lanham, MD: Rowman & Littlefield.

Crockett, Clayton, 2022, *Energy and Change: A New Materialist Cosmotheology*, New York: Columbia University Press.

Haraway, Donna, 2016, *Staying with the Trouble: Making Kin in the Chthulucene*, Durham, NC: Duke University Press.

Latour, Bruno, 2007, *Reassembling the Social: An Introduction to Actor-Network-Theory*, Oxford: Oxford University Press.

Neimanis, Astrida, 2017, *Bodies of Water: Posthumanist Feminist Phenomenology*, London: Bloomsbury.

Park, Hee-Byung (박희병), 1999, *Ecological Thoughts in Korea* (『한국의 생태사상』), Pajoo, Kyung-gi: Dolbegae.

Sen, Amartya (아마티아 센), 2013, *Development as Freedom* (『자유로서의 발전』), trans. Won-Ki Kim, Seoul: Galapagos.

Sheldrake, Merlin, 2021, *Entangled Life: How Fungi Make Our Worlds, Change Our Minds, and Shape Our Futures*, London: Vintage.

Tatsushi, Fujihara (후지하라 다쓰시), 2022, *Philosophy of Decomposition: Thinking of Decomposition and Fermentation* (『분해의 철학: 부패와 발효를 생각한다』), trans. Sung-Kwan Park, Goyang, Kyungi: Book of April.

Whitehead, Alfred North, 2007 (1920), *The Concept of Nature*, New York: Cosimo.

unending

15

freedom is for freeing

MICHAEL N. JAGESSAR

You build your world on lies and illusions ... The truth is [now] showing. (Peter Tosh, 1982)

I do not film with my camera. I fix things ... I attempt, in my modest way, to heal the gaping wounds of history. (Euzan Palcy, 2023)

There is nothing with which poverty coincides so absolutely as the colour black – small or large population, hot or cold climates, rich or poor in natural resources – poverty cuts across all of these factors in order to find black people. (Walter Rodney, 1969, p. 13)

Jione Havea (editor) in the opening chapter of this book describes the essays as engaging the dynamics of release in the multiple contexts and shades of liberation theologies, with the intention to deliberately 'stir up the doing of liberation theologies, mindful of the dynamics of re(l)ease and struggles that have recently invaded our world, our mind, our neighbours and our being'. That calling could not be more timely as mega goliaths continue to trample on the poor and vulnerable with impunity.

Even David, Goliath's nemesis, has turned into a 'goliath', internalizing the habits of colonial occupiers, perfecting the art of apartheid, killing with impunity, while the voices of the religious and political status quo remain silent and complicit in the face of excessive reprisals. Lest we forget, excessive reprisal is the modus operandi of colonial warfare and state consolidation. As A. Dirk Moses observed:

> Mass state violence against civilians is not a glitch in the international system; it is baked into statehood itself. The natural *right* of self-defense plays a foundational role in the self-conception of Western states in particular, the formation of which is inseparable from imperial

expansion. ... [Hence settlers and occupiers will find all necessary means to justify] their reprisals against indigenous resistance as defensive 'self-preservation'. If they felt their survival was imperiled, colonizers engaged in massive retaliation against 'native' peoples, including non-combatants. (Moses, 2023)

necropolitics

The African intellectual Achille Mbembe has coined the term 'necropolitics' as an apt descriptor for the above. The first sentence of Mbembe's article titled 'Necropolitics' begins with the assertion that: 'The ultimate expression of sovereignty resides, to a large degree, in the power and the capacity to dictate who may live and who must die' (Mbembe, 2003). A select group continue to dictate which populations should be left to die.

There is nothing new here as the armoury and full might of the 'goliaths' (babylon shitstems), directed at the oppressed and their opposition (which threatens their righteous 'interest'), will ensure that the status quo stays in place at all costs. No available sling-shots and the abundance of stones from bombed-out concrete seem able to match the impunity of empire's ongoing avatars. And in their struggle for liberation the protests and collective 'rising-up' of oppressed and marginalized peoples are then labelled as violent and brutal by the status quo and the dominant. Surely any violence has to be the insistence by the powerful and hand-washing Pilates that the oppressed should remain nonviolent, quietly acquiescing to occupation.

What more then can we expect from and of liberation theologies in the overthrowing of 'goliaths' as the corners of the dying and the dead continue to multiply (within and between nations)? What sort of re-inventing will liberation theologies or liberating God-talk deploy given this urgent need to uncover lies, undress truth and overthrow Babylon (Tosh, 1982), offering more than balm to 'the gaping wounds of history' (Palcy, 2023)?

This collection intentionally deploys a 'playful' and 'signifying' role on the notion of 'release' in terms of the ultimate goal of liberation. In this 'un-ending' and up-ending chapter my play on release as a transitive verb (to make free, slacken, stretch out again, or to lease again) is reflected in the title: 'freedom is for freeing'.[1] It is a call for freeing, seeing that much of our dreams and euphoria around a postcolonial world have turned into nightmares.

freeing

Mindful of the radical Christian context of this collection, I am drawn to Galatians 5.1 as an orientating text that speaks to this 'freeing' vocation, habit and method. It is said that in the Caribbean when the enslaved people finally received their so-called 'free-paper', 31 years after the British 1807 Abolition Act, they gathered in the nonconformist chapels and their village spaces reading this very text: 'It is for freedom that Christ has set us free. Stand firm, then, and do not let yourselves be burdened again by a yoke of slavery' (Gal. 5.1 NIVUK).

Given their history, people who continually fought for their freedom from coloniality knew that to be free is to be themselves and not become some imitation of what others want them to be, hence the evolving chants of Garvey, Tosh, Marley and Fanon about freeing ourselves from 'mental slavery' – none but ourselves can free our minds from mental slavery. Or as a line by Ginger in the cartoon film *Chicken Run* (2000) went: 'You know what the problem is? The fences aren't just round the farm. They're up here, in your heads.'

Coloniality took things from our ancestors and continues to take from their progeny: things that it will not be able to restitute. We are learning to live with that loss. At the same time, greater responsibility must be taken for the act that coloniality and the church sought to relieve themselves *of* and *from*. Failure to give an account of themselves while doing remedial restitutions here and there means that they will conclude that having said sorry is enough, that having said sorry (with words) makes restitution complete and absolves them from the need to be reminded of what they have done and what they have established – especially the ongoing legacies of coloniality. And so enslavement will continue. Hence Sylvia Wynter's call in the 70s for 'a practice of rethinking and unravelling dominant world views', specifically the concept of the Human and its epistemological underpinnings, which has reached all the way into modernity and postmodernity, and is still relevant (see McKittrick, 2015).

Sadly, coloniality has enough worshippers of all hues. We must not be fooled: the forces in our society and within each one of us that are seeking to enslave and imprison us are very pervasive, persuasive, subtle and strong.

Life lived in freedom has to become a personal and collective responsibility otherwise release will quickly turn into another set of chains. It is therefore imperative to grasp freedom as a vocation – a calling to which the people who walk the Jesus Way must respond to daily, continuously and with extreme vigilance. Freedom in Christ is not something static: it is a way of living. It is not a licence to do what we like individually or nationally, unmindful of the effects it has on ourselves and others. It is liberation to be our true selves and that means to be for others. The calling is to continue to work for release from all forms of enslavement, ensuring vigilance against empire's guile and cunning reach.

So alongside the four 'theological traps' highlighted by the editor in the opening chapter, there must be an intentional self-interrogating habit and method for all who engage in doing liberation theologies, especially given the locations wherein we dwell, live and do our theologizing. Empire, goliaths and babylon shitstems and their extractive capitalist motivation will never easily give up their 'interest'. Co-option and the convergence of interest are among their strategic moves from which even the most vocal liberation theologians are not immune.

elite capture

With regard to the foregoing, *elite capture* (see Taiwo, 2022) and interest convergence continue to entrap and be stumbling blocks to the liberating/releasing calling. The Black British historian and cultural commentator David Olusoga offers a helpful insight and transferable learning point from personal experience. In a piece for *The Guardian*'s Cotton Capital Series, Olusoga writes:

> If you know how a trick is done, if you have peered through the smoke and looked past the mirrors, if you have figured out how the illusion is accomplished, surely you can no longer be fooled by it? Surely? The smoke-and-mirrors trick … like all the best illusions draws your eyes in one direction, away from the details the illusionist does not want you to see. It is carefully designed to frame and delineate our understanding of the past by focusing our attention away from certain linkages and connections. (Olusoga, 2023)

Olusoga goes on to explain how the illusion/trick marginalizes, lures, conceals, distorts, silences, having been 'constructed over centuries' by the elites with one aim in view: 'to create a highly romanticised version of our national story' and 'assisted in this task by generations of historians who were equally determined to construct' such a history of 'the nation's supposed exceptionalism'. Consequently, 'The illusion is effective because we are all subconsciously schooled in it.'

The hold of this illusion is powerful, as Olusoga discovered 'in triggering a form of cognitive dissonance'. He thought he was immune to it as he has researched, written on, lectured about the silenced Black voices in British history – that he could not fall for such a trick and how the illusion works. So when he was asked to serve on the board of the Scott Trust (owner of *The Guardian*) he 'completely failed to recognise the crucial and obvious connections between the founders of the Guardian and the history of slavery' (Olusoga, 2023).

Translated to/for our ecclesial-theological context/purpose, Olusoga's insight highlights the existential lure of *elite capture* as a challenge and stumbling block in re-configuring liberation theologies. A liberating spirituality that facilitates extreme heightened awareness, suspicion and *suspension* of our inherited deposits of biblical hermeneutics, mission history and theological traditions/deposits is a necessary constant throughout our decolonial moves towards liberating theologies. Freedom is for freeing!

remembering

Linked to the above is the need to invest in remembering well, as empire thrives on creating/encouraging amnesia and, in subtle ways, throws up barriers to new knowledge production. This has become more evident to me through my immersion in the LMS/CWM mission archives held at SOAS (London) researching the 1823 Demerara Slave Rebellion in the then British Guiana. Elsewhere I have equated the journey as entering a space not only full of skeletons but that of a 'bloody' crime scene in need of much more decolonial forensic work. There is, of course, a curious link between blood and Christianity, and the wealth-extracting colonial projects past and present. No wonder Christianity loves cross, death, murder and its own innocence, but that most of all it loves blood (Anidjar, 2016).[2] And not to mention that it is upon the liquid flow of the blood of the enslaved and the impoverished of today that extractive capitalism is built. Freedom is for freeing!

A few years ago, our youngest son introduced me to a book he had just finished reading. It was written in 1994 but only recently translated from its original language. *The Memory Police* by Yoko Ogawa is a dreamlike story of dystopia, set on an unnamed island that is being engulfed by an epidemic of forgetting. When objects disappear from memory, they disappear from real life. The disappearances are enforced by the Memory Police, a squad that sweeps through the island, ransacking houses to seize lingering evidence of what has been forgotten.

For our purpose, I note the components of forgetting that the author flags up: the thing disappears, then the memory of that thing disappears, and then the memory of forgetting that thing also disappears. When villagers forget birds and roses, they most definitely erase from memory what these things symbolize: flight, freedom, extravagance, desire and much more. To ensure that the job is thoroughly done, the Memory Police will root out and take away any who do not forget.

Remembering becomes a threat and an act of subversion. A telling line for our purpose of archival memories (what is on display and what is locked away) is when the narrator says: 'If it goes on like this and we can't compensate for the things that get lost then the island will soon be nothing but absences and holes, and when it's completely hollowed out, we'll all disappear without a trace' (Ogawa, 2019, p. 43).

The late Derek Walcott compares this disappearing without trace to Caribbean people tracing their names on the sand with a stick 'which the sea erased again, to our indifference' (Walcott, 1986, p. 306). Alberta Whittle's recent exhibition titled 'deep dive (pause) uncoiling memory' takes on what the artist describes as the 'luxury of amnesia'; that is, 'a state of privileged communal memory loss in which we are able to forget and overlook the atrocities of the past, allowing us to drift into a state of lethargy and inertia' (Dinsdale, 2022). The title has an intentional pause to lead viewers into giving thought to what they may have forgotten as part of the 'process of unlearning' towards 'intervening into what we understand of as history'.

Freedom is for freeing, is an imperative to end amnesia and indifference and remember well. And to do so we need to grapple with the reach of whiteness, elite capture, and how we may be unwittingly lured into perpetuating the virus.

(re)leasing

(Re)leasing liberating God-talk, like decolonizing, is both habit and method geared towards the transformation of social, economic and ideological systems of oppression against marginalized communities. At best it offers a life flourishing alternative to the rapacious greed of the capitalist modern-colonial world system, actualizing another way of living. It is a costly calling. Justice takes sacrifice. Justice also takes faith for Christians – that Christ's way of peace, healing, non-judgemental and acceptance is the way, even though it led him to imprisonment and death. Justice also takes vision and hope: for to act justly is to act out of a profound belief that the future can change. Only those who believe that change can happen, will act.

This vocation and journey need a spirituality to nourish us for such transformative work, modelling a world where the lure of other worlds is real, especially since many of us operate within the 'belly of the beast'.

Notes

1 Drawing on Galatians 5.1 and 13, the late Philip Potter re-read in the context of freedom as an ongoing vocation (see Jagessar, 1997, p. 260).

2 Anidjar (2016) offers an incisive interrogation of the central role of blood in Christianity and its circulating (fluid) omnipresence in the history of Christianity and of Europe, defining and redefining what it means to be human.

References

Anidjar, Gil, 2016, *Blood: A Critique of Christianity*, New York: Columbia University Press.
Chicken Run, 2000, https://www.imdb.com/title/tt0120630/characters/nm0001363.
Dinsdale, Emily, 2022, 'Why artist Alberta Whittle is imploring us to "invest in love"', on Alberta Whittle's 'deep dive (pause) uncoiling memory', *Dazed*, 26 April, https://www.dazeddigital.com/art-photography/article/55947/1/why-artist-alberta-whittle-is-imploring-us-to-invest-in-love (accessed 08.04.2024).
Jagessar, Michael, 1997, *Full Life for All: The Work and Theology of Philip A. Potter: A Historical Survey and Systematic Analysis of Major Themes*, Zoetermeer: Boekencentrum.
Mbembe, Achille, 2003, 'Necropolitics', translated by Libby Meintjes, *Public Culture* 15 (1), https://muse.jhu.edu/article/39984 (accessed 08.04.2024), pp. 11–40.
McKittrick, Katherine (ed.), 2015, *Sylvia Wynter: On Being Human as Praxis*, Durham, NC: Duke University Press.
Moses, A. Dirk, 2023, 'More than Genocide', *The Boston Review*, 14 November, https://www.bostonreview.net/articles/more-than-genocide/ (accessed 19.04.2024).
Ogawa, Yoko, 2019 (1994), *The Memory Police*, trans. Stephen Snyder, New York: Pantheon.
Olusoga, David, 2023, 'Slavery and the Guardian: the ties that bind us', *The Guardian*, Cotton Capital Series, 28 March, pp. 1–2, https://www.theguardian.com/

news/ng-interactive/2023/mar/28/slavery-and-the-guardian-the-ties-that-bind-us (accessed 08.04.2024).

Palcy, Euzan, 2023, *Rétrospective*, Le Festival d'Automne à Paris, https://www.festival-automne.com/en/edition-2023/euzhan-palcy-retrospective (accessed 08.04.2024).

Rodney, Walter, 1969, *The Groundings with my Brothers*, London: Bogle-L'Ouverture.

Taiwo, Olufemi O., 2022, *Elite Capture: How the Powerful Took Over Identity Politics and Everything Else*, London: Pluto.

Tosh, Peter, 1982, 'Glass House', https://www.jah-lyrics.com/song/peter-tosh-glass-house (currently inaccessible for security reasons).

Walcott, Derek, 1986, 'Names', in *Collected Poems 1948–1984*, London: Faber & Faber, pp. 305–8.

Names and Subjects Index

activism 47, 52, 157
adultery 111
advocacy 23, 60, 63, 64, 80, 81
agape 192
agency 11, 80, 117, 118, 121, 123, 125, 127, 128, 143, 192, 197, 198, 206, 208
agribusiness 43, 44, 45, 52
amnesia 215, 216
ancestors 17, 29, 34, 58, 59, 61, 122, 143, 213
animism 200
annunciation 6, 69, 70, 71, 76
Anthropocene 203–8
anthropocentrism 197
anti-racism 164
anti-sexuality 42, 51
apartheid 6, 71, 72, 74, 75, 78, 124, 125, 126, 132, 134, 138, 139, 142, 211
apocalypse 169, 170
apology 55, 57, 58, 59, 60, 61, 63, 64
artificial 12, 198
atmosphere 199
avatars 212

barriers 10, 154, 156, 161, 168, 215
beauty 9, 10, 169–83
being 11, 197, 198, 200, 202, 206

biocentrism 197, 198, 199
bioethics 203
black 6, 23, 42, 45, 48, 51, 56, 57, 71, 73, 75, 76, 77, 78, 81, 126, 131, 135, 137, 139, 140, 144, 157, 164, 211, 215
boat 106, 109, 209
body 10, 11, 45, 81, 118, 123, 131, 169, 175, 185, 186, 188, 189, 190, 191, 198, 204
breast 204
budget 9, 158, 159, 163, 166

camera 211
capitalism 5, 7, 15, 17, 44, 71, 154, 215
choreography 11, 186, 187, 190, 192, 193, 194
class 6, 9, 16, 19, 29, 43, 52, 69, 71, 73, 74, 76, 77, 80, 81, 171, 205
cleaner 159
climate 197, 198, 205, 206, 207, 208
climate change 11, 134, 183, 204
colonialism 4, 8, 10, 15, 43, 52, 86, 169, 176
coloniality 43, 213
communion 25, 172
communism 17
consumerism 161

contrapuntal 103
conversion 10, 169, 171, 173
Covid-19 6, 7, 11, 15, 17, 58, 69, 71, 81, 84, 88, 91–6, 98, 99, 102, 134, 198, 200
crises, crisis 11, 35, 36, 37, 69, 72, 96, 122, 137, 183, 190, 192, 197, 204, 205, 206, 207, 208
crusades 3, 15
cyborg 198, 201

dance(s) 3, 9, 10, 11, 33, 47, 174, 175, 182, 185–92
decolonial 5, 27, 28, 56, 215
decolonization 8, 28, 61, 62
decomposition 203
denunciation 6, 69, 70, 71
depression 9, 36, 137, 138, 140, 181, 192
device(s) 198, 201, 204
diaspora 101, 144, 191
dignity 10, 22, 40, 52, 143, 169
discrimination 27, 33, 38, 58, 73, 75
dissonance 215
divest 157
Doctrine of Discovery 1
doctrine 1, 22, 177, 178
dreams 60, 175, 181, 182, 189, 212
dualism, dualistic 198, 203, 205, 206
dystopia 215

eating 107
echo theology 103
ecology 182, 197, 205
economic liberation 91
ecosystems 10, 169, 199

elite capture 214–15, 216
emancipation 5, 55, 56, 61, 62, 63, 132
empire 3, 4, 5, 17, 29, 55, 64, 105, 106, 110, 119, 120, 135, 177, 180, 212, 214, 215
empowerment 47, 88, 89, 96, 121, 126, 127
energy slaves 170, 171
enslavement 2, 59, 62, 63, 170, 180, 213, 214
entanglement 11, 197–9, 202, 203, 206
epistemic 171, 174, 179, 190
equality, social 43
eros 192
eschatology 17, 18, 21, 22
ethics 4, 21, 143
ethnicity 11, 186, 190, 205
eurocentrism 4, 16, 25
Eurochristians 15, 20, 21, 22
Eurochristianity 16, 21
exploitation 43, 44, 52, 179, 190, 191, 193

finance, church 156, 160, 161, 163, 165
food 7, 15, 41, 44, 49, 51, 52, 73, 75, 85, 87, 88, 90, 91, 92, 93, 94, 95, 104, 106, 107, 111, 180, 182, 186, 202
forgiveness 5, 21, 55, 56, 63, 108
fossil fuel 157, 204
freedom 2, 12, 41, 48, 51, 73, 74, 75, 89, 133, 170, 173, 174, 211–16
freeing 1, 2, 12, 211–16
fundamentalism 43, 44, 51, 52

gender(ed) 11, 33, 38, 40, 42, 45,

222

46, 48, 51, 72, 4, 80, 85, 90,
  135, 136, 138, 139, 142, 143,
  165, 186, 189, 190, 191, 205
genocide 15, 20, 21, 24, 43, 134
goliaths 211, 212, 214
green energy 183

haunting 112
healing 96, 107, 108, 109, 110,
  125, 126, 136, 137, 140, 145,
  176, 217
heteropatriarchy 98
HIV/AIDS 80, 91, 133, 144
holocaust(s) 10, 12, 20, 21, 169
homophobia 76, 134
hunger 15, 22, 73, 94, 105, 107,
  190
hybrid 191, 198, 201

identity 8, 21, 52, 107, 119, 120,
  122, 125, 128, 137, 143, 145,
  153, 156, 157, 158, 160, 180,
  189, 191
illusion 211, 214, 215
imperialism 43, 60, 62, 203
incarnation 190, 193
inclusion 71, 96, 153
indecencies 11, 186, 190
indifference 7, 191, 216
indigenous 10, 20, 61, 169, 171,
  174, 175, 177, 181, 191, 212
industrial complex 10, 153–68
injustice(s) 16, 19, 41, 58, 78, 80,
  81, 205
integrity 128

joy 4, 86, 194
justice
  climate 205
  economic 80, 81, 155

gender 42
racial 153
reparatory 59, 63
restorative 58, 64
social 4, 9, 41, 51, 63, 127, 131,
  153, 155, 156, 157, 160, 163,
  165, 166, 168, 190
justice, worker 159

Kairos Document 6, 76
kenosis 193
kindness 136, 141, 146
kyriarchy 134, 138

labour 5, 79, 85, 86, 87, 88, 89,
  99, 105, 110, 159, 180
landless 5, 40, 41, 44, 45
leftovers 11, 106, 107, 108, 111
leper 109
leprosy 33
limits 1, 4, 19, 22, 28, 70, 98, 99,
  138, 164
limitations 22, 156, 180
liturgy, liturgies 9, 48, 49, 144,
  145, 146
lockdown 7, 84, 92, 94

Manifest Destiny 20
marginalized 5, 6, 16, 17, 28, 74,
  76, 78, 79, 80, 102, 131, 132,
  162, 205, 212, 216
markets 7, 12, 74, 84–96, 175
masculinity 135, 142, 143
massacre, massacred 21, 43, 178
mediator 34, 36, 37
memoria miserabilis 135
memorialization 135
mental health 8, 9, 132, 133, 134,
  136–41, 145
mental slavery 213

messianic complex 102
migration 11, 101, 103, 104, 105, 106
mimicry 110, 111
minjung 7, 98–112
modernity 4, 17, 18, 135, 169, 176, 213

natives 2, 20, 175–83, 212
necropolitics 107, 212
neighbour(ing) 12, 207–8
neocolonialism 61
neoliberalism 15, 69
non-profit(s) 154, 158, 163, 168
nurture 94

occupation 2, 30, 212
ochlos 7, 98–111
oppression 4, 16, 19, 21, 22, 23, 24, 37, 42, 46, 47, 51, 70–4, 76, 77, 78, 80, 96, 100, 128, 134, 140, 177, 216
ordain, ordained 27, 34, 153
organic 198, 206
organic intellectuals 6, 81

pagan 175
Palestine 2, 106
palm tree 34, 35
paradigm(s) 56, 61, 100
paradigm shift 77, 165, 173
patriarchy 3, 5, 15, 45, 72, 91
peasant 5, 41, 44, 45, 52, 103, 177
perichoresis 192
perseverance 24, 146
pilgrimage 34
poets 32, 34, 60, 207
positionality 154, 166, 167
postcolonialism 144

poverty 6, 7, 16, 19, 23, 69–81, 89, 140, 143, 211
praxis 4, 6, 7, 21, 23, 24, 25, 62, 69–81, 131, 136, 141
pride 153
pride flag 157
priestesses 32, 33, 34
priesthood 3, 4, 27–38
primitive 30, 175, 176
profit(s) 5, 10, 19, 44, 154, 158, 167
progress 19, 87, 171, 176, 179, 180
progressive 18, 48, 69, 76, 79, 153, 154, 155, 156, 167, 179
prophetess 33, 34, 37
prosperity 201, 203, 205
protest 59, 60, 63, 80, 99, 117, 118, 123, 124, 127, 128

queer 10, 11, 112, 131, 166, 185–94

racism 8, 15, 43, 52, 63, 135, 139, 140, 164
rainbow 153
Rastafari 56, 57, 61
rationalism 179
reconciliation 36, 37, 38, 118, 124
reform 5, 41, 43, 44, 45, 50, 51, 52
refuge 94
rejection 4, 6, 11, 45, 52, 56, 69, 128, 186, 191
remembering 143, 215–16
remittances 7, 98, 101, 106, 107, 110
reparations 5, 55–9, 62–4, 114
resilience 34, 80, 96, 101, 131

resistance 16, 24, 27, 43, 46, 52, 80, 160, 193, 212
response-ability 199–202, 206
restitution 62, 127, 213
rural (areas, struggles, women, workers) 5, 41, 43, 44, 52, 72, 155, 176

sacred places 10, 169
sacrifice 19, 37, 90, 91, 95, 158, 217
salvation 4, 7, 11, 17, 18, 20, 22, 23, 24, 179
saviourism 102, 110
secular 17, 165, 174
see, judge, act 8, 132
sex for fish 89–91
sexuality 11, 42, 48, 142, 186, 189, 190
shame 135, 145
shitstems 7, 212, 214
silence, silenced 8, 33, 37, 46, 47, 63, 80, 90, 112, 117, 118, 119, 121, 123, 127, 128, 136, 138, 145, 214, 215
single mothers 91, 96
skeletons 215
slaughter 15, 21, 23
slavery 3, 4, 15, 57, 58, 60, 71, 78, 139, 140, 164, 170, 213, 215
solidarity 15, 19, 23, 24, 34, 59, 118, 126, 128
sorry 5, 55, 59, 64, 146, 213
sovereignty 62, 64, 212
space
  invented 79
  invigorated 79
  invited 71, 76
spirituality 40, 78, 138, 143, 178, 179, 215, 217

status quo 211, 212
street vendors 7, 84, 89, 91
stress 8, 9, 89, 92, 95, 118, 120, 131–47
struggle(s) 6, 7, 8, 9, 12, 15, 19, 24, 25, 31, 33, 40, 41, 43, 44, 47, 48, 50–3, 69, 79, 92, 95, 99, 100, 102, 111, 118, 120, 124, 126, 131, 132, 133, 136, 143, 145, 155, 211, 212
subversion 216
suicide 9, 137–40, 144, 146
survival 23, 49, 52, 84, 90, 91, 93, 94, 111, 118, 161, 162, 170, 179, 203, 204, 212
sympoiesis 202, 203, 204, 206

terra 40, 48, 49, 50, 52
terra nullius 178
theodicy 21, 121, 122, 123, 124
tokenism 6
tools 1, 59, 118, 176, 180, 198, 201
torment 173
transformation 6, 52, 56, 69, 70, 71, 79–81, 180, 199, 202, 203, 216
transgressions 101, 172
trauma 6, 8, 9, 10, 133–7, 141–5, 169
  collective 119
  cultural 8, 117, 118–23, 125
  individual 8, 117–21, 122, 125
trick 214, 215

Ukraine 15
underdogs 76, 77
unemployment 69, 71, 72, 73, 140
urban 43, 44, 50, 52, 155

utopia 17, 18, 23, 69

vegetables 85, 87, 88, 89, 94
virtuosity 189
visceral 166, 187, 191, 199
vocation 32, 38, 157, 191, 213, 217
voice(s) 5, 28, 37, 46, 47, 62, 72, 80, 99, 102, 108, 112, 117–28, 131, 132, 188, 194, 208, 211, 215

warfare 181, 211
weaving 171, 174, 181
well-being 84, 201, 203, 205
West Papua 1, 2

white supremacy 20, 57, 63, 124, 125, 140
whiteness 4, 216
widow(s) 89, 91, 95, 96
wisdom 10, 36, 61, 63, 126, 165, 169, 185
work, theology of 85–6, 95
workers 5, 6, 7, 40–53, 86, 87, 88, 98–112, 179, 205
worship 29, 30, 34, 46, 122, 155, 178
wounds 135, 146, 172, 211, 212
wretched 15, 144

young people 9, 74, 131–46
youth 71, 74, 131–46, 160

www.ingramcontent.com/pod-product-compliance
Lightning Source LLC
Chambersburg PA
CBHW032336300426
44109CB00041B/1061